Safeguarding Children Across Services

Safeguarding Children Across Services Series

Series editors: Carolyn Davies and Harriet Ward

Safeguarding children from abuse is of paramount importance. This series communicates messages for practice from an extensive government-funded research programme designed to improve early recognition of child abuse and neglect as well as service responses and interventions. The series addresses a range of forms of abuse, including emotional and physical abuse and neglect, and outlines strategies for effective interagency collaboration, successful intervention and best practice. Titles in the series will be essential reading for practitioners with responsibility for safeguarding children.

Carolyn Davies is Research Advisor at the Thomas Coram Research Unit at the Institute of Education, University of London.

Harriet Ward is Director of the Centre for Child and Family Research and Research Professor at Loughborough University.

other books in the series

Safeguarding Children from Emotional Maltreatment
What Works
Jane Barlow and Anita Schrader McMillan
ISBN 978 1 84905 053 1

Recognizing and Helping the Neglected Child
Evidence-Based Practice for Assessment and Intervention
Brigid Daniel, Julie Taylor and Jane Scott with David Derbyshire and Deanna Neilson
Foreword by Enid Hendry
ISBN 978 1 84905 093 7

Adolescent Neglect
Research, Policy and Practice
Gwyther Rees, Mike Stein, Leslie Hicks and Sarah Gorin
ISBN 978 1 84905 104 0

Caring for Abused and Neglected Children
Making the Right Decisions for Reunification or Long-Term Care
Jim Wade, Nina Biehal, Nicola Farrelly and Ian Sinclair
ISBN 978 1 84905 207 8

Safeguarding Babies and Very Young Children from Abuse and Neglect
Harriet Ward, Rebecca Brown and David Westlake
ISBN 978 1 84905 237 5

Safeguarding Children Across Services

Messages from Research

Carolyn Davies and Harriet Ward

Jessica Kingsley *Publishers*
London and Philadelphia

First published in 2012
by Jessica Kingsley Publishers
116 Pentonville Road
London N1 9JB, UK
and
400 Market Street, Suite 400
Philadelphia, PA 19106, USA

www.jkp.com

Library of Congress Cataloging in Publication Data
A CIP catalog record for this book is available from the Library of Congress

British Library Cataloguing in Publication Data
A CIP catalogue record for this book is available from the British Library

ISBN 978 1 84905 124 8
eISBN 978 0 85700 290 7

Printed and bound in Great Britain

Contents

LIST OF TABLES AND FIGURES

Preface

Safeguarding Children Across Services: Messages from Research brings together a wide-ranging body of government-funded research on safeguarding children from neglect and abuse in England and Wales. It provides a succinct Overview of 15 research projects and highlights the main implications for all professionals and policymakers involved in the safeguarding process.

For many years non-technical summaries of research programmes and initiatives in children's social care, funded by the Department of Health and the Department for Education, have been produced. The intention is to make the messages of research useful and intelligible to practitioners, clinicians, service providers and policymakers. There is a distinctive process through which these Overviews are developed. They are written by academic experts with the support of an outside advisory and implementation group, consisting of clinicians, practitioners, managers and others with expertise in the subject area. Each Overview incorporates the comments of practitioners, clinicians and policymakers on the projects and on the draft text. Each Overview also tries to ensure that the individual researchers agree with the synthesis produced, although the writers have the responsibility of drawing out the messages that they think are warranted by the research.

The Advisory and Implementation Group saw the production of this Overview as one key element in a rather larger exercise that would involve the various stakeholders in safeguarding children, the research community and others specifically concerned with training and dissemination. The key aims have been to bring to a wider audience material that is relevant, evidenced and accessible.

In order to ensure relevance, each study was read by two or more members of the Advisory and Implementation Group who contributed both a summary and an assessment of its main implications. In order to ensure accuracy, the researchers involved in the core studies also read the resulting draft Overview to ensure that their own work had been properly represented. They also contributed the research summaries of their work. The authors, Carolyn Davies and Harriet Ward, then took final responsibility for redrafting the Overview as a whole.

Thanks are due to the many people who have helped support both the programme of research and the preparation of this publication.

We would like to extend our thanks to the Department for Education and the Department of Health for their support in funding and overseeing the preparation of this Overview and particularly Isabella Craig, Julie Wilkinson, Jenny Gray (who chaired the Advisory and Implementation Group), Sandra Williams, Zoltan Bozoky, Christine Humphrey and Alison Elderfield.

Thanks are also due to the following members of the Thomas Coram Research Unit (TCRU) at the Institute of Education and the Centre for Child and Family Research (CCFR) at Loughborough University: Penny Mellor, who supported the commissioning and progress of the Safeguarding Children Research Initiative and developed and maintained the website; Suzanne Dexter and Debi Maskell-Graham, who provided multi-faceted support in preparing the Overview; and Harriet Lowe, who finalized the presentation of the text.

We would also like to express our appreciation to the research teams who conducted the studies on which this Overview is based. They have been very committed and helpful throughout the process and their input is much appreciated.

We are very grateful for the support of our multi-disciplinary Advisory and Implementation Group, whose names are listed in Appendix 1. The group were exceptionally helpful in reading and commenting on drafts, advising on the selection of key messages and providing wisdom from their respective disciplinary perspectives. The Overview has been much improved by their contributions.

Finally the authors would like to extend their thanks to their husbands, respectively Nigel Davies and Christopher Ward, for their patience and support throughout the preparation of the publication.

1
Introduction

This chapter covers:

- the evolving policy context within which the research messages need to be implemented

- prevalence of abuse and neglect

- issues concerning definitions of emotional abuse and neglect and their implications

- details of the studies in the Safeguarding Children Research Initiative

- the strengths and the weaknesses of the evidence they provide.

It can both be read as an introduction to the Overview as a whole and/or be used as a resource by readers looking for more information about these issues.

Introduction

> Any society, any nation, is judged on the basis of how it treats its weakest members – the last, the least, the littlest.[1]

On 25 February 2000 an eight-year-old child, Victoria Climbié, died following weeks of appalling maltreatment and neglect at the hands of the great-aunt who had been entrusted with her care, and the man with whom she was living. On 3 August 2007, a 17-month-old boy, Peter Connelly, died following similarly appalling treatment by his mother and two men who were living in her household. Victoria Climbié and Peter Connelly are by no means the only children to have died in deeply troubling circumstances in England over the last decade or so. However, these deaths both captured the public imagination and have served as catalysts for change. Although all the adults who were directly involved served prison sentences for murder or causing or allowing the death of a child, the ensuing public outcries focused on the professionals who hold responsibilities for preventing such tragedies. The reports that followed the deaths of both these children[2,3] called for an extensive programme of change in both the structure and the delivery of services aimed at safeguarding and promoting the welfare of children suffering, or likely to suffer, significant harm.

The Safeguarding Children Research Initiative

The Safeguarding Children Research Initiative[4] is an important element in the government response to the Inquiry following the death of Victoria Climbié. Its purpose is to provide a stronger evidence base for the development of policy and practice to improve the protection of children in England in three specific areas that have been identified as requiring particular attention:

* identification and initial response to abuse

* effective interventions after abuse or its likelihood have been identified

* effective inter-agency and inter-disciplinary working to safeguard children.

In each of these areas the research has encompassed a specific focus on neglect and emotional abuse, significant elements in the maltreatment of Victoria Climbié.

Research of the depth and quality covered by the Initiative takes time to commission and to execute. During the period in which the studies were undertaken, another significant tragedy, that of Peter Connelly, occurred. Regular annual meetings between researchers and policymakers during the course of the Initiative made it possible for emerging findings to be fed into ongoing national policy development, much of which has been shaped first by Lord Laming's progress report[5] following Peter Connelly's death and more recently by Professor Eileen Munro's report on child protection.[6]

Before introducing the reader to the studies, this introductory chapter sets the scene by examining some of the background issues against which they should be understood. These include: the evolving policy context within which the messages need to be implemented; the prevalence of abuse and its consequences; issues concerning how maltreatment should be defined; the nature of the studies; and the strengths and weaknesses of the evidence base they provide.

Who should read this Overview?

Safeguarding Children Across Services: Messages from Research provides an Overview of the key messages from 15 studies, distilled to meet the needs of those professionals who seek to utilize such research findings to shape their day-to-day work. These include strategic and operational managers and practitioners, commissioners and providers of services, and policymakers in all those agencies that are required to work together to safeguard children: although these are primarily those who work in children's and adults' social care, health, education, the police and the family justice system, the messages are relevant to staff in many other agencies in both the statutory and independent sectors.

The evolving policy context

Initiatives to promote the welfare of children and to protect those likely to suffer harm have been central elements in government policies for children and families over many years. They form part of a wider agenda for improving outcomes for all children, tackling child poverty and reducing social exclusion.

The inquiry following the death of Victoria Climbié made it clear that a number of long-standing problems, repeatedly raised by numerous child abuse inquiries over the preceding 30 years, had still not been overcome. These included poor co-ordination between services; a failure to share information between agencies; the absence of anyone with a strong sense of accountability; and the numbers of front-line workers trying to cope with staff vacancies, poor management and inadequate training.[7] These were not new issues,[8] although the Victoria Climbié Inquiry brought them into sharper focus.

The Green Paper *Every Child Matters*[9] that followed the inquiry accelerated a number of strands of policy development that were already under way.[10] It covered four main areas: supporting parents and carers; early intervention and effective protection; accountability and integration; and workforce reform. One of its most significant features was the articulation of a set of five outcomes which all children should achieve: be healthy, stay safe, enjoy and achieve, make a positive contribution and achieve economic wellbeing. This outcomes framework set child protection within a wider agenda of improving the wellbeing of all children. All children's services would now be required to work together towards the achievement of these outcomes and to provide evidence of progress across a set of performance indicators for which they could be held accountable.

The Children Act 2004[11] delivered the legislative changes to support the new agenda. These included the duty to promote co-operation between the children's services authority and its relevant partner agencies with a view to improving the wellbeing of children in the authority's area; provisions for integrating education and children's social services departments; and the introduction of Local Safeguarding Children Boards, whose purpose is to co-ordinate and ensure the effectiveness of member agencies in safeguarding and promoting the welfare of children.

These structural changes were also reflected in the strengthening or introduction of a number of programmes designed to improve practice. These included: more widespread implementation of the existing, holistic *Framework for the Assessment of Children in Need and their Families*;[12] the development of a Common Assessment Framework[13] to be used by all agencies in identifying and assessing children's additional needs; the updating of statutory guidance for all professionals with responsibilities to safeguard and promote the welfare of children;[14] and the development of practice and recording tools designed to support social work practitioners and managers in undertaking the key tasks of assessment, planning, intervention and review.[15]

The *Every Child Matters: Change for Children* agenda was reflected in the *National Service Framework for Children, Young People and Maternity Services*, a ten-year programme to stimulate long-term and sustained improvements in children's health and welfare, through setting standards to ensure fair, high-quality and integrated children's health and social care from pregnancy through to adulthood.[16]

Five years later, the recommendations for change made in the report triggered by the death of Peter Connelly[17] focused on many of the same issues. These included a call for greater strategic co-ordination, improvements in the recruitment, training, management and supervision of front-line social workers, reduced and better managed caseloads and for all agencies with a safeguarding role to have clear duties and responsibilities to work together and share information.

Emerging policy developments under the Coalition Government and their implications

Many of these innovations remain key priorities for the current Coalition Government. There is a continuing commitment to the principle of early intervention to counter the adverse effects of socio-economic disadvantage and diminished life chances.[18,19] There is a renewed commitment to the reform of social work and the strengthening of social work training.[20] A number of major new policy developments are also being introduced, the purpose of which is to introduce greater autonomy and innovation at both the levels of professional practice and strategic management and delivery of services. These are likely to bring changes which will significantly impact on the manner in which the welfare of children is safeguarded and promoted. Policies which at present appear most likely to have such an impact are the substantial cuts to public services funding set out in the 2010 Public Spending Review,[21] the reshaping of local authority responsibilities for partnership arrangements, the reforms to the delivery of NHS services and the forthcoming changes to approaches to delivering child protection services at the front line.

Cuts to public spending may be necessary to reduce the financial deficit but they will inevitably have an impact on the manner and extent to which children are safeguarded. They could produce incentives for positive and imaginative changes, but they could also exacerbate existing tensions and reduce the availability of high-quality services for families where there is a likelihood of maltreatment. For instance, the evidence from the studies in this Overview indicates that already too many children are left for too long in abusive families where there is insufficient support, and that more, rather than fewer, would benefit by being looked after away from home. Yet budgetary pressures will make it hard to resist *raising* the threshold for access to children's social care and *reducing* the numbers of looked after children even though, in the long run, these may be false economies.

Whilst the Coalition Government continues to support the need for local partnerships as central to meeting the needs of children, it argues that the role of central government should be reduced, that a one-size-fits-all approach will not work and that co-operation will be better achieved by freeing local bodies to adopt their own approaches to local problems than by defining partnership arrangements.[22] The previous requirement for local authorities to set up a Children's Trust Board and to produce an annual Children and Young People's Plan has been withdrawn, on the grounds that:

> Strong integration of services leads to better services for children, young people and families – especially the vulnerable – and … the core principles enshrined in the duty to cooperate on local strategic bodies remain as important as ever, but Children's Trusts are not critical to achieving this.[23]

However, it remains to be seen how such a duty to co-operate will be met under these new arrangements, particularly as other reforms are increasingly pointing towards greater fragmentation of services.

For instance, new policies to give local authorities greater freedoms and to encourage more schools to become independent from their oversight by taking Academy or Free School status have now been introduced.[24] The duty placed on schools to co-operate with the local authority through Children's Trusts is also being removed.[25]

Similarly, the main thrust of reforms to the NHS[26] is to reduce central direction and introduce more local autonomy in the delivery of services. The major responsibility for commissioning health care will move to GP-led consortia. The policy of 'any qualified provider' is intended to introduce diversity of services and service providers.

These new developments are intended to produce more opportunities for innovation and creativity in local authorities and the NHS. There are, however, plans to promote integration between the NHS and social care through the establishment of Health and Wellbeing Boards, which will allow local authorities to take a strategic approach across services including safeguarding children.

Although the new Health and Wellbeing Boards will have a duty to encourage integrated working, it may nevertheless prove problematic to withstand the challenges to inter-agency collaboration that increasing diversity may produce. In times of economic stringency it is likely to be particularly difficult to promote successful multi-agency practice and to share safeguarding responsibilities, especially when these entail pooling budgets. A number of studies in the Research Initiative show significant differences between authorities in the effectiveness of measures to safeguard children, and these may increase as autonomy grows.

The Munro Review of Child Protection

The *Munro Review of Child Protection* has recommended extensive changes to the day-to-day delivery of child protection services. Following the death of Peter Connelly, concerns were raised by social workers and others about the nature and amount of guidance and the potentially adverse impact of performance indicators, both of which were thought potentially to stifle their ability to exercise professional judgement or to prioritize time with children and families. In addition, the public anger directed at social workers following the media furore surrounding the deaths of Victoria Climbié and Peter Connelly has been extreme; one consequence has been an increasingly defensive professional culture that may have further reinforced dependency on rules and processes at the expense of professional judgement. The *Munro Review* adopted a systems approach to analyse why the current problems have arisen, to set out the characteristics of an effective child protection system and to outline the reforms that might help the current system get closer to the ideal.[27] The Government response[28] has taken forward many of its recommendations. Statutory guidance will be revised to achieve a better balance between professional judgement and central prescription and to make child protection services less procedurally driven. There will be reductions in performance indicators as drivers of service quality and the use of standardized formats and rigid timetables for assessment. There will be more emphasis on supervision and professional support of social workers with new senior professional roles at central and local level. There will be less emphasis on adherence to procedures in the inspection process. There are also plans to formalize shared responsibility with the NHS and public health services for 'early help' services and to clarify the relationship between Local Safeguarding Children Boards and Health and Wellbeing Boards which may well, in practice, come to fulfil a similar role to that of Children's Trust Boards.

These measures are intended to raise professional standards, promote shared responsibility with health services, and give more time for direct work with children. Their impact on day to day practice is not yet clear but they are likely to address some of the issues identified by the research covered by this Overview.

Emerging findings from the Safeguarding Children Research Initiative have already informed key policy areas such as social work training,[29] and the organization and responsibilities of Local Safeguarding Children Boards,[30] identified as central to reform. They also informed the *Munro Review of Child Protection*, and will no doubt continue to provide an evidence base for the development of policy in this area.

How much maltreatment is there?

It is not easy to find out how many children are subject to abuse and neglect. The numbers vary substantially according to the sources of information, the time-span over which it is collected and the ways in which maltreatment is defined. The most recent government statistics show that, in 2009–10, 88,700 children and young people aged under 18 were the subject of a Section 47 enquiry, but only about half that number (44,300) were made the subjects of child protection plans. Nevertheless, the numbers of children for whom child protection plans are made, and are therefore considered to be suffering or likely to suffer significant harm, have been rising annually since 2005, culminating in an increase of 30 per cent over the two years following the furore when the circumstances surrounding the death of Peter Connelly emerged in 2008–9.[31,32]

However, these figures show the numbers of children assessed as being likely to suffer significant harm in the future and therefore requiring a plan to protect them. The numbers who are thought to be maltreated each year are much larger, for many are not referred to children's social care, and many referrals for abuse or neglect are not substantiated.[33] The most recent prevalence study in the UK,[34] undertaken in 2009, found that 2.5 per cent of children aged under 11 and 6 per cent of young people aged 11–17 had experienced some form of maltreatment from a caregiver within the previous year. Experience of maltreatment *at some time* during childhood is understandably higher: the same study found that 5 per cent of children aged under 11, 13.5 per cent of young people aged 11–17 and 14.5 per cent of young adults aged 18–24 had experienced serious maltreatment by a parent or caregiver at some time during their childhood. Evidence from this study suggests, however, that since 1997 there has been a significant drop in self-reported experiences of harsh emotional and physical treatment and in experiences of physical and sexual violence. So it could be that, while increasing awareness of maltreatment has meant that more children are referred to children's social care, in the population as a whole, fewer children are being abused. Such a trend may well be an artefact, relating to the manner in which data were collected rather than reflecting any true changes; however, it has been replicated in studies from the US.[35] Whatever the current trends, there is ample evidence that, in England and Wales today, far too many children and young people are abused or neglected by their parents and caregivers.

Uncertain definitions and their consequences

One reason why it is not easy to calculate the prevalence of abuse and neglect is that definitions vary. For instance, in view of emerging evidence concerning their long-term impact on children and young people's welfare, it could be argued that greater attention should be given to bullying by peers and siblings, teenage intimate partner violence and neighbourhood violence.[36] If the numbers of children experiencing these types of maltreatment were routinely included in calculations, the apparent prevalence would greatly increase, as the statistics shown above only refer to abuse and neglect by parents and caregivers.

Definitions also vary between cultures. In the UK, for instance, the physical abuse of children was not recognized as a form of maltreatment until the 1880s, and smacking was considered to be acceptable parental behaviour for at least another century. It is still legal in this country, although it has been outlawed in much of the rest of Europe. Witnessing intimate partner violence has only relatively recently been recognized as a cause for concern. The parameters have changed as the impact on children's welfare has become better understood. In some cultures both the physical abuse of children and intimate partner violence are still regarded as normative adult behaviours, with the result that identifying maltreatment and developing an appropriate response becomes a complex issue in a multi-cultural society. Nevertheless, it is possible to make too much of cultural differences: abuse is often defined as a failure to meet the child's developmental needs, and there is a very significant cross-cultural consensus about the basic needs for healthy child development.[37]

Understanding how abuse and neglect should be defined is not simply an academic issue. Maltreatment is known to have a negative impact on children's physical, cognitive, emotional and social development; it is linked with conduct disorder, emotional disorders, delinquency and criminal behaviour, risk-taking behaviours, addiction and suicide. The consequences may persist into adulthood and be linked to adverse outcomes such as physical and mental health problems, reduced employment opportunity, social exclusion, intimate partner violence and abusive parenting.[38] Abuse is therefore a public health issue, in that its prevalence has a negative impact not only on the individuals concerned, but also on the welfare of society as a whole. At a population level, understanding what constitutes abuse is a prerequisite to first calculating its prevalence and then developing universal, targeted and specialist services that aim to reduce it. At an individual or familial level, understanding what constitutes abuse is a necessary step in identifying whether a child is being subject to maltreatment, and taking appropriate action.

Focus on neglect and emotional abuse

The severity and persistence of neglect and emotional abuse were key factors in the death of Victoria Climbié. One of the questions raised by the subsequent inquiry was how a large number of professionals from a range of disciplines had been in contact with this child and yet failed to recognize the extent of her maltreatment. This is why, although some cover a wider range of maltreatment, many studies in the Research Initiative have a specific focus on these two types of abuse. Moreover, while there is considerable consensus both nationally and in other Western societies concerning what constitutes physical and sexual abuse, there is much less common agreement concerning the definitions and the thresholds for emotional abuse and neglect.[39] Both the systematic reviews of literature[40,41] that explored the evidence in this area concluded that neglect and emotional abuse are associated with the most damaging long-term consequences, yet they are also the most difficult to identify. Studies in this Overview provide evidence of the consequences of failing to understand these issues. However, maltreatment is often multi-faceted, and there are many messages which apply equally to the identification and response to physical and sexual abuse.

Defining neglect and emotional abuse

Government guidance provides descriptions of both emotional abuse and neglect.[42] Emotional abuse is described as:

> The persistent emotional maltreatment of a child such as to cause severe and persistent adverse effects on the child's emotional development. It may involve conveying to children that they are worthless or unloved, inadequate, or valued only insofar as they meet the needs of another person. It may include not giving the child opportunities to express their views, deliberately silencing them or making fun of what they say or how they communicate. It may feature age or developmentally inappropriate expectations being imposed on children. These may include interactions that are beyond the child's developmental capability, as well as overprotection and limitation of exploration and learning, or preventing the child participating in normal social interaction. It may involve seeing or hearing the ill-treatment of another. It may involve serious bullying (including cyber-bullying), causing children frequently to feel frightened or in danger, or the exploitation or corruption of children. Some level of emotional abuse is involved in all types of maltreatment of a child, though it may occur alone.

Neglect is described as:

> The persistent failure to meet a child's basic physical and/or psychological needs, likely to result in the serious impairment of the child's health or development. Neglect may occur during pregnancy as a result of maternal substance abuse. Once a child is born, neglect may involve a parent or carer failing to:
>
> • provide adequate food, clothing or shelter (including exclusion from home or abandonment)
>
> • protect a child from physical and emotional harm or danger
>
> • ensure adequate supervision (including the use of inadequate caregivers)
>
> • ensure access to appropriate medical care or treatment.
>
> It may also include neglect of, or unresponsiveness to, a child's basic emotional needs.

We have quoted these descriptions in full to demonstrate how comprehensive and detailed they are. Yet even with such precise guidelines, professionals find it difficult to identify these types of abuse and to decide when a threshold for action has been reached. The difficulties arise for a number of reasons:

- Both types of maltreatment are heterogeneous classifications that cover a wide range of issues as is evident from the descriptions above.

- Both emotional abuse and neglect are chronic conditions that can persist over months and years. Professionals can become accustomed to their manifestations and accepting of the lack of positive change: the serious case review into the death of Peter Connelly, for instance, found that professionals were too accepting of low parenting standards.[43] These can include poor supervision resulting in numerous 'falls' and bruises; poor cleanliness of the house and poorly cared-for animals; persistent and recurrent infestations such as head lice; loss of weight and failure to thrive; poor dentition; skin problems and nappy rashes; delayed motor and speech development; and self-harm and running away in teenagers.

- Both types of maltreatment can persist for many years without leading to the type of crisis that demands immediate, authoritative action. Without such a crisis it can be difficult to argue that a threshold for a child protection plan or court action has been reached.

- Both types of maltreatment are also closer to normative parental behaviour patterns than physical or sexual abuse, in that most parents will, on occasion, neglect or emotionally maltreat their children to a greater or lesser degree. It is the persistence, the frequency, the enormity and the pervasiveness of these behaviours that make them abusive. However, such factors are difficult to pin down with any degree of clarity and this makes it difficult both for practitioners and the courts to determine when a threshold has been reached.

The neglect of adolescents is a major issue that frequently goes unnoticed.[44] Adolescents can be neglected by services as well as by their families. Better understanding of what constitutes adolescent neglect might lead to prompter identification and service response.

It is clear that neglect is age-related, and as children grow older it is defined not only by parental behaviours but also by the way in which young people experience them. However, some of the fundamental questions have barely been considered. For instance, there is little consensus as to what constitutes an acceptable level of supervision as children grow older. At what ages can young people be safely allowed out on their own? Be left alone for the day? Be left alone overnight? When should a GP be worried about a request for contraceptives? When should they ask the identity of the person accompanying the child? Although at a familial level appropriate responses to such questions will be shaped by young people's levels of maturity and experience, nevertheless at a societal level neglect would be better understood if there were some open discussion concerning what is acceptable and what is not.

Introduction to the studies

Eleven studies were commissioned as part of the Safeguarding Children Research Initiative. This Overview focuses on the findings from these studies, but also refers extensively to a further four important research studies that also reported during the same time period. Brief resumés of all 15 studies are given in Appendix 3, which also includes details of how the full reports can be accessed. In order to make it easier for the reader to identify them – and to make this Overview more readable – these studies are referred to by their abbreviated titles in the following pages. The studies are listed in Table 1.1.

Training materials

The evidence from the studies has also been used as the basis for developing the following training materials:

Daniel, B., Taylor, J. and Scott, J. (forthcoming) *Training Resources on Child Neglect for a Multi-Agency Audience.*

Hicks, L. and Stein, M. (2010) *Neglect Matters: A Multi-Agency Guide for Professionals Working Together on Behalf of Teenagers.* London: Department for Children, Schools and Families.

Hicks, L. and Stein, M. in collaboration with the Children's Society and the NSPCC (2010) *Neglect Matters: A Guide for Young People about Neglect.* London: ChildLine.

Carpenter, J., Patsios, D., Szilassy, E. and Hackett, S. (2011) *Connect, Share and Learn: A Toolkit for Evaluating the Outcomes of Inter-Agency Training to Safeguard Children.* London: NSPCC.

Table 1.1: Studies included in the Safeguarding Children Research Initiative (all available at www.education.gov.uk/researchandstatistics/research/scri)*

Study		Full title	Authors
Identification and initial response to abuse or neglect			
1	Recognition of Neglect Review[†]	Noticing and Helping the Neglected Child: Literature Review	B. Daniel, J. Taylor, J. Scott
2	Recognition of Adolescent Neglect Review[†]	Neglected Adolescents: A Literature Review	M. Stein, G. Rees, L. Hicks, S. Gorin
3	Emotional Abuse Recognition Training Evaluation Study[†]	Does Training and Consultation in a Systematic Approach to Emotional Abuse (FRAMEA) Improve the Quality of Children's Services?	D. Glaser, V. Prior, K. Auty, S. Tilki
Effective interventions after abuse or neglect has been recognized			
4	Neglected Children Reunification Study[†]	Case Management and Outcomes for Neglected Children Returned to their Parents: A Five Year Follow-Up Study	E. Farmer, E. Lutman
5	Home or Care? Study[†]	Maltreated Children in the Looked After System: A Comparison of Outcomes for Those Who Go Home and Those Who Do Not	J. Wade, N. Biehal, N. Farrelly, I. Sinclair
6	Significant Harm of Infants Study[‡]	Infants Suffering, or Likely to Suffer, Significant Harm: A Prospective Longitudinal Study	H. Ward, R. Brown, D. Westlake, E.R. Munro
7	Emotional Abuse Intervention Review[†]	Safeguarding Children from Emotional Abuse: What Works?	J. Barlow, A. Schrader McMillan
8	Physical Abuse Intervention Review[†]	Systematic Reviews of Interventions Following Physical Abuse: Helping Practitioners and Expert Witnesses Improve the Outcomes of Child Abuse	P. Montgomery, F. Gardner, P. Ramchandani, G. Bjornstad
Effective inter-agency and inter-disciplinary working to safeguard children			
9	Inter-Agency Training Evaluation Study[†]	Organisation, Outcomes and Costs of Inter-Agency Training for Safeguarding and Promoting the Welfare of Children	J. Carpenter, S. Hackett, D. Patsios, E. Szilassy
10	Information Needs of Parents at Early Recognition Study[†]	Understanding Parents' Information Needs and Experiences where Professional Concerns Regarding Non-Accidental Injury were not Substantiated	S. Komulainen, L. Haines

11	General Practitioner Tensions in Safeguarding Study[†]	The Child, the Family and the GP: Tensions and Conflicts of Interest in Safeguarding Children	H. Tompsett, M. Ashworth, C. Atkins, L. Bell, A. Gallagher, M. Morgan, P. Wainwright
12	Local Safeguarding Children Boards Study[†]	Effectiveness of the New Local Safeguarding Children Boards in England	A. France, E.R. Munro, A. Waring
13	Analysis of Serious Case Reviews 2003–5[‡]	Analysing Child Deaths and Serious Injury through Abuse and Neglect: What can we Learn? A Biennial Analysis of Serious Case Reviews 2003–2005	M. Brandon, P. Belderson, C. Warren, D. Howe, R. Gardner, J. Dodsworth, J. Black
14	Analysis of Serious Case Reviews 2005–7[‡]	Understanding Serious Case Reviews and their Impact: A Biennial Analysis of Serious Case Reviews 2005–07	M. Brandon, S. Bailey, P. Belderson, R. Gardner, P. Sidebotham, J. Dodsworth, C. Warren, J. Black
15	Sure Start Local Programmes Safeguarding Study[‡]	Understanding the Contribution of Sure Start Local Programmes to the Task of Safeguarding Children's Welfare. Report of the National Evaluation	J. Tunstill, D. Allnock

[*]   See Appendix 3 for summary information about each study. All unpublished reports and research briefs can be downloaded from the website, which also has full details of all published material. Some of the titles have changed from their originals upon publication, as indicated in the Appendix.

[†]   Studies commissioned as part of the Initiative.

[‡]   Studies that reported during the time period.

The nature of the evidence

What topics do the studies cover? How far do they complement one another?

All the studies covered by this Overview aim to identify how children might be better safeguarded in the three key areas of recognition, effective intervention and inter-agency working. However, within these areas they cover a wide range of subjects and employ a number of different methodological designs:

- Two studies explore the question of how maltreatment might be recognized and responded to more promptly and effectively. These are *systematic reviews of evidence* gathered from other, primary, sources. The *Recognition of Neglect* and the *Recognition of Adolescent Neglect Reviews* focus specifically on neglect; as well as exploring the effectiveness of interventions, these studies also raise questions concerning definitions and thresholds.

- The *Sure Start Local Programmes Safeguarding Study* focuses on the impact of an initiative to provide targeted services to prevent abuse and maltreatment. This is an issue that was also touched on by many other studies in the Research Initiative. This is a *mixed methods* study utilizing qualitative data from documents and interviews and quantitative data from a study of referrals.

- Three *longitudinal cohort studies* explore the impact of general interventions from social workers and their colleagues. The *Neglected Children Reunification*, the *Home or Care?* and the *Significant Harm of Infants Studies* all use designs that are mainly *prospective*. All three studies follow a *mixed methods* design, making use of both quantitative and qualitative data.

- Two studies, the *Emotional Abuse Intervention Review* and the *Physical Abuse Intervention Review*, focus on the impact of more specific interventions. These are *systematic reviews* of primary evidence.

- Two studies explore the impact of training: the *Emotional Abuse Recognition Training Evaluation Study* utilizes a *quasi-experimental* design to assess the impact of a new framework for the recognition, assessment and management of emotional abuse on professional practice. The *Inter-Agency Training Evaluation Study* assesses the impact of a number of training modules for Local Safeguarding Children Boards, using a *before and after* design.

- The *Local Safeguarding Children Boards Study* is an evaluation of the impact of new structures and processes for safeguarding and promoting the welfare of children, utilizing a *mixed methods* approach that includes surveys, case studies and social network analysis.

- Two other studies focus on specific issues. The *Information Needs of Parents at Early Recognition Study* is a small qualitative study that explores parents' experiences following unsubstantiated professional concerns about non-accidental injury to a child. The *General Practitioner Tensions in Safeguarding Study* is a qualitative study that analyses the complex factors that come into play when a GP has both a child and an alleged perpetrator as patients in child protection cases.

- The two *Analyses of Serious Case Reviews* utilize the same transactional ecological approach to analyse data from the reports of serious case reviews (2003–5; 2005–7). A third study, exploring data from 2008–9, was not published in time to be reviewed by the steering group, and is referenced, but not formally included, in the Research Initiative.[45]

Although the studies focus on specific topics, their subject matter overlaps and intertwines. Putting them all together is like viewing a building through many different windows, each showing a different perspective, but each shedding a different light on the wider picture. While each of the chapters in this Overview focuses on a selection of the studies, they are all informed by the full range of messages from the Research Initiative.

While the studies provide a wide range of research messages on the topics they cover, none of them focused specifically on the role of fathers or on ethnic and cultural diversity in relation to safeguarding issues. The studies provide a small number of messages that shed some light on these issues, but these are clearly areas where further research is required.

The Safeguarding Children Research Initiative focuses on government-funded research, commissioned by the Department of Health and the Department for Education. This type of research tends to be applied rather than theoretical, for it is intended to provide evidence that can have a direct impact on policy and practice. The studies inevitably reflect the government priorities for research, and are by no means representative of all research in this field in England and Wales, or indeed further afield. Where appropriate we have referenced the wider body of research that provides a context for these studies.

Strengths and weaknesses of the evidence

How strong is the evidence? Are the messages transferable to other contexts and settings? How valid are they? Can they be relied on?

Readers will want to understand what weight to give to the findings from the studies and how far they are relevant to a particular context. Both the research proposals and the final reports for all studies included in this Overview were subject to rigorous peer review. The messages drawn out from the reports were then identified and discussed by the Advisory and Implementation Group, whose role was to ensure that the implications of the findings were presented in such a way as to be properly understood by the different professional groups to which they apply. The reader should therefore regard this Overview as presenting robust research findings whose relevance to practice has already been extensively scrutinized. The events that led to the Research Initiative raised a large number of questions concerning the effectiveness of the full spectrum of structures, processes and services in place to safeguard children from abuse and neglect. Numerous questions were asked about the evidence base; as the preceding paragraphs show, a wide variety of methodologies has been utilized in trying to answer them.

The four *systematic reviews of evidence* explored extensive secondary data on trials and evaluations conducted on a variety of programmes to identify those which appear to be most likely to promote change. They were commissioned in the place of primary evaluations on the grounds that the Research Initiative would provide a more useful evidence base if it included information on a wide range of interventions rather than shedding an intense light on the effectiveness of one or two. These reviews utilized an accepted hierarchy of evidence to identify interventions that had been rigorously evaluated. This is discussed further in Chapter 5.

The evidence from the reviews demonstrates that there has been, as yet, very little methodologically sound evaluative research to identify 'what works' in safeguarding children from abuse and maltreatment. While such reviews initially identify relatively large numbers of studies within the subject area, the vast majority are of insufficient methodological rigour and are filtered out of the final selection. For instance, the initial search strategy in the *Recognition of Neglect Review* identified a total of 20,480 studies that originally appeared to meet the inclusion criteria, yet only 63 papers represented primary studies of sufficient quality to merit further scrutiny. However, if the criteria for inclusion are relaxed, less dependable evidence, that may be of limited validity, reliability and generalizability, may be included.

Even those studies that are sufficiently sound methodologically to merit inclusion in the systematic reviews may still have their weaknesses. Some of the best conducted randomized controlled trials are only able to recruit very small numbers and/or suffer considerable attrition at follow-up. Many fail to clarify their terms: neglect and emotional abuse are particularly poorly defined, and are often conflated with other forms of maltreatment. There is also a tendency for studies to use a range of proxy measures rather than directly observe the most relevant outcomes, such as continuing maltreatment or its impact on the child. Moreover, a vast array of different outcome measures are employed and this can restrict attempts to compare findings. Studies also generally focus on one discipline, thereby ignoring the many factors at play as services become more closely integrated.

The *systematic reviews* also demonstrate that even well-conducted interventions which can be shown to produce positive changes do not necessarily have a lasting impact. Those evaluations that include a later follow-up often find that initial improvements are subsequently lost over the following six months or so. Thus where the evidence base is sound, the data are not always encouraging.

While formal trials of specific interventions are common in the area of health, evaluations of broader interventions from social workers and their colleagues are still very much in their infancy in the UK. At the time of writing, randomized controlled trials of specific interventions such as Multi-Dimensional Treatment Foster Care[46] and Multi-Systemic Therapy[47] are under way, but interventions such as returning children home from care or accommodation or placing infants for adoption cannot be easily evaluated in this way. Randomly assigning children to such interventions, which will have a far-reaching impact on the rest of their lives, is difficult to justify ethically unless we are certain that we genuinely do not know which are likely to be the most beneficial not just for one child but for the whole group of potential participants. Moreover, there are substantial differences within such interventions and between the children concerned, so that it is difficult to compare like with like. Until relatively recently, studies in this area were largely descriptive. However, the three empirical studies in the Initiative that focus on these issues all improve on the existing evidence base and produce sophisticated, robust findings. The *Home or Care?* and the *Significant Harm of Infants Studies* both introduce comparative elements, demonstrating how outcomes for children who return home differ from those who remain looked after, or showing how infants in families where there are different degrees of risk of significant harm follow different life trajectories. The small sample in the latter study reflects the huge ethical and practical obstacles to accessing the very vulnerable population studied; the key findings would merit further testing with a larger database.

Understanding effective inter-agency and inter-disciplinary working is a multi-faceted issue, and research in this area is still under-developed. The mixed methods and the small qualitative studies that explore this area either identify themes that should be tested out with larger quantitative studies, or, as in the *Local Safeguarding Children Boards Study*, use a variety of methods to explore several different issues within a wide area of service development.

Conclusion

This Overview explores the messages from a programme of 15 research studies and discusses their implications for the development of policy and practice in identifying and responding to maltreatment (Chapter 2) and in the development of: universal and targeted services to prevent its occurrence (Chapter 3); social work interventions to keep children safe (Chapter 4); and specific interventions for children and families with additional or complex needs (Chapter 5). Policy and practice for safeguarding children will only develop successfully within a context of effective inter-agency working, an issue that runs through all the chapters, but is explored in depth in Chapter 6.

Key messages from Chapter 1

- 'Children', as discussed here, means those unborn, babies, children and young people under 18 years old, all of whom may be subject to maltreatment. The group may also include maltreated young people and their own children.

- Emotional abuse and neglect are far-reaching and malignant in their effects, and may or may not accompany physical or sexual abuse. Early detection and long-term support can make an enormous difference to children's developmental progress.

- Many more children are maltreated than come to the attention of statutory services.

- Reduction of the role of central government and increased diversity at local level will have implications for safeguarding children in the future.

- The 15 studies covered by the Overview cover a wide range of topics in the themes of: identification and initial response to abuse and neglect; effective interventions after maltreatment has been identified; and effective inter-agency and inter-disciplinary working to safeguard children.

- The range of different research methodologies reflects the diversity of the questions they seek to answer.

Identification and Initial Response

- This chapter draws largely on the evidence from the *Recognition of Neglect Review*,[48] the *Recognition of Adolescent Neglect Review*[49] and the two *Analyses of Serious Case Reviews (2003–5 and 2005–7)*.[50,51]

- This chapter has important messages for all those who have responsibility for safeguarding and promoting the welfare of children.

- It also has specific messages for the following professional groups:

  o Local Safeguarding Children Boards (all sections)

  o policymakers, commissioners and operational managers in adult health and social care; children's health and social care; the police; and education (sections on consequences of neglect and emotional abuse; risk factors associated with neglect and emotional abuse; recognition by professionals; professional responses: to refer or not to refer)

  o practitioners in adult health, mental health and social care; children's health, mental health and social care; education; the police; and the family justice system (all sections).

Introduction

Chapter 1 explored some of the issues that make it difficult to define both neglect and emotional abuse. It is not always easy to distinguish between these two types of maltreatment because they often overlap. Neglect cases almost always have an element of emotional abuse because parents who ignore their children's basic needs for food, warmth and safety are also indicating that they do not understand or care about them. However, emotional abuse can occur without neglect: children who are singled out and rejected are sometimes physically well looked after.

There are two reasons why it is important to recognize emotional abuse and neglect early and intervene appropriately. First, there is very robust evidence that both types of maltreatment have serious long-term consequences across all areas of children's health and development. The effects appear to be cumulative and pervasive, making early recognition and intervention necessary if the likelihood of longer-term harm is to be minimized. The impact of emotional abuse and neglect can be particularly severe when they occur during early childhood, because the first three years of life are critical to children's later development. Emotional abuse in a child's early years is thought to have such a far-reaching adverse impact because it compromises the infant's ability to resolve the primary developmental tasks of forming a secure attachment with an adult caregiver, learning to trust others and developing a sense of self-worth. Success in completing later developmental tasks in latency and adolescence is dependent on the extent to which the child has been able to complete the earlier tasks of infancy and toddlerhood.[52]

Second, prevalence studies conducted in many countries, including Great Britain and North America, suggest that the numbers of children and young people experiencing these forms of abuse may be up to ten times as many as those who come to the attention of professionals and receive services.[53] The *Analysis of Serious Case Reviews (2003–5)* found that only a small number (12%) of children who die or are seriously injured as a result of neglect are the subjects of child protection plans. Although the majority (83%) are known to them, little more than half of these children are receiving services from children's social care at the time of the incident. Emotional abuse and neglect only rarely result in specific incidents which prompt attention from those outside the family group; this makes it particularly important for practitioners in front-line services to be alert to the signs and symptoms they need to look out for.

Neglect and emotional abuse have received limited attention in the past. Both forms of maltreatment are particularly challenging for professionals to recognize because of their pervasive and long-term nature and the lack of physical signs and symptoms. But the long-term damage may be at least as serious as that from physical and sexual abuse. In fact these may be the most damaging forms of maltreatment because their consequences are the most far-reaching and difficult to overcome.[54] Before considering the evidence about how better recognition by professionals can be promoted, we shall briefly consider what the studies say about the impact of these forms of abuse on the child.

Consequences of neglect and emotional abuse

Why is it important for members of the community and professionals to be alert to the possibility of neglect and emotional abuse and to respond in appropriate ways? What do the studies tell us about the consequences and impact of these types of maltreatment?

Neglect and its impact

The *Neglected Children Reunification Study* provides a valuable summary of the impact of neglect on the child. We have drawn out the key points in the following paragraphs, but readers may wish to turn to the original for more comprehensive information.[55]

Whilst the psychobiology of neglect is not yet fully understood, it is likely that all forms result in serious, pervasive effects on a child's neurological and endocrine development. The neglected child's system of response to stress, through the hypothalamic-pituitary-adrenal axis (HPA), develops abnormally and this in turn results in increased vulnerability to a range of psychological, emotional and, probably, physical health problems throughout the lifespan. Both structural and functional abnormalities are found in maltreated children's brains. Changes are seen in the prefrontal cortex, corpus callosum and hippocampus – all areas concerned with emotional life and its regulation. Physical, behavioural, emotional and attachment systems are dependent on these structures functioning normally. There are therefore potentially highly damaging and long-term effects for those suffering neglect.[56]

These changes are thought to represent adaptations to the extreme stress of maltreatment, enabling the child to cope with an abusive and/or neglectful parenting environment to some degree. However, such resilience is accompanied by a greater likelihood of misperceiving and responding disproportionately to everyday encounters in social situations and problems in managing emotions such as fear and anger. Although research is still at an early stage, there is encouraging evidence that some maltreatment effects can be modified if the child's caretaking environment improves.[57]

Neglectful parenting

Neglectful parenting can also affect the essential processes of children's early attachment and subsequent development. Children who receive care which is unpredictable, rejecting or insensitive are more likely to develop attachments which are less secure.

Children who have experienced neglectful parenting may have poorer emotional knowledge and be less able to discriminate between different kinds of emotions. They may have lower self-esteem and higher levels of emotional problems. Neglected children tend to be more aggressive than children who are not neglected and are also more uncooperative and noncompliant. There is also a related impact on children's social development: the evidence suggests that neglected children are more withdrawn and socially isolated and less socially competent than their peers. Data from the large American longitudinal LONGSCAN sample[58] show that at the age of eight 'general neglect', as identified by child protection services, continues to be associated with behaviour problems, impaired socialization and problems with daily living skills.

The stage of life at which a child experiences neglectful parenting is important, as is the duration of the experience. Neglected children may experience a lack of stimulation in early childhood, resulting in delayed speech and language problems.

This means that these children start school at a disadvantage, and may be one reason why neglect has been shown to have a serious impact on educational achievement and cognitive development.[59]

The *Recognition of Adolescent Neglect Review* found that neglect is most damaging in both the early stages of life and in the teenage years. By adolescence 'neglect and/or neglectful parenting are associated with poorer physical and mental health, risky health behaviours, risks to safety including running away, poorer conduct and achievement at school, and negative behaviours such as offending and anti-social behaviour'.[60] Adolescents who have experienced neglect have shown higher ratings on measures of depression and hopelessness.

Risk of fatalities

The risk of fatalities from neglect is by no means negligible, and may be as high as that from physical abuse.[61] *The Analysis of Serious Case Reviews (2003–5)* found that neglect features in a third (52/161) of cases where children die or are seriously injured, although it is not always identified as the primary cause and this figure is likely to be a serious under-estimate.[62] Although children die from neglect primarily as a result of negligence (for instance from house fires, accidentally ingesting poison or overlying), persistent neglect may also feature in adolescent suicides.

Emotional abuse and its impact

Many authorities consider that emotional abuse is a component of all forms of child maltreatment.[63] There is powerful evidence of its harmful effects whether alone or associated with other forms of maltreatment. The *Emotional Abuse Intervention Review* provides a valuable summary of this evidence.[64] Emotional abuse is known to be particularly harmful when experienced in the first three years of life. It affects an infant's ability to form a secure attachment with an adult caregiver and to develop trust in others to provide a stable environment. Toddlers who experience rejection of their bids for attention will have difficulty in developing a sense of self-worth and belief in the availability of others. Emotional abuse may be the most damaging of all forms of maltreatment because it represents a direct attack on the child's needs for safety, love, belonging and wellbeing from their primary carer – the person who should be responsible for nurturing them and helping them to fulfil key developmental tasks. Children who are emotionally abused show early signs of problems through a steep decline in performance from as young as 9 to 18 months. One prospective study found that by 18 months of age emotionally abused children were showing evidence of anxious attachments, by 42 months they were observed to be 'more angry, non-compliant, lacking in persistence and displaying little positive affect', and in early school they were 'more socially withdrawn, unpopular with peers and in general exhibiting more problems of the internalizing type'.[65]

In adolescence emotionally abused children may display higher levels of social problems, such as delinquency and aggression; they may also be more prone to eating disorders. Retrospective studies have also identified specific and unique types of problem associated with emotional abuse compared with other forms of maltreatment, particularly aggression in later childhood and dissociation.

Emotionally abusive parenting

Emotional abuse results from the interplay of a variety of factors including parental issues. These may include learned behaviours, psychopathology and/or unmet emotional needs, and are often linked with mental health problems, drug and alcohol misuse and domestic violence.[66] Parents experiencing these problems can be cold and insensitive, emotionally unavailable and even hostile. The effect is harmful across all areas of children's development, affecting security of attachment, emotional development, behaviour, educational achievement and social and physical development. Emotionally abusive parenting is associated with a range of negative long-term outcomes for children such as anxiety and depression, shame and anger/hostility.

Risk of fatalities

Whilst emotional abuse on its own may be less likely than other forms of maltreatment to result in fatality as a result of carer action, it is known to be linked with children attempting suicide and suffering multiple mental health problems. One prospective follow-up study found that children who had been emotionally abused in early childhood reported more attempted suicides by adolescence. The majority received at least one diagnosis of mental illness and 73 per cent had two or more disorders.[67]

Thus both emotional abuse and neglect have potentially highly damaging consequences across all areas of children's development. Professionals (and members of the general public) need to be aware of them because they demonstrate the importance of recognizing and responding early to indicators of these types of maltreatment or the likelihood of their occurrence.

Risk factors associated with neglect and emotional abuse

What factors should alert practitioners to an increased likelihood of neglect and emotional abuse?

There are now a number of well-recognized factors in both children themselves, and their wider family and environment, that adversely impact on parental capacity and make emotional abuse and neglect more likely. Such risk factors do not mean that maltreatment is inevitable, but their presence, particularly in combination, increases its probability and should alert practitioners to look out for indicators that a child is suffering significant harm. There is common agreement across the studies that an ecological model is relevant to assessing both the likelihood of emotional abuse and neglect and the indicators that a child may be suffering significant harm. This is because an ecological framework encompasses a constellation of both positive and negative factors and therefore offers a valuable methodology for helping professionals to recognize the inter-relationship between them. The next section summarizes the evidence from the studies concerning risk factors and indicators, using domains from one such model: the *Framework for the Assessment of Children in Need and their Families*.[68]

Family and environmental factors
Family history and functioning
Parental problems such as mental illness, alcohol and drug misuse, domestic violence and learning disability are all known to increase the likelihood of children experiencing emotional abuse and neglect, particularly when they appear in combination. Cleaver, Unell and Aldgate[69] have brought together and analysed a comprehensive body of evidence of the ways in which these factors adversely affect parenting capacity. We have tried to draw together the key messages in the following paragraphs, but readers may wish to turn to the original for more detailed information. Several of the studies in the Research Initiative, notably the *Neglected Children Reunification Study*, also summarize these issues.[70]

Parental mental health
Two thirds of adults who have been diagnosed with psychiatric disorders are parents of children and young people who are less than 18 years old. However, the research makes it clear that the risk of children being harmed is not inevitable and that not all mentally ill parents neglect or emotionally abuse their children.[71]

Nevertheless, parental mental health problems can lead to a deterioration in parenting capacity. For example, parents may become preoccupied and depressed and be unresponsive to their children's physical and emotional needs. Therefore those offering adult mental health services should be highly alert to the possibility of neglect and emotional abuse and be ready to ensure that children's needs are actively addressed. There is evidence that risk of harm can be mediated by appropriate psychiatric treatment; it can also be reduced by protective factors in the environment such as strong social and family support systems or the absence of financial worries, as well as individual children's coping skills. On the other hand, the absence of social and family support and the presence of financial stressors and/or inter-partner conflict increase the likelihood of children being harmed.

The ways in which parents' mental health problems may impact on their children also vary with age. The adverse effects of maternal caregiver depression on the wellbeing of children, and in particular the under-fives, is well documented[72] and has specifically been shown to be linked to physical neglect, neglect more generally and emotional abuse. On the other hand, adolescents may be more likely to take on caring roles in addition to not always being adequately cared for themselves, and may lack support and supervision at critical phases in their development.

The *Emotional Abuse Intervention Review* provides more specific information about the impact of maternal depression, anxiety and psychotic disorders on parenting behaviour in relation to emotional abuse.

Maternal depression

Maternal depression is associated with lower levels of maternal sensitivity and, to a lesser degree, the mother's disengagement with the child. Lower maternal sensitivity may result in less empathetic understanding of toddlers, higher intrusiveness, negative regard and harshness, lower warmth, more negative perceptions of infants' behaviour and more hostile feelings towards them. The timing and severity of the depression is important. It affects all age groups but seems to be most harmful in the first five years of a child's life. However, the impact on older children should not be under-estimated as maternal depression is also associated with fewer positive and more negative behaviours toward adolescents.

Anxiety disorders

Amongst the most widespread mental health problems are anxiety disorders, including panic disorder and phobias. Whilst there has been little research specifically on the effect of anxiety disorder on parenting behaviour, parents who suffer from severe anxiety have been observed to display some behaviours which may result in emotional abuse of their children. For instance, such parents have been observed to be highly critical, to express less affection, smile less, be more likely to over-react during interactions with their children, and appear to be less likely to encourage emotional autonomy, by not soliciting their child's views or tolerating differences of opinion.

Psychotic disorders

At the most serious end of mental health problems, psychotic disorders which involve distortions of thought, perception and communication, and significant restrictions in the range and intensity of emotional expression, are associated with greater difficulties in fulfilling daily parenting roles. Such disorders are highly significantly associated with social services supervision and practitioners' concerns about emotional responsiveness, practical baby care, and perceived risks of harm to the baby.[73]

Substance and alcohol misuse

An estimated 250,000 to 350,000 children in the UK have parents who are problematic drug users.[74] About four times as many (1.3 million) children live with parents who are thought to misuse alcohol. Drug and alcohol misuse are widely recognized as serious risk factors in child maltreatment. They can impact on children before birth, and in extreme cases result in foetal alcohol[75] or neonatal abstinence syndrome.[76] Infants who have been exposed to drugs or alcohol *in utero* may experience withdrawal symptoms and distressed behaviour after birth, as well as possibly long-term consequences for their future health and wellbeing.[77]

Substance and alcohol misuse may have an adverse impact on parenting capacity because parents become preoccupied with their own needs and are unable to focus consistently on the needs of their children. Living standards can be adversely affected if family income is used to sustain excessive alcohol or drug consumption. In order to increase their income, substance-misusing parents may also become involved in criminal activities such as shoplifting, drug dealing and prostitution; as a result children may become exposed to violence and to inappropriate sexual activity. Studies have shown an association between parental substance misuse and neglect, for children's basic needs for food, warmth and hygiene may go unnoticed or unmet. Used needles and syringes may pose a risk of harm to small children, and a lack of supervision may encourage experimentation. There is some evidence that those parents whose 'principal attachment is to a substance' may have difficulty in forming attachments with their children.[78] Older children report the significant impact of parental substance misuse on their lives and can often find themselves caring not only for themselves but also for their parents.[79] Unsurprisingly, substance misuse is prevalent in families who come to the attention of services. Two thirds of the children in the *Neglected Children Reunification Study* had parents who misused substances. Parents in this study who misused alcohol often very severely neglected their children and supervised them inadequately; there was also evidence of a considerable shortfall in services for these parents, with only 16 per cent of those who needed it receiving help. Parental substance misuse problems also feature in serious case reviews, highlighting that these difficulties can put children at risk of serious injury or death.

Substance misuse rarely occurs without other problems, such as those relating to mental health, family relationships and socio-economic circumstances. Rather than the drug use *per se*, it is the impact of inter-relationships between these risk factors in families where substance misuse is an issue that should be regarded as a signal of potential need for help.

Parental learning disability

There is no foundation for assuming that parents with learning disabilities will inevitably neglect or abuse their children. Most available research suggests that the majority of learning-disabled parents can provide adequate care, and that, with sufficient support, parental learning disability does not affect child outcomes. Where care is inadequate it is often the product of a constellation of factors, of which learning disability is just one among many others.

However, the presence of learning disability is a risk factor, especially when it is associated with difficulties such as a shortage of money, chronic housing problems and fraught relationships. Many adults with learning disabilities will have experienced difficulties in their childhood, which have left them with a poor sense of self-esteem and a low sense of their own worth. These may make them vulnerable to being entrapped into relationships with child sex abusers.[80] Learning disability also affects opportunities to learn how to parent. Some learning-disabled parents will have experienced poor parenting themselves or been brought up in a very sheltered and protected environment. Their life experiences may also have left them feeling powerless to deal effectively with negative attitudes and prejudices.

Neglect is the most common form of concern raised about children cared for by parents with learning disabilities. Neglect is more likely if the mother's resources, knowledge, skills and experiences are insufficient to meet the needs of her child and if she receives inadequate support in overcoming these adversities. Parents with learning disabilities may need long-term support over many years if they are to provide adequate care for their children. These parents often experience other problems such as mental ill health, social disadvantage and deprivation: the inter-relationship between these factors may lie behind evidence that parents with learning disabilities may be more likely than others to have their children removed from their care.[81]

Domestic violence

Children are twice as likely to have neglect confirmed within their first five years if there is domestic abuse in the household. Domestic violence has been found to be present in the homes of just over half of those children who are identified by the NSPCC as child protection cases, or who are the subject of care proceedings or become the subjects of serious case reviews.[82]

Domestic violence is rarely confined to physical assaults but includes a mixture of physical and psychological violence. Female victims can be exposed to emotional abuse, constant criticism, undermining and humiliation, all of which can have a profound impact on their mental health. There is considerable evidence that women exposed to domestic violence suffer a loss of confidence, depression and feelings of degradation. They become isolated, suffer sleep loss and use medication and alcohol more frequently.

Domestic violence also affects parenting skills. It is closely associated with depression, and this can make parents irritable and angry with children and less likely to be emotionally available and affectionate. They may have difficulty in organizing day-to-day living. When parents are preoccupied with their own feelings they may experience greater difficulty in responding to their child's needs. Cues are missed and the parent seems withdrawn and disengaged. In cases of maternal depression, children may be perceived as having behaviour problems that affect their parents' capacity to provide adequate guidance and boundaries. Feelings of inadequacy can affect parents' interactions with their children.

There is also a relationship between domestic violence and physical abuse of children. The *Analysis of Serious Case Reviews 2003–5* found that seven out of eight young children who are the subject of serious case reviews following physical assault come from families where domestic violence is an issue. Such parents are often known to probation, the police or adult services, but not to children's social care.

While the presence of domestic violence increases the risk of physical abuse and neglect, *witnessing domestic violence* is, in itself, a form of emotional abuse. Attacks on a parent almost always frighten children even if the child is not the direct or indirect target, and a parent (most frequently, but not invariably, the male partner) will sometimes exploit a mother's or child's fears for each other and use threats or actual violence as part of a pattern of aggression. Witnessing domestic violence undermines children's emotional wellbeing and healthy development; there is evidence that even babies are adversely affected by this particularly harmful form of abuse.

Economic and neighbourhood factors

Widespread poverty, housing stress (e.g. residential instability, vacant housing), and drug and alcohol availability are all known to add to the stresses of living in a particular neighbourhood, and increase the likelihood of abuse and neglect. Areas where these factors are prevalent are consistently shown to have higher rates of child maltreatment, irrespective of the way this is measured.[83]

The *Recognition of Neglect Review* emphasizes the pervasive impact of poverty on parents' neglectful behaviour. Poverty is a stressor that makes neglect more likely, but it is not, in itself, a causal factor: not all poor parents neglect their children, but the majority of neglectful families who come to the attention of children's social care are poor.

The *Recognition of Adolescent Neglect Review* found that approximately 2 per cent of the population of young people in England have been forced to leave home for one night or more before their 16th birthdays.[84] Poverty is one of the many stressors identified amongst young people running away or being forced to leave home during the teenage years, for it can lead to or exacerbate tensions between teenagers and birth parents or their partners.[85]

Social isolation/informal support

Informal support from family, friends and neighbourhood networks is recognized to be a protective factor in reducing the likelihood of maltreatment. The converse – social isolation and lack of social support – is a further risk factor that makes neglect, in particular, more likely. Neglectful mothers have been found to have fewer members in their social networks and to perceive themselves as being less supported (and more often excluded) than those who do not neglect their children. These perceptions appear to be an accurate reflection of reality, and it seems probable that neglectful parents are the most socially isolated of all types of maltreating parents.[86]

The *Significant Harm of Infants Study* suggests that one reason why mothers who have had previous experiences of care or accommodation may neglect their children is that they lack informal support from either their birth families or from substitutes such as previous foster carers. Many of the abusive or neglectful parents in this study had been maltreated in their own childhood. They frequently had dysfunctional relationships with their own parents, who in turn had often been perpetrators or had failed to protect them from abuse. They also had diminished opportunities for supportive relationships within their extended families, as contact had been severed with other family members who had also sometimes been perpetrators.

Child's developmental needs: disabilities

Whilst factors within the child's family and environment may increase the risk of maltreatment, some children are also more likely to be abused or neglected than others. All the studies draw attention to the greater likelihood of disabled children being maltreated. The *Recognition of Adolescent Neglect Review* found that disabled children are more vulnerable to abuse and neglect because inadequate or poorly co-ordinated services can leave their families unsupported and isolated. Maltreatment of disabled children is also easier to conceal, as communication difficulties may prevent them from revealing what is happening and indicators of abuse or neglect may be mistakenly attributed to their impairment.[87] The associations identified between disability and maltreatment do not imply a one-directional causal link. A US national incidence study indicates that, based on professional assessments, disability can be both a risk factor for, and a consequence of, neglect.[88]

Child development indicators of emotional abuse or neglect

While constellations of the risk factors discussed above should alert professionals to an increased likelihood of emotional abuse or neglect, the studies also identify several symptoms and signs that may indicate that maltreatment is taking place. Indicators of maltreatment may be evident in all aspects of children's development.

However, just as risk factors are not indicators or necessarily predictors of emotional abuse and neglect, so indicators are often non-specific and may be the result of a wide range of underlying problems of which maltreatment is one possibility;[89] there is also some overlap between those indicators that suggest that abuse is taking place and those discussed at the beginning of this chapter that show the longer-term outcomes of maltreatment on children's health and development.

> How may neglect and/or emotional abuse be indicated in children's physical development?

Faltering growth

Faltering growth was previously known as non-organic failure to thrive. It is a complex issue and maltreatment is one of many potential causes. However, it can be an indicator of emotional abuse or neglect. In such circumstances, acts of omission, specifically in terms of meeting a child's emotional as well as physical needs, may result in an infant falling to the bottom 5 per cent or lower on established growth charts.[90] In the months before his death Peter Connelly's weight plummeted from the 75th to the 9th centile. His dramatic weight loss was noted on two separate occasions by the health visitor and by a school nurse, but did not result in immediate action.[91]

Very small children who are not fed eventually cease to cry, as did two of the babies in the *Significant Harm of Infants Study*: this is probably a dissociative reaction to anxiety, but may be falsely regarded as a sign of contentment.

Burns

Burns are an important physical indicator associated with neglect and maltreatment. The *Recognition of Neglect Review* identified two studies conducted by burns units, respectively in the US and the UK, which offer a sobering perspective on ways in which neglect may be signalled. The American evidence shows that burns due to both abuse and neglect are likely to be scalds. The majority of the neglected children who suffer burns have been identified as at risk of harm before their injuries, yet are returned to their original environments. Where children suffer neglect, families often delay seeking help; neglected children are less likely than other maltreated children to keep appointments or to receive adequate wound care.[92]

The UK evidence corroborates these findings, but also indicates that where neglect is an issue it is more likely that:

- the child will not have been given first aid at the time

- the parents/carers will have put off seeking help for over 24 hours
- the burns will be deeper.[93]

How may neglect and/or emotional abuse be indicated in children's cognitive, emotional, behavioural and social development?

The evidence suggests that indicators of possible emotional abuse or neglect can be manifest quite early in life. Problems with infant attachment behaviour can be an early sign of emotional maltreatment. Disorganized/disoriented attachment patterns in young children are revealed through odd behaviours, such as repeated incomplete approaches to parents and failing to seek contact when very distressed. These appear to reflect fear and confusion on the part of the infant.[94] This pattern of attachment is thought to occur when the person from whom the infant seeks secutiry also becomes a source of fear.[95]

Neglect may be one of the many possible causes of delays in language and communication, socio-emotional adjustment and behavioural problems. The *Recognition of Neglect Review* suggests that neglect may be manifest in behavioural patterns of children as young as three – a point corroborated by the *Significant Harm of Infants Study*, which found that several children who had suffered neglect since birth were showing signs of developmental delay and/or behavioural problems by their third birthday. These factors are likely to compromise children's early experiences at nursery and school, as they will adversely impact on the early stages of literacy and numeracy and on children's acceptance by their peers. However, the findings from a range of studies suggest that there are opportunities in the school setting for teachers to be alert to these possible indicators of neglect and emotional abuse.

Drawings by maltreated children are also significantly different from those by non-maltreated children. Although these differences are not sufficiently distinctive to provide a 'diagnosis', the evidence suggests that drawings could be usefully included as part of an assessment of possible neglect.[96]

Adolescents signal neglect by behaviours which are harmful to them and are considered anti-social. For example, there is strong evidence of a relationship between neglectful parenting and the kinds of risk-taking behaviours that are likely to affect young people's health, such as drug and alcohol use in early adolescence, although this is less evident as young people grow older.[97] Maltreatment during adolescence increases the chances of arrest, violent offending and drug use. Neglect has the strongest association with violent behaviour in late adolescence, although the impact dissipates somewhat in early adulthood. On the other hand physical neglect at home is associated with children and young people being stigmatized and bullied.

Assessing risk factors and indicators of maltreatment

Interplay of multiple factors

It is rare for there to be a single clear pathway leading to either emotional abuse or neglect. If practitioners are to recognize the signs of both types of abuse, they need to be alert to the interplay of the multiple risk and protective factors that make such forms of maltreatment more – or less – likely. Practitioners should therefore be cautious about making assumptions about the impact on children of a single issue such as parental mental health or learning disability, because it is the cumulative impact of combinations of factors that has been found to increase the likelihood of harm for children.[98] This makes the task of recognizing and responding to these types of maltreatment particularly challenging, as does their pervasive nature and the lack of clear signs or specific incidents.

Frameworks and models for conceptualizing neglect and emotional abuse

We have already seen that an ecological model is relevant in helping professionals to make assessments of emotional abuse and neglect. The model provided in the *Framework for the Assessment of Children in Need and their Families*[99] offers practitioners a conceptual framework which covers relevant multiple dimensions to assess individual children's and families' cases. The dimensions of the assessment are presented in the form of a triangle with three inter-related domains: the developmental needs of children, the capacity of parents or caregivers to respond appropriately to these needs and the impact of wider family and environmental factors on both parenting capacity and the child's development. The Core Assessment Records intended to facilitate recordings from assessments using the Assessment Framework offer a set of age-specific indicators, covering a range of dimensions relevant to all forms of maltreatment including neglect. These support assessments of levels of care and of the extent to which children's needs are met. They thus offer the potential for a consistent method of defining neglect and emotional maltreatment in relation to individual cases. They have been found to be particularly useful in assessing neglect in adolescents. However, while the Core Assessment Records offer a tool that should be valuable in identifying neglect, the *Significant Harm of Infants Study* found that in practice they are often missing from case files or poorly completed.

Building on the ecological model underpinning the Assessment Framework, the *Analysis of Serious Case Reviews 2003–5* suggests that practitioners might adopt an 'ecological transactional' perspective in analysing their assessments. This approach permits an analysis of accumulating risks of harm.

Such an approach would involve:

- good-quality social and family history taking, including information about parents' childhood relationships and behavioural background

- analysing the interactive effect of vulnerabilities and risks
- better understanding of the ecology of child abuse and neglect.

Their recommendations are as follows:

> Information and evidence should be collected…based on clearly understood developmental and psychosocial theories, including the relationship and developmental histories that have shaped parents, families and children.

> The ecological developmental framework should also provide a conceptual structure and language for presenting a case formulation that should include (i) a clear case summary and synthesis of knowledge brought together by the assessment, (ii) a description of the problem/concern, (iii) a hypothesis about the nature, origins and cause of the need/problem/concern, and (iv) a plan of the proposed decisions and/or interventions.[100]

Two important training packs designed to help practitioners identify and respond specifically to neglect have been commissioned within this Initiative. Both *Training Resources on Child Neglect for a Multi-Agency Audience*[101] and *Neglect Matters*[102] are multi-agency resources for professionals working together on behalf of neglected children and young people; *Training Resources* covers all aspects of neglect, while *Neglect Matters* focuses specifically on teenagers.

Signalling the need for help: direct approaches

In what ways do families directly and indirectly signal their need for help?

We know that emotional abuse and neglect (as well as other forms of maltreatment) arise in families where there are multiple difficulties that may not be recognized by professionals until problems have accumulated and become severe. Some families may be aware of their growing problems and signal their need for help either directly or indirectly. This is an under-researched area.

The indicators of neglect and emotional abuse and their outcomes discussed above are one way in which children indirectly signal a need for help. Direct approaches are less common, for most children tend to protect their parents and do not talk about their family affairs easily. However, professionals should be aware that children often consult the school nurse more frequently when problems begin to arise. Young children often speak more openly than older age groups, and will more readily respond to questioning, but there are great individual differences.[103]

The *Recognition of Neglect Review* found that we do not know whether neglectful and emotionally abusive parents try and fail to seek help from professionals, or whether they tend not to do so. Nor do we know if they want help, but not on the terms in which it is offered. It is evident from the *Significant Harm of Infants Study* that such parents may have few friends or family members to whom they can turn for support, and may conceal their difficulties from professionals for fear that their children will be removed from their care – particularly if they have already had such an experience with an older child. This corroborates other evidence which suggests that, far from seeking help, neglectful families may be low users of universal services. Persistent failure to attend appointments for routine services such as immunization and hospital appointments should be seen by professionals as a sign of potential neglect. More than a third of the children whose cases were scrutinized in the *Analysis of Serious Case Reviews 2005–7* had a history of missed appointments for immunizations and developmental checks, while nearly half of their mothers had only sporadically attended antenatal appointments if they had gone at all.

The *Significant Harm of Infants Study* found that cases are often closed by social workers in the expectation that parents will contact the local Sure Start children's centre if problems recur. However, interviews with parents show that many are lacking in self-confidence and do not have the courage or the ability to make the effort to attend support services such as play groups, and, as noted above, are more likely to hide their difficulties than ask for help. The *Recognition of Neglect Review* found that, although the views of parents are important, this is another area where we have little information. The evidence suggests that substance-misusing parents, for example, understand how their addictive behaviour impacts on their children. They are also aware of what good parenting is but feel unable to fulfil this role adequately and may be unwilling to signal this to service providers. Likewise the *Emotional Abuse Intervention Review* found that, contrary to what is sometimes assumed, substance-misusing women often desire to be good mothers and can be aware of what good parenting involves, but feel unable to fulfil this role.[104]

The *Significant Harm of Infants Study* includes evidence from a group of parents whose children were likely to suffer significant harm, often as a result of their substance misuse. Many of these parents had been unable to acknowledge the harm their actions were causing their children at the time of the abuse, but in retrospect, after a child had been placed for adoption, some were able to accept the reasons for the separation.

Practitioners must work to determine levels of risk of harm that parents themselves can identify and use this information to inform their actions. A simple chart that would graphically demonstrate to neglectful parents the reasons why a child is considered to be likely to suffer significant harm and the actions they need to take to reduce this likelihood might be useful here. However, more evidence is needed to find out what kind of services such parents would be willing to access and what forms of help would enable them to move beyond having anxieties about their children's wellbeing to doing something about it.

Practitioners need to be alert to indicators which help them identify those parents who have the capacity and motivation to overcome adverse behaviours in order to meet the needs of their children. A useful model is provided by Morrison[105] who describes seven sequential elements of this process:

1. I accept that there is a problem.

2. I have some responsibility for the problem.

3. I have some discomfort about the impact, not only on myself, but also on my children.

4. I believe things must change.

5. I can be part of the solution.

6. I can make choices about how I address the issues.

7. I can see the first steps to making changes/can work with others to help me.

Recognition by professionals

How well equipped are professionals to recognize maltreatment and what judgements do they make when deciding what action to take in relation to concerns? What do we know about the ways professionals respond to concerns about abuse and neglect? What action do they take? Does this vary between professions? What seem to be the barriers and facilitators to action?

We have seen from the above short review of the evidence how constellations of risk factors as well as signs and symptoms from parents and children provide indicators of both the likelihood and the presence of neglect and emotional abuse that might be recognized by professionals. There is also some evidence about how families signal their need for help. But how well equipped are practitioners to recognize these factors? Do they act on their concerns and, if so, how? What do the studies tell us about factors which inhibit or encourage recognition and response?

Professional perspectives and a reluctance to act

It is evident from a number of the studies that professionals often have high thresholds for recognizing emotional abuse and neglect and are reluctant to act in response to suspicions in cases that are not clear cut.[106] The *Recognition of Neglect Review* identified a number of studies which compared the views of professionals about what constitutes neglectful parenting with those of the general public. Two American studies asked subjects to rate neglectful behaviours in terms of seriousness; in each case professionals indicated a higher threshold of concern than members of the public.[107,108] An English study also found that social workers consistently rated statements indicating neglect as less serious than a group of mothers.[109]

Absence of incidents

There are also other problems. We have already noted that clearly abusive incidents which precipitate a crisis are rare in cases of emotional abuse and neglect, making it difficult to decide when to take action. Moreover, neglected and emotionally abused children may not attract attention in the same way as those subject to physical or sexual abuse, so that despite the threats to their wellbeing, the maltreatment they experience may often pass unnoticed. Even when emotional abuse is suspected, workers often feel 'impotent in the face of problems which [unlike sexual abuse, physical violence or physical neglect] are difficult to tabulate'.[110] These difficulties may be compounded by the tendency of child protection services to focus on risks, rather than to assess children's needs and explore how parenting capacity might be strengthened.

Particular groups of children: adolescents and disabled children

It is particularly difficult to recognize neglect and emotional abuse amongst certain groups of children. For example, there is no common understanding concerning what constitutes neglect of adolescents – especially what is appropriate supervision at what age. This gives rise to obvious difficulties in identifying when adolescents are being neglected. Adolescents may also be neglected by services, as those who are rejected by their own families may become disengaged and ignored by professionals because their behaviour is challenging, and there are very few interventions that meet their needs.

Agencies may fail to recognize indicators of neglect in disabled children, or be reluctant to act in the face of concerns, as is powerfully illustrated by the case study of a 12-year-old disabled boy in the *Analysis of Serious Case Reviews 2003–5*. This boy had articulate, well-qualified, professional parents who severely neglected him. He was fully dependent on his parents or others for all his self-care needs and his appearance was described by professionals as grubby and unkempt. The house was clean and tidy except for his room, which was messy and unhygienic. His parents did not take him to appointments at the Child Development Centre; at the age of eight he was taken out of school and educated at home where he became increasingly isolated. Several agencies assessed that this child needed to be cared for outside the family home, but there was a year's delay before this happened. Finally, at the insistence of a senior health professional, he was admitted to foster care, by which time his severely neglected state led to a serious case review. It was evident that this child had been allowed to live in conditions which, for any other child, would have been considered degrading and unsuitable; however, his disability, rather than his unmet needs, was held responsible for his state:

> There was clear evidence of neglect in this case yet agencies failed to follow these pointers consistently or effectively. The model of neglect used was based on defining the concern in relation to parental action or omission rather than viewing neglect as a set of needs for care and protection regardless of the efforts of those caring for the child concerned.[111]

Recognition and response amongst specific professional groups

Different professional groups vary in their capacity to take note of the multiplicity of risk factors and indicators that a child is suffering, or likely to suffer, significant harm and respond to them. This section considers what the studies tell us about the specific issues they face.

Health visitors

The *Recognition of Neglect Review* found that health visitors stand out as one group who are well equipped to recognize the parental characteristics associated with neglect and the developmental signs in children. However, they find it difficult to act on their concerns because they perceive that thresholds for access to services are high. One UK study indicated that a high proportion of health visitors working with vulnerable families see themselves as referral agents but many perceive the lack of social services resources as a barrier to referral. They describe themselves as:

> …angry and frustrated over the lack of social services input with families, particularly in those areas of 'high concern' often described as 'grey areas'.[112]

These findings from a literature review are corroborated by the evidence from focus groups attended by health visitors in the *Significant Harm of Infants Study*. There were numerous comments concerning the difficulties of getting referrals accepted by children's social care, particularly if a case had been (prematurely) closed.

Differences in thresholds and difficulties in identifying likelihood of harm in cases of chronic neglect can lead health visitors to feel frustrated that their concerns are not adequately acknowledged:

> 'We've got, I can think of three families on our caseload that we have got grave concerns about, and we must make a referral probably every other week…at least once a month. But because it's little bits of things it just goes "Oh, we're not going to take it forward, the case is closed."' (Health Visitor, Local Authority A)[113]

Evidence about health visitors' unwillingness to act on signs of neglect suggests that they see their role as one of deciding whether or not to refer a case to children's social care rather than of considering alternative responses, such as developing or arranging access to targeted services that might obviate the need for referral.

Differences in the concept of response may relate to how practitioners perceive their role in supporting and caring for families and children where there is abuse or neglect. For instance, a Finnish study of 20 interviews with school nurses identified two operational modes: a passive and uninvolved mode and an active and firm mode. Those nurses who adopted a passive and uninvolved mode equated responding to family or child problems with referral to other professionals. These nurses collaborated minimally with other professionals and viewed home visits as unnecessary. In contrast, those nurses who adopted an active and firm mode focused less on referral. Instead, they were confident about their role in supporting families, made home visits, were clear about their concerns and saw themselves as active members of a collaborative network:

> Active and firm school nurses were not afraid of interfering and did not wait needlessly, expecting things to turn out right by themselves. They searched for these families and supported them also by making home visits. Many of the nurses sent a letter to the child's home or telephoned the family as problems arose. The school nurse might also ask the whole family to visit him or her; they showed interest in their clients and cared for their wellbeing.[114]

Schools

Schools are settings in which there are particular opportunities for practitioners to be alert to constellations of problems. Indeed, in recent years national policy has placed schools at the heart of early intervention, although it is at present unclear whether this emphasis will remain as strong under the Coalition Government. While practitioners in the law, social care and the health services are more likely to identify maltreatment that manifests itself in crises, people working in schools tend to be more alert to chronic issues, a major factor in the identification of neglect and emotional abuse.[115]

The *Recognition of Neglect Review* found that there is a paucity of evidence concerning effective ways for schools to undertake such responsibilities, and a striking absence of rigorous studies into the role of schools, teachers and also the police in safeguarding children. However, one important study has shown that, where teachers and educational psychologists are offered specific training in child protection, together with online support, guidance and consultation, recognition improves and appropriate referrals increase. Training in this area may be particularly effective if it addresses professionals' fears and doubts about what would be best for the child, and also their lack of confidence and knowledge about the contribution they can make in safeguarding children.[116]

Adult mental health, substance misuse and domestic violence services

The association between parental problems, such as poor mental health, domestic violence and substance misuse, and emotional abuse and neglect is well established.[117] We might therefore expect that practitioners in these services would be highly alert to risks of harm to the children of their clients/patients who are parents. However, evidence of referral rates suggests that workers in all three services are missing opportunities to recognize these risks or to respond to concerns. For example, despite the high incidence of mental health and addiction amongst their parents, only 1 of 50 children in the *Significant Harm of Infants Study* was referred by drug and alcohol services, and none by adult mental health.

The *Emotional Abuse Intervention Review* considered that mental health practitioners were chary of recognizing or acting on concerns:

> Practitioners are perhaps understandably reluctant to describe the often erratic, inconsistent and even frightening behaviours that can result as a consequence of severe mental illness as emotional maltreatment, and there is currently very little attention paid to the needs of children whose parents have severe mental illness.[118]

The problems stem partly from understandable concerns about the wellbeing of the parent as client/patient but also from a lack of collaboration and indeed some hostility between, for example, mental health and child protection services. There may be poor communication between those professionals who focus on the risks to children posed by emotional maltreatment, and those who are more concerned with treating the parental behaviour that gives rise to it. However, there is some evidence that early recognition and intervention can influence such interaction and improve outcomes for children.

The *Emotional Abuse Intervention Review* found that opportunities for recognizing abuse that should be routinely considered as part of normal practice are missed by practitioners working with adults. Children are at increased likelihood of suffering emotional abuse where one parent, particularly if this is the main carer, is experiencing mental health and drug/alcohol problems, and in families where domestic violence is taking place. In the case of substance misuse, the dangers also need to be recognized prenatally. The rate of substantiated maltreatment, mostly neglect, is much greater in infants who have been exposed to drugs or alcohol *in utero*.

Amongst all these services an assessment of the impact of parents' problems on child wellbeing should be a routine part of normal practice. Appropriate tools to undertake such assessments include standardized psychological tests; assessments of parent–child interactions; Goal Attainment Scaling; ongoing evaluations of the impact of tailored interventions; and standardized tests showing progress over time.[119]

Police

Many factors associated with neglect are also likely to entail police contact. The *Analysis of Serious Case Reviews 2003–5* found the police to be the agency most involved with families in neglect cases, as the parents were often involved in community and domestic violence. However, some branches of the police force are insufficiently aware of the link between domestic violence and the risk of harm to children. The *Recognition of Neglect Review* found that the role of the police in identifying and responding to neglect had not been researched.[120]

Professional responses: to refer or not to refer

> What happens when professionals have concerns about maltreatment and neglect? How do they respond and what action do they take?

The *Recognition of Neglect Review* explored how professionals other than social workers respond to their own concerns about maltreatment. Response tends to be conceptualized as 'referral' or 'reporting' and this is where the bulk of evidence lies. Professionals outside social care are reluctant to take direct action other than to refer to social care agencies. They appear to be frozen by the decision to refer or not to refer rather than to consider what other forms of action might be useful and appropriate.

There is far less evidence about the stages following recognition, or about what universal services might be able to offer to support neglected children.

However, there is evidence concerning those factors that make referral more likely, although it comes from the US, and may not translate easily into a UK context. These factors are:

- *Family-related factors*, including: the age of the child; whether they are at a primary school where more children take free school meals and 'perception of maltreatment' is high; whether there is strong evidence of concern for safety; whether the child and parent are white rather than Afro-Caribbean.

- *Practitioner factors*, including: being white (Asian practitioners are least likely to refer); having knowledge or personal experience of being abused.

- *System factors*, including: mandatory reporting; having fewer concerns about the process of investigation; knowing that previous reporting has led to a good outcome for a child; the absence of a range of system barriers.[121]

We have already seen that adolescents can be neglected by services. The *Recognition of Adolescent Neglect Review* and the *Analyses of Serious Case Reviews* both found that they are also the age group least likely to be referred.[122]

Response from the wider community

What happens when members of the wider community have concerns about maltreatment and neglect? How do they respond and what action do they take?

Although we know that the general public tends to have a lower threshold for determining maltreatment, there is only minimal evidence about how ordinary community members act when they have concerns about a child in their neighbourhood. This comes from two studies undertaken with different populations in different societies, and we do not know how far it would be relevant in a UK context. Members of a South Asian Canadian community have been shown to be quite able to identify neglect, but to be reluctant to approach child protection services about their concerns.[123] A general population survey in a southern state in the US found that the majority of the general public would help if they became aware of a child being abused or neglected as a result of substance abuse; however, the help they would offer would be to contact child protection agencies.[124] We do not know the extent to which reported intention in this study is translated into action if the occasion to refer arises.

Conclusion

The evidence discussed above carries a number of messages concerning how maltreatment – and specifically emotional abuse and neglect – can be better identified and responded to by all those who have responsibility for safeguarding the welfare of children. While all of these have general relevance, some are of specific value to professionals from the numerous agencies involved.

Key messages for all who work together to safeguard children

- Emotional abuse and neglect have long-term adverse consequences for children's future wellbeing.

- The risk of fatalities from neglect may be as high as that from physical abuse.

- Ten times as many children experience emotional abuse and neglect as come to the attention of child welfare services.

- Neglect and emotional abuse often manifest themselves early and have a corrosive impact throughout childhood.

- The consequences of neglect and emotional abuse are particularly severe *in utero* and in the first three years of life because of the child's developmental stage.

- Adolescent emotional abuse and neglect are widespread and associated with numerous adverse consequences, including suicide and death or serious injury from risk-taking behaviours.

- Approximately 2 per cent of the population of England have been forced to leave home for one night or more before their sixteenth birthdays.

- There is no common understanding of what constitutes supervisory neglect of adolescents. However, there is much evidence that inadequate supervision and monitoring is associated with adverse behaviour patterns.

- Assumptions about impairment, inadequacies in service provision and impairment itself may all render disabled children more vulnerable to abuse.

Key messages for front-line practitioners in education, health, social care and the police

- Neglect and emotional abuse only rarely result in crises, so practitioners need to look for evidence of long-term, chronic maltreatment.

- Not all mentally ill parents neglect or emotionally abuse their children, but parental mental health problems can lead to a deterioration in parenting capacity and the failure to meet the child's physical and emotional needs.

- Substance and alcohol misuse can be associated with severe neglect.

- When compounded with other parental difficulties, learning disability may be associated with neglect and emotional abuse.

- Police need to be aware that, not only is domestic violence harmful to children, it is also often associated with physical abuse. Moreover parents of neglected children may also often be involved in community and domestic violence. Such parents may be known to the police and probation, but not always to children's social care.

What to look for
In adult health, mental health and social care

- The impact of parental problems such as poor mental health, alcohol and substance misuse, or domestic violence on child wellbeing. This should be routine practice where adult service users have parenting responsibilities.

In health and social care settings

- Persistent failure to attend appointments for routine services such as immunization and hospital appointments.

- Disorganized/disoriented attachment patterns in young children, revealed through odd behaviours, such as repeated incomplete approaches to parents and failing to seek contact when very distressed.

- Frequent consultations with the school nurse.

- Passivity and sudden weight loss in very young children.

- Children who suffer burns or scalds who are not given first aid immediately; whose parents or carers have put off seeking help for over 24 hours; whose burns are unusually deep; who receive inadequate wound care; whose parents fail to keep appointments.

In nursery, preschool and school

- Children who show a steep decline in performance (this can be from as young as nine months).

- Children who become more socially withdrawn and unpopular with peers as well as more aggressive and less attentive.

- Delays in language and communication, socio-emotional adjustment and behavioural problems. These may be indicators of neglect in children as young as three.

Response and referral

- Teachers are well placed to identify neglect and emotional abuse. Where teachers and educational psychologists are offered specific training in child protection, together with support, recognition of maltreatment improves and appropriate referrals increase.

- High thresholds for access to children's social care may deter referrals. Those front-line practitioners in universal/primary-level services who adopt an active and firm mode of operating may be more confident about their role in supporting families and less likely to need to refer cases on.

- It is unrealistic to expect very vulnerable parents to refer or re-refer themselves to children's social care – or to access targeted services without support.

- It is important for social workers and health professionals to assess whether parents do or do not have the capacity to change: a number of indicators, such as recognition of the impact their problems have on their children, can be looked for as a basis for decision-making.

Universal and Targeted Services to Prevent the Occurrence of Maltreatment

> - This chapter draws largely on the evidence from the *Emotional Abuse Intervention Review*,[125] the *Recognition of Adolescent Neglect Review*[126] and the *Sure Start Local Programmes Safeguarding Study*.[127]
>
> - The chapter has important messages for all those who have responsibility for safeguarding and promoting the welfare of children.
>
> - It also has specific messages for the following professional groups:
>   - policymakers (section on prevention before occurrence)
>   - strategic managers and commissioners of services (all sections)
>   - operational managers (sections on targeted approaches to prevention; assessment tools; parent-training programmes)
>   - practitioners (sections on targeted approaches to prevention; assessment tools; parent-training programmes).

Introduction

The last chapter explored the risk factors associated with maltreatment, and considered how abuse and neglect can occur as a result of a complex interaction between these and the positive factors in a child's life. Emotional abuse and neglect pose particular challenges to recognition because of their long-term nature and the absence of specific events or evidence of physical harm that might prompt attention.

Programmes that prevent the occurrence of abuse are likely to be more effective than those that aim to address its consequences. There is evidence of the effectiveness of some well-designed, early intervention, preventive programmes. This chapter explores what the studies have to say about these. However, first we shall briefly consider the different stages at which effective intervention is possible.

A framework for intervention

A three-level model of prevention is often used to map both medical and social interventions. In this model *primary* prevention covers universal approaches to reduce the potential incidence of abuse and maltreatment; *secondary* prevention covers targeted approaches towards families where there is a greater likelihood of abuse and neglect, but before maltreatment has taken place; whilst *tertiary* prevention is designed to prevent further deterioration in cases where abuse or neglect has been identified.

Another way to look at this is to distinguish conceptually between preventive interventions, designed to reduce the likelihood of maltreatment, and therapeutic interventions, designed to prevent its recurrence and/or address the often extensive psychosocial consequences. This is shown in Figure 3.1. The diagram provides a useful framework for considering the timing and types of intervention which can be provided.

The left-hand side of Figure 3.1 maps preventive interventions before the occurrence of maltreatment, and distinguishes between universal (primary) and targeted (secondary) prevention. The right-hand side maps interventions which take place after maltreatment (tertiary prevention). In including tertiary prevention, the diagram demonstrates how interventions designed to prevent maltreatment and its recurrence differ from those designed to prevent long-term impairment to the child's health and development.

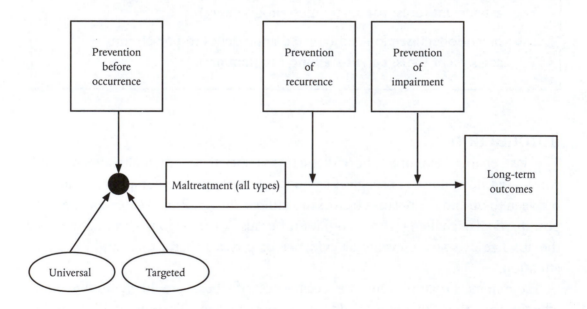

Figure 3.1: Framework for intervention and prevention of child maltreatment[128]

In this chapter we focus on primary and secondary interventions designed to prevent maltreatment before it has occurred. Many of these interventions are introduced as part of public health programmes. Some are *universally provided*, and aimed at a total population, while others are *targeted* towards families where there is a greater likelihood of maltreatment. In Chapters 4 and 5 we look at both long and short-term specific or tertiary interventions, introduced at a familial or individual level, after abuse (or a high risk of harm) has been identified. Chapter 4 focuses on social casework, while Chapter 5 covers complementary specialist interventions, designed to prevent the recurrence of maltreatment and to help children overcome its consequences.

Prevention before occurrence of maltreatment

Why are universal or population-based interventions a good idea?

There are several reasons why it makes sense to adopt a universal or population-based approach to prevention. The evidence from a number of population-based surveys shows that the prevalence of both moderate and severe forms of maltreatment is high. They indicate that every year 4–16 per cent of children in high-income countries are physically abused, 10 per cent are neglected or emotionally abused and at least 15 per cent are exposed to some form of sexual abuse.[129] We have already seen in Chapter 2 that the most recent UK population-based survey shows that 2.5 per cent of children aged under 11 years and 6 per cent of young people between the ages of 11 and 17 years had experienced some form of maltreatment in the previous year.[130] The proportion of children and young people who are known to children's social care, or are the subject of child protection plans, is much lower. The latest statistical data for England indicate that, in the year 2009–10, about 3.14 per cent were regarded as children in need (i.e. requiring support from social services if they are to achieve a reasonable standard of health and development), but only 0.32 per cent were the subjects of child protection plans.[131] In other words, the population-based surveys show that well over ten times as many children may experience abuse or neglect as the official statistics would indicate.[132]

The contribution of population-based approaches may be to reach children whose maltreatment has not yet been brought to the attention of services, or whose situation does not meet the threshold for statutory intervention. By reaching these families early, such approaches can reduce the number of parents who might otherwise later abuse or neglect their children.

A second advantage of population-based approaches is that they are non-stigmatizing. Maltreating families are often low or inconsistent service users and therefore hard to reach. They are more likely to be reached through programmes that are provided through services that are accessible to all, such as health care, education with a broad-based curriculum and public leisure and recreation facilities, which offer a safe environment for older children and young people.[133] In recent years much effort has been directed at increasing the number of non-stigmatizing access points through which potentially useful approaches such as parenting programmes can be made more easily available. Other approaches include mass media public education programmes; outreach services such as those provided by health visitors; increased monitoring, surveillance and support through primary health care; building up the school health provision; and support through Sure Start children's centres.

Many universal approaches aim to shift the norms of parenting behaviour and thus change extreme patterns that are harmful to children. If we assume that parenting behaviour follows a normal distribution pattern then the majority of behaviour falls in the middle of the graph. The argument is that, by shifting the normative behaviour of a whole population, extreme, abusive behaviour patterns will also be influenced to change in the same positive direction.

Universal or population-based approaches to prevention in the UK

What universal approaches in the UK can impact on maltreatment? How do these apply to different age groups?

The studies in this Research Initiative did not explicitly review evidence evaluating the effectiveness of population-based approaches. However, several comment on their general applicability and suggest it is likely that they have an impact on factors related to maltreatment. For example, the *Emotional Abuse Intervention Review* found that the application of parenting programmes on a universal basis improves many factors known to be associated with child maltreatment, such as family functioning, parental depression, stress, conflict, efficacy and competence.[134,135]

The *Healthy Child Programme and Inter-Disciplinary Framework (HCP)* is a nationally implemented health-based preventive initiative provided universally under the NHS, designed to reach both children and their families.[136] It comprises a health promotion and surveillance programme that incorporates a range of universal strategies which can be used by primary care professionals to promote the type of sensitive and attuned parenting that is recognized to be important to the wellbeing of young children. The programme includes screening, health and development reviews, immunizations, and health promotion, all of which might prompt a series of inter-disciplinary interventions critical to safeguarding the child's welfare: for example, a failed hearing test or detection of developmental dysplasia of the hip will need urgent, preventive intervention. In addition, the programme recommends the use of a range of interventions to support early parenting including the use of media-based tools, books supplied to every mother in a choice of languages,[137,138] strategies such as promotional interviewing, and group-based early interventions (e.g. infant massage and parenting programmes). Every family is entitled to these services,[139] which are offered in GP surgeries, clinics and Sure Start children's centres. Making these services available in a range of settings maximizes opportunities for families who may be disengaged from services to access them and for front-line practitioners to recognize and encourage such families to make use of them.

Sure Start children's centres are an example of a primary programme relevant to the prevention of neglect.[140] Their role is:

> To help link services provided for fathers, mothers and their children from the antenatal period through to when a child starts nursery school. They are intended to help to provide a source of easily accessible advice about how parents may help their child's early learning development and mental health. In doing so they can help with the early identification of children with specific developmental difficulties.[141]

Sure Start has been designed as a broad-based, non-stigmatizing, universally available service. The number of Sure Start children's centres has increased in recent years, and there were plans to make them available in every community by 2010 as part of the national health promotion strategy.[142] However, they also have a particular focus on improving support to families who have been less ready to access traditional services. In this sense they may also be seen to have a targeted focus. This targeted approach may become more pronounced: under current financial stringency plans, Sure Start centres may be reduced or charging may be introduced for middle and higher-income parents.[143]

Many of the primary programmes are aimed at younger children. The *Recognition of Adolescent Neglect Review* found that there are very few services available that are relevant to the needs of neglected adolescents. Preventive interventions aimed at improving parenting for this age group are particularly limited. A particular issue for young people as they move towards independence is the extent to which they should be supervised or monitored when not in school. One of the key developmental issues for adolescents is the need to have the opportunity to exercise autonomy in their transition to adulthood. Parents and carers may need support in achieving the right balance between setting appropriate boundaries and acknowledging young people's increasing independence and potential for self-determination.[144]

As Chapter 2 has shown, the relationship between levels of parental supervision and monitoring and the likelihood of adolescents engaging in a range of risky or anti-social behaviours is well established.[145] There is some evidence that the most effective mode of supervision for this age group is one in which young people keep their parents informed of their activities through an open relationship, rather than through one in which parents insist on being given detailed information about the young person's whereabouts at all times.[146] However, there is little consensus as to what might be appropriate levels of parental supervision for this age group. There is a case for a national debate to be engendered through the media, and for programmes to be introduced in Personal, Social and Health Education (PSHE) classes in schools to take this issue forwards. The *Neglect Matters* guide for young people[147] (see Figure 3.2) has been produced as part of the Safeguarding Children Research Initiative, and is already initiating such a debate, through its widespread utilization in schools, youth clubs and health centres.

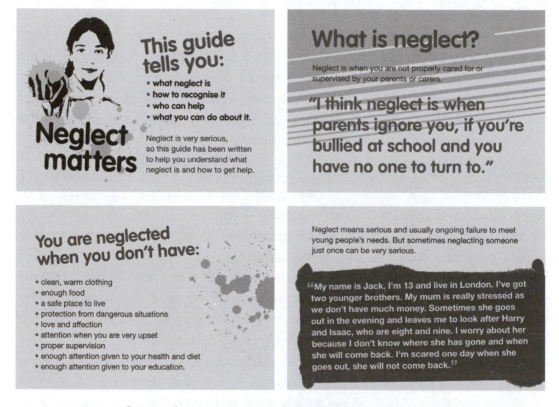

Figure 3.2: Extract from Neglect Matters: A Guide for Young People about Neglect

Preventive interventions might also be piloted and introduced as part of parenting support programmes. Their purpose would be to change societal norms about appropriate forms of parental monitoring and supervision of adolescents. If successful, such approaches could play a similar role to those addressed at the parenting of younger children, namely to change normative behaviour and therefore shift extreme behaviour in a more positive direction.

The reviews have found no validated interventions aimed at the perpetrators of intimate partner violence; the *Significant Harm of Infants Study* found that very few services were available, and the common response was to exclude perpetrators from the family home, with the result that many went on to abuse another family. One way of beginning to address this issue might be to develop preventive, universal programmes designed to raise awareness and change adolescent perceptions of intimate partner violence and its consequences; this is another area where extreme behaviour might well be shifted by a change in normative patterns.

Evaluated universal/population-based preventive interventions

> Which universal/population-based preventive interventions have been shown to be effective?

Not all population-based interventions have been formally assessed. However, the two approaches described below have been subject to rigorous evaluation, which has shown them to be effective. The first example shows how the introduction of new legislation can provide an effective means of changing public attitudes and reducing the maltreatment of children, while the second describes an effective, universally introduced parenting programme.

An evaluation of the Swedish ban on physical chastisement

In 1979, Sweden became the first nation to introduce legislation that banned mild forms of physical chastisement including smacking. The ban's aims were threefold: to alter public attitudes; to increase early identification of children likely to suffer significant harm; and to promote earlier and more supportive interventions with families. It was accompanied by an associated national public education campaign designed to change parenting behaviour. This included the distribution of a public education brochure, and a two-month publicity campaign that included printing information about the change in law on milk cartons.[148] More than 15 years after the ban was introduced, its impact was evaluated. The evaluation was based on an extensive examination of officially held statistics in three key areas: public attitudes, crime prevention and child welfare. It also drew on a series of cross-sectional studies of the use of physical punishment by parents, including children's reported experiences. The findings showed that public support for such punishment had declined. By 1994 only one third of middle school children reported having received physical punishment from their mother or father, and of these most had experienced only its mildest forms (arm grabbing or mild slaps). Of the population surveyed, only 3 per cent had received a harsh slap and 1 per cent had been hit with an object. Young adults whose own childhoods had largely been spent under the protection of this legislation were also less likely to be suspected of physical abuse. Moreover, for a period of 11 years after the introduction of the ban, no child died as a result of physical abuse in Sweden.

While it is difficult to be confident about the extent to which these positive shifts can be attributed to legislative reform, it seems likely that the ban will have played some part in the changes witnessed not only in the attitudes and behaviours of 'average' parents in the population, but also in a noted reduction in the more extreme forms of those parenting behaviours that are the concerns of child protection agencies.

The Triple P-Positive Parenting Programme: A validated population-based approach

The Triple P-Positive Parenting Programme (Triple P) is a population-based approach that has been rigorously and extensively evaluated. This is a multi-level parenting and family support strategy that aims to prevent severe behavioural, emotional and developmental problems in children by enhancing the knowledge, skills and confidence of their parents.[149]

Triple P incorporates up to six levels of intervention of increasing strength for parents of children from birth to 12. The preventive element consists of three levels. These comprise a public health campaign linked to a more intensive primary health intervention, which includes guidance and help to families with children with mild behavioural problems. These first three levels of intervention can be summarized as follows:

- Level One: A universal parent information strategy provides access to information about parenting through a co-ordinated promotional campaign, using print and electronic media.

- Level Two: A brief one or two-session primary health care intervention provides anticipatory developmental guidance to parents of children with mild behavioural difficulties, with the aid of user-friendly parenting advice sheets and videotapes that demonstrate specific parenting strategies.

- Level Three: A four-session primary care intervention targets children with mild to moderate behavioural difficulties and includes active skills training for parents.

This programme has been formally evaluated in the US.[150] The evaluation consisted of a population trial in which 18 medium-sized counties in a south-eastern state were randomly assigned to either dissemination of the Triple P Programme or a services-as-usual control condition. The sample was controlled for county population size, poverty rate and county child abuse rate. The evaluation was undertaken after a two-year period of intervention and employed a holistic approach, exploring the impact on a range of factors at the individual, environmental and family level. It found that the dissemination of Triple P, alongside the use of universal media and communication strategies, and professional training to the relevant childcare workforce, was effective. When compared with standard services, Triple P produced large changes in three independently derived population-based predictors of child abuse: the number of substantiated official reports of child maltreatment; the number of out-of-home placements; and the number of identified child maltreatment injuries. The overall findings appear to be very promising, however, by public health standards, the evaluation used a relatively small sample (an estimated 8883–13,560 families participated) and we do not know whether Triple P is equally effective in a UK setting. However, Triple P is currently being trialled on a population-wide basis in Glasgow, and if successful, the results may further strengthen confidence in its effectiveness.[151]

Targeted approaches to prevention

Targeted approaches to prevention have a number of benefits. First, they facilitate a more efficient and cost-effective delivery of services through their focus on those sectors of the population which have the highest need. For example, the evidence suggests that the long-term cost-effectiveness of one such approach, home-visiting programmes, is dependent on careful targeting of the service to socio-economically deprived, first-time, teenage, parents.[152]

One of the most commonly used criteria to target interventions is that of demographics or geography. This approach can be justified in designing interventions to prevent the occurrence of abuse, as this is more prevalent amongst families living in highly stressed, socio-economically deprived, areas. While this type of approach might be appropriate in terms of the delivery of broad, preventive interventions, further criteria can be applied to identify families where there is a greater likelihood of child maltreatment. In this way, more sharply targeted interventions may be designed and delivered to meet the specific needs of small sectors of the population. However, it is necessary to have reliable ways to recognize and target such families.

The best way to target services may be for practitioners in universal services to identify and assess need. For instance, The *Healthy Child Programme*[153] provides for assessments to be undertaken *routinely* by primary care professionals, such as midwives, health visitors and GPs, all of whom have regular contact with parents. In addition, GPs see children under five an average of five times a year for minor illnesses: these consultations can provide occasions for opportunistic surveillance, especially for those who miss out on routine appointments. They also provide opportunities to relate to the child and parent or caregiver and observe their interaction, forming the basis of a more holistic assessment and reflection.

Assessment tools to identify families who might benefit from targeted preventive interventions

What tools exist to help front-line workers to identify families whose children are considered to be likely to be maltreated?

As Chapter 2 has shown, the coexistence of factors such as parental substance misuse, intimate partner violence or severe mental health problems increases the likelihood of maltreatment, particularly if protective factors such as the presence of a supportive extended family or evidence of parents' capacity to change are absent.[154] Parental problems such as these need to be assessed formally by appropriate specialists. Such assessments need to be undertaken alongside more broad-based assessments of parent–child factors including parent–child interaction.

Good assessment may be as much part of an intervention as the intervention itself; both require the same core practice skills of being able to interact and communicate with parents and children, and utilizing knowledge and expertise to promote relationships. This is an important point to bear in mind when conducting any type of formal assessment or manualized intervention, as without intelligent sensitivity and engagement, professionals risk falling into the trap of allowing these to become mechanistic, and ultimately counter-productive, tick-box exercises.

A broad-based assessment tool: the Common Assessment Framework

The Common Assessment Framework (CAF) has been developed to help target preventive services towards children and families where there may be multiple problems or an increased probability of maltreatment. This tool is designed to help workers in universal services identify and assess children's additional needs. Government practice guidance explains that the CAF should be used where children in ordinary settings have additional needs.[155] The purpose of the CAF is to help practitioners from a range of sectors assess children's additional needs for services earlier and more effectively; develop a common understanding of these needs; and agree a plan for working together to address them.

Some common assessments might conclude with the identification of a lead professional to co-ordinate the implementation of the plan. This is someone who acts as a single point of contact for a child and their family when a range of services is involved and an integrated response is required. The CAF process has the advantage of being suitable for use with families with children of all ages, from infants to adolescents. Needs are considered in consultation with the family and/or young person and recorded on shared forms which may be held electronically.

An evaluation of the implementation of CAF has been conducted, using a mixed methods model.[156] The findings suggest that parents, young people and practitioners are generally positive about the process. The role of lead professional is found to be helpful in co-ordinating service inputs when needs have been identified. When supported by good multi-disciplinary training and support systems, the process of implementation helps consolidate inter-agency and inter-professional working. However, there are also some obstacles to effective implementation. These only occur in some authorities and are related to poorly conducted training, poor support systems for staff, and insufficiently developed or unsuitable IT systems. Some practitioners find the process time-consuming and some find the role of lead professional stressful and are reluctant to take it on. No evaluation of the outcomes of the CAF in terms of its possible contribution to the prevention of maltreatment has yet been undertaken, although this would obviously be valuable.

The challenges of effective implementation may inhibit the capacity of CAF to deliver fully on its objectives. Initiatives to reduce the burden of recording by practitioners[157] may result in retrenchment and the rolling back of plans for the national implementation. However, it would be regrettable if this were to result in the jettisoning of a tool which can be used across disciplines and that provides a valuable means of identifying and assessing the needs of families whose children may not be achieving their optimal outcomes.

As we saw in Chapter 2, the quality of early parenting, including parent–child interactions and the development of secure infant attachment, is fundamental to a child's early development. The task of assessing the parenting of very young children is a more difficult and skilled undertaking. At a more specialist level than the CAF, a number of tools are available to assess the quality of parent–child interaction. Some examples are described below.

A sharply focused approach to assessment: tools to assess child–parent interaction
Infants and toddlers

The Alarm Distress Baby Scale (ADBB)[158] and the Crittenden CARE Index (CARE-Index)[159] are both valuable in assessing parent–baby and parent–toddler interaction. Both scales can be utilized by social workers or health visitors who have received specialist training, or by a specialist professional such as a parent–infant psychotherapist. Training for using the Crittenden CARE Index is now available in the UK.

The Alarm Distress Baby Scale (ADBB) is designed to assess social withdrawal behaviour in infants under three years of age. It is undertaken by assessing the infant's social responses to the clinician (rather than the parent). Social withdrawal behaviour is evident in infants from as young as two months old, and is indicated by 'a lack of either positive (for example, smiling, eye contact) or negative (for example, vocal protestations) behaviours'.[160] The scale requires practitioners to assess eight items, with low ratings being considered as indicators of unusually low social behaviour. This instrument is a useful resource in assessing social withdrawal behaviour, which should alert practitioners to problems with the infant's environment. However, although this can be an indicator of emotional abuse (see Chapter 2), there may be other reasons; the potential of the ADBB to differentiate between abusing and non-abusing parents has not yet been tested.

However, the Crittenden CARE Index (CARE-Index)[161] *has* been shown to differentiate abusing from neglecting, abusing-and-neglecting, marginally maltreating, and inadequate (i.e. providing seriously suboptimal parenting) dyads, and is recommended for use as part of a broader assessment of functioning. Using three minutes of videotape of parent–infant/toddler interaction, trained practitioners analyse seven aspects of behaviour, assessing both parental actions and infant responses. This enables the clinician to assess factors such as sensitivity, control and unresponsiveness in parents, and co-operativeness, compulsiveness, difficultness and passivity in infants and toddlers.[162] This assessment provides the practitioner with some indication of both the severity of the problems, and the nature of the intervention required. Assessments are rated on a 14-point scale, with low scores indicating negative behaviour patterns and the possibility of maltreatment. The CARE-Index is short and can be used across a range of settings including the home and clinic. It can also be used as an intervention to improve maternal sensitivity.

The strength of tools such as the CARE-Index is that they can be used not only to target or identify parents who show an increased likelihood of maltreating very young children, but also to focus intervention. Recent research points to the value of such tools when employed as part of a broader procedure for assessing parents' capacity for change.[163]

Older children

Assessments of parent–child interaction involving older children can be undertaken using other structured methods including the Parent–Child Interaction Coding System II.[164] This records the frequency of discrete parent and child behaviours and can distinguish abusive from non-abusive parenting. The Emotional Availability Scales[165] rate several dimensions of parenting for older children, including parental sensitivity, parental non-intrusiveness, parental non-hostility, child responsiveness and child involvement. As with the CARE-Index, such instruments can be introduced both as part of a broader clinical assessment of functioning[166] and to identify actual maltreatment or seriously suboptimal parenting in order to target costly interventions more effectively.

An actuarial approach to assessing risk

The *Significant Harm of Infants Study* used an inventory of risk and protective factors that have been shown to be associated with a greater or lesser likelihood of maltreatment or its recurrence[167] to create an independent, four-level index of the likelihood of the babies in the study suffering harm. Families were classified both at the time of identification, and also two to three years later, at the children's third birthdays. This proved to be a useful method of identifying, at a very early stage, those families that would not be able to provide a nurturing home within a child's timescale – by the end of the study all but one of the children in the severe risk category had been permanently removed, although there had been damaging delays in making some of the decisions.

Such an actuarial approach has considerable value, and indeed there are plans to pilot this methodology in a practice setting. However, its limitations should be acknowledged. First, even using the best evidence we have, the current state of knowledge does not allow for a reliable and accurate use of numerical scoring of relative risk. Moreover the issues are more complex than can be reflected in a numerical score or simple actuarial table. Individual cases will all have their own idiosyncrasies and risk factors may interact with one another in different ways. Even if valid estimates of the probability of future harm could be calculated for groups of children, they will not necessarily be accurate for individual cases. Decisions made about these children have permanent, life-changing consequences, and it is not ethically defensible to make them on the basis of mathematical probabilities without exploring the qualitative information about each child's individual circumstances. On the other hand, estimates of probability can be extremely useful in providing a baseline against which decisions which ignore them have to be justified. Therefore, while actuarial approaches have considerable potential as *an aid to* decision-making, there are dangers in introducing them *in place of* professional judgement.[168]

Similar caveats hold for the use of validated inventories and assessment tools, such as the CARE-Index: they have considerable potential to support decision-making, but should not be allowed to become tick-box exercises that replace analysis and judgement. Findings from both the implementation of the Integrated Children's System,[169] and the Assessment Framework[170] that preceded it, suggest that decision-makers need to develop the ability to analyse and understand the implications of complex constellations of risk and protective factors and indicators of maltreatment, supported by the practice tools available to them.

Notwithstanding these issues, validated tools are a valuable resource in helping practitioners and clinicians assess the likelihood of a child being maltreated, or the evidence that this may be happening, and make decisions about the delivery of targeted interventions. In the next section we look at two examples of such targeted interventions that have been shown to be effective.

What targeted approaches to prevention have been shown to work?

Overall, the most effective targeted approaches to preventing child physical abuse or neglect appear to be home-visiting schemes and multi-component interventions of the type used in parent training.[171]

Home-visiting (or visitation) programmes

Home visiting for very young children and their parents through the health visitor service has existed in the UK and most European countries for decades. However, some more intensive home-visiting interventions have been developed which are targeted at those children identified as being at greatest risk of being maltreated.[172]

Intensive programmes are very different in nature from those provided routinely as part of a universal service. They vary both in terms of their nature and their intensity. Some meta-analyses of evaluations of home-visiting programmes have concluded that early childhood home-visiting schemes are effective in improving a range of outcomes for children;[173] however, they are not uniformly effective in reducing child physical abuse, neglect and outcomes such as injuries.[174] Moreover, there are important differences both in the models of service delivery, content and staffing, and in the design and methods, including outcome measures, used in evaluations.

Nevertheless, one targeted home-visiting programme, the Nurse Family Partnership (the Family Nurse Partnership (FNP) in the UK), has been the subject of rigorous evaluations (including pilots in the UK) and shown significant benefits, including reducing physical abuse.

The Nurse Family Partnership is a home-visiting programme provided by nurses to low-income, first-time mothers, commencing at the prenatal stage and continuing during pregnancy. The aim is to improve pregnancy outcomes through better health-related behaviours and to improve parenting both in the short and long term by facilitating the development of better skills both in the care of the child, planning and economic self-sufficiency. The programme employs a model based on theories of human ecology, self-efficacy and human attachment. Nurses develop trusting relationships with mothers and other family members to review their childhood experience of being parented, to help them decide how they themselves want to parent, and to promote sensitive, empathetic care of their children.

The Nurse Family Partnership was first developed in the US, where it has been shown to have lasting and wide-ranging impacts, including a reduction in children's injuries and in adolescent anti-social behaviour.[175,176,177] Rigorous evaluations have also shown that the programme reduces physical abuse and neglect, as measured by official child protection reports, and associated adverse outcomes such as injuries to the children of first-time, disadvantaged mothers.

A 15-year follow-up has found child abuse and neglect to have been identified significantly less often over this extended period in home-visited families, except where there were moderate to high levels of reported intimate partner violence.[178]

Before considering whether such a programme should be implemented in the UK, it is important to discover whether the results can be replicated. The model is therefore being tested to see whether it can be delivered in a UK context in a way that fits with NHS universal services. This is considered to be one of the most important developments for vulnerable families.[179] A formative evaluation of Family Nurse Partnerships has now been undertaken in ten sites across England with promising indications, and the programme is now being tested in 55 sites. A randomized controlled trial is currently being carried out in 20 sites in the UK and is due to report in 2013. The aims of this trial will be to test the effectiveness of Family Nurse Partnerships in England compared with existing universal services and consider costs, savings and any variations in impact between sites and subpopulations.[180] Further evaluations are also being undertaken in the Netherlands[181] and Canada.[182]

As many as two thirds of the babies in the *Significant Harm of Infants Study* were identified as suffering, or likely to suffer, significant harm before they were born, and cases were frequently closed prematurely and later reopened. FNP is delivered from pregnancy until the child is two years old; had it been available, these infants and their parents would have benefited greatly from this type of intensive, long-term intervention.

Parent-training programmes

The Triple P-Positive Parenting Programme was described earlier. This multi-level programme has modules of increasing intensity to be applied both as a population-based approach and also on a targeted basis to families where there is an increased likelihood of maltreatment. The first three levels, designed to prevent risk of maltreatment or other forms of harm, were described above. Further, more intensive, levels are available to targeted families where there is a risk of their children being maltreated or where maltreatment has been identified. We shall describe the more intensive programmes in Chapter 5.

The Webster-Stratton Incredible Years programme has also been shown to be effective in reducing problems associated with maltreatment. This is a series of three interlocking training programmes for parents, children and teachers. The parenting programme spans the age range of 0–12 years. It is based on cognitive social learning theory. The training is based on principles of video modelling, observation and experimental learning. Aims of the parenting programmes include improving parent–child interactions, building positive parent–child relationships and attachment, improving parental functioning, promoting less harsh and more nurturing parenting and increasing parental social support and problem-solving. The programme is delivered by group leaders drawn from professionals with qualifications in psychology, psychiatry, social work or counselling and knowledge of child development. The programmes have been recommended by Sure Start, particularly for children under five years, and there is training available for group leaders in the UK. The Incredible Years has been extensively and rigorously evaluated and found to reduce harsh parenting, increase positive discipline and nurturing parenting, reduce conduct problems and improve children's social competence. Programmes have been widely implemented in the UK in both parenting and schools-based forms.[183,184]

Most parenting programmes are directed towards families with young children. The *Recognition of Adolescent Neglect Review* found little material of direct relevance to neglected adolescents; however, it did identify a number of interventions with troubled adolescents that might be relevant to this group.[185] For example, some parenting programmes are designed to promote more vigilant approaches to adolescent monitoring in order to protect troubled young people from self-harming behaviours.

The Informed Parents and Children Together (ImPACT) programme is designed to promote increased parental monitoring as a means of reducing a range of risky behaviours, including reducing substance misuse. It involves an intervention with the parents to promote greater awareness and monitoring. A rigorous evaluation of the ImPACT intervention utilized a randomized controlled trial design with a sample of 817 African-American young people who had already participated in a school-based risk reduction programme, and their parents and carers.[186] The intervention group and their parents received a single session ImPACT intervention (a videotape and discussion), while the control group received only a booster of the school-based programme with no parenting element. The results indicated a reduced risk in 6 out of 16 behaviours for the ImPACT intervention group. The reduction in risky behaviours included: days suspended from school; substance abuse behaviour; and sexual risk behaviour, as measured by completion of a self-report questionnaire at baseline and at 24 months follow-up. The evidence suggests that a parental monitoring intervention can significantly broaden and sustain protection beyond that conferred by an adolescent risk reduction programme.

Dangerous driving is another highly risky form of behaviour amongst adolescents with time on their hands. A further initiative, the Checkpoints Programme, encourages parents to play an active role in discussing driving risks with older teenagers. Again, results are promising and show a positive impact on traffic violations although not on driving accidents.[187]

Conclusion

A wide variety of universal and targeted approaches are available at both primary and secondary level to prevent the occurrence of abuse and neglect. Universal approaches include possible legislative changes and media campaigns, as well as specific programmes that can be introduced on a population basis. Targeted approaches can address whole localities where indicators of poverty and deprivation suggest that there may be a greater likelihood of maltreatment, as well as families where children are at greater risk of suffering significant harm. Most of these programmes originate from other countries (most frequently the US) and there are questions as to how easily they can be transplanted into the UK. However, the most successful are now being trialled in this country and, if effective, may offer valuable approaches to the prevention of abuse and neglect. The findings from the many studies identified in this chapter reinforce the message that early interventions, accompanied by better integration of services, are necessary to reduce the probability of maltreatment at a later stage.

Key messages for all who work together to safeguard children

- Programmes that prevent the occurrence of abuse are likely to be more effective than those that address its consequences.

- Well-designed interventions both at primary level (aimed at whole populations) and at secondary level (targeted on at-risk populations) can be effective.

- A population-based approach to prevention is non-stigmatizing, more likely to reach families early and prevent escalation of abuse, and more likely to reach those children whose maltreatment tends to pass unnoticed.

- Effective approaches include legislative changes, mass media public education programmes and universally accessible parenting programmes. Examples include the introduction of the Healthy Child Programme and Sure Start children's centres.

- By shifting the normative behaviour of a whole population, universal approaches may influence extreme behaviour patterns to move in the same, positive direction.

- The introduction of legislation banning physical punishment in Sweden may have had this type of impact, in that it was followed by a decline in public support for physical punishment, a noted reduction in extreme forms of parenting behaviours, and a 15-year cessation of child deaths from physical abuse.

- There is a strong case for developing and testing public education programmes aimed at raising normative standards of parental monitoring and supervision of adolescents outside of school to address neglect.

Key messages for policymakers, strategic managers and commissioners of services in health, education and children's social care

- The Triple P-Positive Parenting Programme has been shown to be effective in the US in reducing the number of identified child maltreatment injuries as well as the number of substantiated reports of maltreatment and the number of children placed away from home.

- The most effective targeted programmes to prevent maltreatment and neglect are home-visiting schemes and multi-component schemes. Home-visiting schemes vary widely, both in terms of the nature and intensity of service; effective targeted approaches need to be based on tested versions with good models of practice.

- The Family Nurse Partnership now being trialled in the UK is a home-visiting programme offered by specially trained nurses. It has been positively evaluated in the US. Early results from the UK evaluation are promising.

- The Webster-Stratton Incredible Years programme has been shown to be effective in the US. It has been implemented in the UK in both a parenting and schools-based format to tackle issues such as harsh parenting, child conduct problems and early-onset anti-social behaviour.

Key messages for operational managers and practitioners in health, education and children's social care

- The best way to target services may be for primary care professionals to identify need by routinely assessing parents.

- The Common Assessment Framework has been shown to consolidate inter-agency and inter-professional working, and to be acceptable to service users and practitioners, but its possible contribution to the prevention of maltreatment has not been evaluated.

- The Alarm Distress Baby Scale and the Crittenden CARE Index can be used to assess parent–baby and parent–toddler interaction respectively. For older children the Parent–Child Coding System II and Emotional Availability Scales are recommended.

- Programmes such as ImPACT, which involve parents as well as adolescents in initiatives to reduce risk-taking behaviours, are more effective than those which only engage the young people.

Social Work Interventions to Keep Children Safe

- This chapter draws largely on the evidence from the *Neglected Children Reunification Study*,[188] the *Significant Harm of Infants Study*[189] and the *Home or Care? Study*.[190]

- This chapter has important messages for all those who have responsibility for safeguarding and promoting the welfare of children.

- It also has specific messages for the following professional groups as indicated:

  - policymakers (all sections, with reference to social work training, ensuring children are safeguarded, benefits of local authority care or accommodation)

  - Local Safeguarding Children Boards (all sections)

  - strategic managers and commissioners of services in children's social care (sections on services and outcomes of care)

  - practitioners and operational managers in children's social care (all sections)

  - judges, magistrates and local authority solicitors (sections on assessments, plans, court involvement).

Introduction

The previous chapter focused on universal services, such as education and health care, available to all families to improve the wellbeing of children, and targeted services such as Sure Start children's centres, available to all, but providing additional support to more vulnerable families. However, some families will need more intensive support if their children are to be safeguarded from harm. This will include interventions from children's social care such as the provision of family support, social work casework and, for some children, placements away from home, as well as a range of support from practitioners in partner agencies including alcohol and substance misuse teams, psychologists, psychiatrists, health visitors and professionals in education. This chapter focuses on the more general interventions from social workers and their colleagues, while the following chapter explores the more specific interventions that are often required to complement them.

Consequences of child maltreatment

The *Neglected Children Reunification*, the *Home or Care?* and the *Significant Harm of Infants Studies* all explored primary empirical data from social work case files and interviews with practitioners, parents and children that demonstrated the extent of adversity facing some families and the consequences for their children. They provide further evidence of the close relationship between child maltreatment and parental problems such as mental ill health, substance and alcohol problems and domestic violence, particularly when these occur in combination.[191,192] Both the *Significant Harm of Infants* and the *Home or Care? Studies* also found relationships between child maltreatment and parents' criminal convictions for violent offences, often committed under the influence of alcohol. They both confirm that adults who get involved in fights or muggings are more likely to subject their children both to physical abuse and to the emotional abuse of witnessing intimate partner violence – evidence that corroborates the findings from all three *Analyses of Serious Case Reviews 2003–9*, and reinforces the point that the police need to be aware of the link between domestic violence and children suffering harm.

Chapters 1 and 2 have discussed how child abuse and neglect impact on children's development and life chances; they have also shown how difficult it is for professionals to identify that a child is being neglected or emotionally abused and to take appropriate action. Other research that demonstrates that the longer children experience maltreatment, the greater the risk to their long-term wellbeing and the more entrenched are the adverse consequences, is confirmed by all three of the empirical studies in the Research Initiative.

The *Home or Care?*, the *Neglected Children Reunification* and the *Significant Harm of Infants Studies* all found extensive evidence of the consequences of abuse in children's delayed development, poor speech and language, poor school performance, decayed teeth and untreated medical conditions, as well as in numerous emotional and behavioural problems, particularly violence and aggression.

Both the *Home or Care?* and the *Neglected Children Reunification Studies* found that many maltreated and neglected children are identified at a very early age. Over half (56%) of the children in the latter study had been referred to children's social care before they were two, a third before they were born. The children in the *Significant Harm of Infants Study* had been selected on the basis of their having been identified as suffering, or being likely to suffer, significant harm before their first birthdays; nevertheless, it is noteworthy that 65 per cent of this sample had also been identified before birth.

It is therefore clear that swift and decisive interventions are of paramount importance where children are thought to be at high risk of being maltreated or where there is evidence that they are already being abused or neglected. So the first questions we need to ask are, how successful are such interventions, and how could they be improved?

> What do the studies tell us about social care interventions? What obstructs and what facilitates prompt action when maltreatment has been identified?

The studies identified a number of instances where maltreatment, or a serious likelihood of maltreatment, was identified early and appropriate action taken. For instance, a small number of infants, judged by the research team to be at severe risk of suffering significant harm, were swiftly removed from potentially damaging families and apparently never abused. However, such prompt and decisive action is relatively rare. There are few cases where there is unequivocal evidence right from the start to indicate that children either can or cannot be adequately safeguarded at home; moreover, a number of other factors also tend to get in the way of swift intervention when children are being maltreated.

First, there are a number of gaps in social workers' knowledge and understanding that mean that evidence of maltreatment, and particularly neglect, can be overlooked or given too little attention. The implications of exposure to alcohol or substance abuse *in utero* are particularly poorly recognized, and core assessments often give only limited attention to the developmental needs of very young children. Interviews with social workers reveal that child development has often been only a small part of qualifying training – and one that is quickly forgotten. Theories of attachment are sometimes misunderstood – for instance, secure attachment to a birth parent is sometimes used as an argument *in favour* of separation and adoption on the grounds that this can easily be transferred. Child development, attachment and the impact of maltreatment and neglect should obviously be core elements of training for all those who work with children in need and their families. Moreover, new evidence is constantly emerging in this field – these issues should also form an essential component of continuing professional development.[193]

Second, some practitioners do not appreciate the importance of reading case files and gaining a historical understanding of a child's previous experience. Simple chronologies showing, for instance, accumulating evidence of abuse and neglect and mounting concerns expressed by referrals from neighbours and other professionals are rarely compiled or used as a basis for action. Even where accumulating evidence of chronic neglect is available and accessible, it is rarely acted upon without a trigger incident, such as the discovery that a small child is being locked up alone in the house. One problem is that local authority legal departments are reluctant to act in neglect cases without such an incident. This is a serious issue. For example, in the Peter Connelly case the legal team did not feel able to make a decision as to whether the threshold had been met on the basis of the (incomplete) evidence presented to them.[194] Greater understanding of the consequences of *not* acting might be of value both to local authority legal departments and the courts.

The new empirical evidence also confirms findings from earlier research showing that practitioners can become desensitized to evidence of neglect and uncritically accepting of poor parenting standards.[195,196] There are some disturbing examples of children who, as a result, are left unprotected in dangerous and damaging situations. For instance, the *Significant Harm of Infants Study* found a baby whose parents so persistently forgot to feed her that she ceased to cry, a two-year-old left to forage in the waste bin for his food and a three-year-old who could demonstrate how heroin is prepared. All of these children remained with their birth parents for many months without being adequately safeguarded.

Neglect is not the only type of maltreatment to which practitioners can become desensitized: the *Neglected Children Reunification Study* identified 'a number of children [who] suffered continuing physical abuse, which social workers had come to view as "acceptable" in some way, and even on occasions sexual abuse';[197] this study also has an example of a child who passed the social worker a note saying 'help me' – which still did not elicit an adequate response.[198]

Third, the studies also confirm evidence found in earlier research[199] that children's families can face such multi-faceted problems that practitioners can find themselves overwhelmed in the face of so much adversity, to the point where they are unable to take decisive action. The *Analysis of Serious Case Reviews 2003–5* found that:

> One common way of dealing with the overwhelming information and the feelings of helplessness generated in workers by the families, was to put aside knowledge of the past and focus on the present in what we have called the 'start again syndrome'. In this respect a new pregnancy or a new baby would be seen to present a fresh start. In one case the child's mother had already experienced the removal of three children because of neglect, but her history was not fully used in considering her and her partner's capacity to care for this child. Instead, agencies were more focused on supporting the mother and the family to 'start again'.[200]

There is ample evidence of the 'start again syndrome' in the three empirical studies. Moreover, interviews with practitioners undertaken in the *Significant Harm of Infants Study* found that this tendency to 'start again' could sometimes be underpinned by ethical concerns about not allowing their judgement to be prejudiced by parents' previous abusive behaviour. For instance, it was policy in one team to reallocate the case to a different social worker if a mother became pregnant after her older children had been placed for adoption. The new social worker was deliberately kept in ignorance of the past.

All three studies of social work interventions found extensive evidence of thresholds for access to children's social care being too high and of professionals giving parents 'too many chances' to demonstrate that they could look after a child, often in the face of substantial evidence to the contrary and regardless of the child's timescales. The *Neglected Children Reunification Study* estimated that this had happened in nearly two fifths (38%) of cases. This tendency was not only evident in social workers' decisions, but also in those made by psychologists, psychiatrists, magistrates and judges. Decisions were informed by concepts of parental rights and views about empowerment, so that the child's welfare was not always the paramount consideration. In a climate in which all decisions were made with the expectation that children would remain at home, it was exceptionally difficult for professionals to identify the few who could not safely do so. Some practitioners appeared to consider that their role was to safeguard the family rather than the individual children within it.

Both the *Analyses of Serious Case Reviews* demonstrate the serious consequences of getting the threshold wrong for children living in families with multiple problems. Some of the serious case reviews were of children who had been living in overwhelmed families and were known to be neglected but whose circumstances were not judged to reach the threshold for services to be provided by children's social care. Similarly, the *Significant Harm of Infants Study* raises questions about how bad parenting has to become to be identified as unacceptable. Judging by the continued presence of recognized risk factors, just under half of the children in this study who remained with birth parents were not considered to be safeguarded at age three. The main issue was neglect, often as a result of parental alcohol or substance misuse. Although none of the sample children died in the course of the study, some of the cases might well have had a fatal outcome. However, about half of the children for whom evidence was available were displaying considerable developmental and behavioural problems by the time they were three. These included delayed speech and language development, very aggressive behaviour towards other children or pets, and destruction of property. One child required one-to-one care at nursery, another had attacked the carer's grandchild and a third was considered so aggressive that she was not taken to the park for fear that she would hurt another child. The children's difficulties were already jeopardizing some placements, and were likely to cause major problems once they started school. A further follow-up of this sample is currently exploring these issues.[201] There was evidence that almost all of these children had experienced maltreatment in their first few months of life, many of them *in utero*, because some parents misused substances or alcohol throughout the pregnancy as well as after they were born.

The findings indicate that practitioners need much clearer guidance and training as to what constitutes acceptable and unacceptable levels of parenting, and that this should also be spelled out to parents – a point made by the parents themselves in this study as well as by the Peter Connelly serious case review.[202]

> What do the studies tell us about supporting maltreated children at home? Are assessments adequate? Are plans viable? Do parents and children receive appropriate help, for long enough to meet their needs? Is such support effective?

Action following referral

Where children are suffering, or likely to suffer, significant harm, effective social care interventions require careful assessment and planning, with clear articulation of changes that need to be made, and specific goals and timescales explicitly agreed between families and professionals with safeguarding responsibilities. Support has to include the provision of a package of services tailored to meet the needs of children and their families. The complex issues facing such families indicate that these services must address the multi-faceted needs of both adults and children; careful co-ordination between several agencies will therefore be necessary. The issues raised by such inter-agency working are discussed further in Chapter 6. In this chapter we consider what the studies tell us about assessment, planning and overall case management within children's social care.

Assessments

The majority of assessments undertaken immediately following referral are completed by social workers. Specialist assessments, undertaken by a range of experts, may later be commissioned by local authority children's social care services, in preparation for legal proceedings, or by order of the courts.

There is some evidence that social work assessments sometimes fail to focus sufficiently on the core question – whether the child can safely remain in their current circumstances. They also reveal some of the gaps in knowledge and understanding, particularly around child development, attachment, and the signs and consequences of maltreatment, discussed in this and earlier chapters. In some authorities social work assessments are left undone, and there is little evidence of any assessments being undertaken until a case comes to court.

However, most of the evidence from the studies concerns the use of specialist assessments, and here the findings are mixed. On the one hand, there appear to be very few expert assessments of specific issues such as the extent to which children will be likely to suffer significant harm if they remain with/return to their families, of the likelihood of parents overcoming substance misuse within a child's timeframe, or of the impact of neglect or maltreatment on children's welfare.

On the other hand, large numbers of expert assessments of more general issues such as the parent's capacity to look after a child are undertaken by psychologists, psychiatrists and specialist practitioners as part of the decision-making process. There are a number of questions about the appropriate use of these assessments. The *Significant Harm of Infants Study* found that they are frequently repeated within very short timeframes, giving parents little opportunity to overcome previously identified problems. Many appear to have been commissioned in order to provide evidence that parents' rights are being duly acknowledged rather than to identify whether adequate changes in parental behaviour have taken place. Both courts and local authorities consider that too many specialist assessments are being undertaken; there are long waiting lists for them, and there is substantial evidence that they delay decision-making to the detriment of children's welfare.

The majority of recommendations from expert parenting assessments are in favour of parents retaining care of their children; these are virtually always followed. All three studies found, however, that these recommendations can often be unreliable. The *Significant Harm of Infants Study* found that over half of them proved to be over-optimistic in that children, who, on the advice of experts, remained at home, later had to be removed following further maltreatment. While expert assessments are obviously valuable in some circumstances, careful thought needs to go into how they could be better timed, and made more reliable.

Plans

Planning matters: where there is evidence of careful planning, outcomes for children tend to be better. Conversely, where planning is weak, there is more evidence of drift, so that children are left too long in abusive circumstances without appropriate services to safeguard them; there is also more evidence of children missing their chances of achieving permanence, of parents removing children from placements at will, and of reunification occurring by default, without clear arrangements for how children will be safeguarded in the future. Planning can deteriorate – or come to a halt – when cases remain unallocated or when practitioners become overwhelmed with the complexity of problems facing families.

The quality of assessment and planning tends to vary significantly between local authorities, and indeed between different teams within them. The *Neglected Children Reunification Study* found that care planning had been inadequate for over a third of all the children (36%) in its sample, and 81 per cent of those from one authority. In ten cases there was very little planning of any sort. Wide variations between authorities were also found in the *Home or Care? Study*. They suggest that authorities have much to learn from one another, and that some of these issues could be addressed by stronger management and supervision of front-line staff. Where there is a likelihood of significant harm, the primary issue to explore is how far children can be adequately safeguarded in different settings. Although both the *Significant Harm of Infants* and the *Home or Care? Studies* found that decisions were often informed by evidence that parental problems had improved and that risks to the child's safety were acceptable, there was also ample evidence of children being left or returned to dangerous situations.

The *Significant Harm of Infants Study* found that social work interventions tend towards the least intrusive option. Thus if the child protection conference considers that a child can be adequately safeguarded through the provision of services under Section 17a of the Children Act 1989, then a child protection plan is not considered necessary. If a child can be accommodated successfully under Section 20 of the Children Act 1989, then a care order (and indeed court proceedings) may be avoided. Although such decisions follow the spirit of the legislation, and are consonant with the aims of empowering vulnerable parents and promoting family cohesion, less intrusive measures do not always ensure that children are adequately safeguarded. There are, for instance, significantly more social work services provided for children who are the subjects of child protection plans[203] than for those who are not. Children who have had some court involvement also tend to receive a more robust overall service than those who have not.

Court involvement

Assessments, planning and case management are all usually more evident for children who are the subject of care orders. Both the *Neglected Children Reunification* and the *Home or Care? Studies* found that less rigorous work is undertaken with children who are accommodated. Where children return from care through placement with parents, every dimension of assessment and planning is stronger than where they are discharged from accommodation. Abrupt and unplanned reunifications occurring as a result of a placement disruption, the lack of suitable alternatives or running away are all more common with children who are accommodated than with those who are the subject of care orders. The *Home or Care? Study* found that, six months after the decision has been made, reunification is judged to have been appropriate for less than half (47%) of the children who return home after being looked after by the local authority. However, children who are the subject of care orders and return home under placement with parents regulations are more likely to re-enter care than those who return home from being accommodated. This may be because care orders make it possible to remove children quickly from unsatisfactory placements; they therefore give local authorities sufficient security to attempt reunification where family circumstances are more difficult and the prospects for a successful outcome less likely. Children and young people who are the subject of care orders may also be more likely to re-enter care because they are under greater surveillance and there is therefore a greater chance that maltreatment will be detected. Accommodated children in the *Neglected Children Reunification Study* were also older than those placed on care orders, another factor that may have had an impact on the extent to which they were monitored following return.

However, although children may be better safeguarded when the courts have been involved, their directions are not always carried out. The *Neglected Children Reunification Study* found that 62 per cent of care plans made by the courts are either not successful or not fully carried out. Moreover, those provisions that are implemented are not always sufficiently robust. Again in line with the tendency to seek the least intrusive intervention, wherever it is thought that a child can be adequately safeguarded through a supervision order, care orders are not made. Where care orders *are* made, there is also a tendency to place children with their parents at the earliest opportunity; indeed many of these children never leave home. However, over three fifths (62%) of supervision orders fail as the situation at home breaks down, as is also the case with 87 per cent of children who are placed with their own parents. It would appear advisable for more robust procedures to be developed whereby the courts routinely receive feedback on the outcomes of their decisions.

Services

The sheer complexity of problems facing families where children are being, or likely to be, maltreated makes it clear that they will not be adequately safeguarded at home without intensive, well-coordinated support services. However, such services are often unavailable. The *Neglected Children Reunification Study* found that only 38 per cent of substance-misusing parents and as few as 16 per cent of those who abuse alcohol receive support. Children and young people also receive insufficient support: after they have returned home from care, only half of those who need it have support with substance misuse, a quarter have help with independent living skills or mental health problems, and only 8 per cent of those who need it receive help with alcohol misuse. The scarcity of support for alcohol-abusing adults and children is rarely acknowledged. There is also too little help with critical issues such as parenting skills, parent–child relationships and children's behaviour problems. All these adversities make maltreatment more likely – if children are to be adequately safeguarded in their homes, then much more needs to be done to ensure that effective services are readily available. Services also need to be provided at sufficient intensity and for a long enough period. Most of the specific validated interventions currently provided are on a short-term basis, and end after six months. Social work support is also often of relatively short duration – half the child protection plans for the babies in the *Significant Harm of Infants Study* were for 32 weeks or less, and almost all for less than a year.

There are diverse reasons for the short duration of service provision. Some services may be most effective in the first few months and then have increasingly diminishing impact. The cost of provision is, and will increasingly be, a significant consideration. There are also concerns about parents becoming too dependent on services and evading their responsibilities towards their children. However, withdrawing services in order to reduce dependency may well be at the expense of children's safety and welfare.

Even where parents apparently succeed in overcoming their difficulties sufficiently to safeguard a child, there is a strong case to be made for continued light-touch monitoring to ensure that their progress is maintained. Those parents in the *Significant Harm of Infants Study* who had overcome substantial adversities and were successfully parenting a child after others had been placed for adoption were surprised that their cases were closed after just a few months. Some of them asked for child protection plans to be extended in order to provide them with the continuing support they felt they needed. Expectations that they would contact social workers if they later ran into difficulties were not fulfilled because none of them were prepared to run the risk of being separated from the new baby. Health visitors appear to be seen as able to offer help with less threatening connotations; their role could be expanded to offer continuing support in such circumstances. At present, considerable thought is given to how the referral process, from universal and targeted to specialist services, might be improved, but too little attention is paid to processes by which children and families might be referred back to less intensive services when social work cases are closed.

A major difficulty is that many parents who maltreat their children have deep-seated and entrenched problems that they are unable to overcome within a child's timeframe. These parents may not be able to safeguard their children adequately without intensive long-term support, sometimes until the children are sufficiently independent to take care of themselves. If policy and practice aims, quite rightly, to ensure that children are adequately safeguarded within their own families, then the need for long-term dependency on services has to be acknowledged. Swift withdrawal of services, and premature case closure, found in all three empirical studies, is of concern.

There is also disturbing evidence of diminishing levels of social work services as children grow older and their problems become more entrenched. The *Neglected Children Reunification Study* found that case management is more proactive with younger children, and tends to drop off as they grow older and there appears less chance of them achieving permanence. The focus of intervention tends gradually to shift from children's experience of maltreatment to their difficult behaviour, which is likely to become more challenging as they remain unprotected. This study found a key turning point when children are as young as *six*. Those over that age who return home unsuccessfully are less likely to settle, and have much less chance of achieving a permanent placement in care or accommodation. This important finding not only demonstrates how necessary it is to act swiftly to ensure that children are properly safeguarded in stable homes as early in their lives as possible. It also indicates the need for robust back-up procedures, such as regular joint visits with senior practitioners, and routine case audits by senior managers, to ensure that case management remains proactive and focused on the child's needs as they grow older.

The *Recognition of Adolescent Neglect Review* and the two *Analyses of Serious Case Reviews* all identify how the process of disengagement continues, so that young people at severe risk of suffering significant harm can become rejected by services as well as by their families as they grow older. In the long run, diminished support, passive case management and premature case closure are not cost-effective. The *Home or Care? Study* provides convincing evidence to show how children who are not safeguarded develop increasingly severe behavioural and emotional problems, engage in risk-taking behaviours and become excluded from school and mainstream society. All of these factors indicate future emotional costs to children and families as well as financial costs to statutory services.[204,205] Moreover, if it later becomes evident that these young people need to be placed away from home, their care episodes may be shorter, but they will be more unstable, and will cost more than earlier intervention (including placement away from home) would have done.[206]

Including parents

Written agreements

Although intensive, long-term packages of services may be necessary, parents should not be supported indefinitely, with few incentives to overcome their difficulties and eventually safeguard their children independently. All the studies identify a need for transparent and time-limited plans, to be agreed between parents and children's services, with clearly articulated goals and well-understood consequences if these are not achieved. At present such plans exist in the form of written agreements made between local authorities and parents. However, when, as often happens, parents break the terms of these agreements, there are frequently no consequences and they are given yet another chance to show that they can safeguard the child. This is both damaging to children and also confusing to parents, who may become resentful at a later date when action is finally taken to enforce agreements that have previously been ignored with impunity. There is scope to develop written agreements further into more formal contracts which both parties expect to see enforced.

Partnership with parents and its limits

Working in partnership with parents is one of the principles of the Children Act 1989, and is seen as the hallmark of successful parenting support. However, repeated failures to honour the terms of written agreements in high-risk families may indicate that a more assertive approach to case management is required. The evidence from serious case reviews and from the three studies of social work interventions demonstrates that there may be some families and situations in which parents cannot be treated as active partners if their children are to be adequately safeguarded. This is an unwelcome finding, but it should be noted that the *Neglected Children Reunification Study* found that as many as two fifths of parents may actively resist or attempt to sabotage interventions from professionals. Where parents are uncooperative, extra vigilance is necessary to ensure that children are adequately safeguarded.[207]

Parents' views

Interviews with parents show that they appreciate social workers who not only have the ability to listen, but are also 'straight-talking' and honest about their problems and the threat that their children may be removed. Practitioners who find it difficult to break bad news or who encourage parents to be over-optimistic about their progress are not so highly valued:

> 'The first [social worker] didn't like breaking bad news, and I said he shouldn't really be doing the job. Yeah, he didn't like saying that she [partner] wasn't going to get [child's older sibling] back. He said she [partner] would have [child's older sibling] back at Christmas, he said, so that's giving someone false hope. But the next, like, two [social workers] we had were really on the ball, they said, "There's no chance," and I found that more respectful than being deceived all the time… I mean, if people aren't there to break bad news, they shouldn't be doing the job… 'Cos that is a tough job, and I mean decisions have to get made, on the spur of the moment, you can't just linger people along and get their hopes up.' (Birth father)[208]

Identifying who can be safeguarded at home

The studies identified a number of factors that make it more, or less, likely that children will be adequately safeguarded while living with birth parents. Virtually all the parents in the *Significant Harm of Infants Study* were struggling with known risk factors for maltreatment[209] or its recurrence. About a third of them succeeded in making sufficient changes to provide a nurturing home for an infant. Indicators identified by this study should be tested out with a larger database, but they appear to point to a number of factors that distinguish between those parents who are likely to overcome adversities sufficiently to care for a new baby from those who are not. Parents who succeed in making sufficient changes appear to be less likely to have experienced abuse (particularly sexual abuse in childhood); to have come to terms with the removal from home of older children and to have developed sufficient insight to acknowledge that their behaviour may have played a part in such decisions; and to make use of the support that both social work and more specialist services can provide. Engagement with services is often regarded as a positive indicator, but the findings from this study suggest that many parents will go through the motions of, for instance, attending appointments and support groups; it is only those who are genuinely motivated to change who will participate thoroughly in the programmes they are offered. Parents appear to find it easier to overcome external factors such as a relationship with a partner who abuses them and/or their children than internal factors such as their own addiction to drugs or alcohol.

Parents who are motivated to change often have a defining moment when they realize that they will need to take substantial action if they are to meet the new baby's needs: for some parents this is the permanent separation from an older child; for others it is the early death of a close relative from alcohol or substance misuse; for others it is the realization that they will need to disengage from an abusive partnership; and some parents become deeply attached to the baby. Parents who do not make sufficient changes do not appear to experience such wake-up calls.

A new baby appears to act as a catalyst for radical changes in parental behaviour patterns; however, if these have not occurred within six months of the birth, then any minor changes parents appear to have made are unlikely to persist or be sufficient to meet the needs of the child within an appropriate timeframe.

Returning home from care or accommodation

The studies also identify a number of factors that make it more – or less – likely that children who return home after a period spent in care or accommodation will be adequately safeguarded and not require readmission.

Reunifications are more likely to endure if children return to a different parent from the one with whom they were living prior to becoming looked after. Children who return early to the same parent are unlikely to do as well as those who return after sufficient time has elapsed for the problems that led to the original admission to have been addressed. For reunification to have some chance of success, there needs to be some evidence that sufficient changes have taken place and that the child will now be safe. For instance, reunification is unlikely to be successful if there are ongoing concerns about parents' substance misuse: the *Home or Care? Study* found that 81 per cent of children who are reunited with parents who are still misusing drugs subsequently re-enter care or accommodation.

Younger children are more likely to return home successfully than those who are older and perhaps have more entrenched experience of maltreatment and instability. Children who return home with other looked after siblings appear to fare better than those who return alone or are reunited with siblings who are already *in situ.*

Looked after children who have experienced chronic and serious emotional abuse and neglect do significantly worse than others if they return home, and plans for their reunification should be considered with great caution. Reunification for these children should not be undertaken unless there is strong evidence of sufficient change in parenting capacity and appropriate long-term services are available. Since one of the major factors that influence successful reunification is the local authority in which the child resides, it would appear that proactive case management plays a major role in the success or failure of reunification.

Readmissions to care or accommodation

The *Home or Care? Study* found that, when placements with own parents are counted as reunifications, the proportion of maltreated children who return home is almost exactly the same as that of other children who have been looked after. However, both the reunification studies found that about two thirds of maltreated children who return home from care or accommodation are subsequently re-admitted.

Both the *Home or Care?* and the *Neglected Children Reunification Studies* show that many children experience repeated attempts at reunification. These should be avoided. Children who move in and out of care or accommodation have the worst overall outcomes. Not only are repeated attempts at reunification damaging to children's welfare, they also increase the risk of their losing the chance of finding an alternative pathway to permanence. Where parental progress is not sustained or parents fail to comply with therapeutic programmes, an early assessment of the impact of return for the child should be made to prevent drift and further deterioration. Most difficulties emerge within the first few months of reunion.

The courts frequently insist on further trials at home before approving a permanence plan – an issue that has been identified as causing increasing instability and delays for very young children, to the detriment of their welfare.[210] Judges and magistrates need to be aware of the frequency with which attempts at reunification with birth families break down, and the detrimental consequences for the children concerned.

What do the studies tell us about the looked after children system? Which children benefit from being separated from their birth families? How do outcomes compare with those for maltreated children who return home?

Who benefits from being looked after?

Timing

Both child development research and the evidence from practice analysis demonstrate the importance of taking early action when children are found to be maltreated. Research on child development indicates that, in the first six months of life, having positive interactions appears to be more important than interacting with specific people.[211,212] More preferential attachment behaviours and stranger anxiety begin to set in at around seven months. From this age, maltreated children may start to develop maladaptive attachments.[213,214] Also at about this age, looked after children in temporary placements may start to develop secure attachments to carers, the loss of which, particularly in the early years, can be sources of enduring distress. An important recent study of attachment in adopted children found that those who were adopted before 12 months of age were as securely attached as their non-adopted peers, whereas those adopted after their first birthday showed less attachment security than non-adopted children.[215] Therefore if children cannot live with their birth parents, early separation and speedy progression towards permanence are likely to be the least damaging courses of action.

The *Significant Harm of Infants Study* also found that all the parents in the sample who successfully overcame problems which represented significant risk factors for maltreatment, and were able to provide a nurturing home for the index child, did so before the baby was six months old – before birth if the problem was substance abuse – an indicator that early action can be fair to parents as well as in the child's best interests.

However, this study also found that about one in five babies identified as suffering, or likely to suffer, significant harm before their first birthdays are doubly jeopardized: both by being left too long in neglectful homes while professionals wait in vain for parents to overcome their difficulties, and then by remaining so long with interim carers that they experience disrupted attachments when they are finally placed for adoption. Frequent references are made to meeting children's timescales, but professionals need to be more aware of what these actually are in terms of children's stages of development.

Based on the evidence of known risk and protective factors,[216] researchers in the *Neglected Children Reunification Study* considered that over a quarter of children (28%) were left for too long in abusive homes before they were removed. This was also true of about half the separated infants in the *Significant Harm of Infants Study*, while it was also evident that the long-term wellbeing of about 50 per cent of those who were still living with their birth parents at the age of three had been compromised by persistent exposure to neglect and emotional maltreatment.

Outcomes of care and accommodation

The studies in the Research Initiative all focus on children who have been identified as suffering, or likely to suffer, significant harm or who have become looked after because they are being abused or neglected by their birth families or other carers. This is the primary reason for entry to care or accommodation for about 60 per cent of looked after children in England, although many others will also have experienced maltreatment. The studies provide incontrovertible evidence that many of these children benefit from being placed away from home.

Stability

While constant moves from one placement to another are seen as a major problem for children looked after away from home, the instability experienced by those who remain with very vulnerable families is less well publicized.[217,218] The *Home or Care? Study* compared the progress and outcomes of a subset of 68 looked after children who returned home at some point within the four-year follow-up period with a matched group of 81 children who did not. Six months after the key decision, children in the care group were more settled than those who had returned to their birth families. Although similar proportions had changed placements, moves for the care group had largely been for positive reasons – for instance, from short-term to long-term placements, or from strangers to kinship carers after assessments had been completed. In contrast, moves for children in the home group had been far less positive, resulting from disrupted arrangements with relatives and/or returns to care or accommodation. About one in five of these children had never settled and had moved continually between relatives and family friends before finally returning to care. This pattern continued into the final follow-up, by which time two thirds of the care group (65%) had been settled for two or more years in their current placement, compared with two fifths (41%) of those at home. The proportion of children who had found stability at home is almost identical to that found in the *Neglected Children Reunification Study* (43%).

Kinship care is, rightly, the placement of choice, but the *Significant Harm of Infants Study* raises a number of caveats concerning its indiscriminate use. Although such placements are often beneficial, and may produce better outcomes than placements with strangers, they are sometimes selected with little regard for the quality of care provided, the carers' previous history of poor parenting, their personal problems or their knowledge of the child. More attention needs to be given to ensuring that children are only placed with relatives who can genuinely offer both the benefits of belonging to a wider family network and the commitment that makes such placements valuable. There are several indications that relatives and friends may need specialist services to help children overcome the consequences of maltreatment – and to manage the relationship with birth parents – but too little of this is forthcoming.[219] Several family and friends carers in the *Significant Harm of Infants Study* were receiving minimal support to cope with the children's often serious behavioural problems; by the time these children were aged three, many of these placements were approaching breakdown.

Wellbeing

Notwithstanding such issues, children who remain looked after tend to do better on measures of wellbeing than those who return home. The *Home or Care? Study* found this to be true even when comparisons were made with those whose reunions with birth families had stayed stable throughout the follow-up period. There is no evidence that this finding can be explained by greater difficulties among children who go home; it suggests that, overall, remaining in care or accommodation is likely to enhance the welfare of maltreated children.

At the final follow-up, those in the *Home or Care? Study* who remained looked after were less likely to have misused alcohol or drugs or to have committed offences than those who returned home; they had significantly better mean scores for health; they were more likely to have close adult ties; and they were considered more likely to have a range of special skills, interests and hobbies. They were less likely to be in pupil referral units, in alternative forms of education, without a school place or to be persistent truants than those who had returned home, although significant differences in school performance were not noted between the two groups. The findings are slightly less positive in the *Neglected Children Reunification Study*, probably because different methodologies and definitions were used, although they point in a similar direction.

Neglected children who are returned prematurely to maltreating families fare worse than those who have experienced other types of maltreatment. Where there has been strong evidence of past neglect, even after taking account of other factors that predict future wellbeing, these children do best if they remain looked after. Amongst those who go home, the stability of the reunion appears to have little impact on their overall wellbeing. Emotionally abused children who go home also tend to fare worse than similarly maltreated children who remain looked after.

Local authority care can be rightly castigated for its low aspirations, lack of stability and insensitivity to some children's needs, and these are all issues that need to be addressed.[220] Nevertheless, the studies provide robust evidence of its benefits. The poor outcomes of care and accommodation that have been so widely publicized[221] are largely the product of children's long-term exposure to abuse and neglect prior to entry, or following unsuccessful returns home. The myth that care will have a negative impact on children's wellbeing has meant that professionals have tended to be reluctant to remove children from abusive situations, to the detriment of their long-term life chances. When children are looked after, placements need to provide more specialist interventions to help overcome the consequences of abuse, but their potential to benefit maltreated children should be better recognized. All the studies that utilized recent, primary data found that, in the absence of intensive, effective packages of family support services, provided on a long-term basis to meet parents' and children's needs, more children should be placed away from home.

Conclusion

The messages from the studies that focus on interventions from children's social care point to the need for considerable improvement. They indicate that, for a number of reasons, too many children are inadequately safeguarded while they remain in the care of abusive and neglectful birth parents. Neglect and emotional maltreatment are not sufficiently recognized and acted upon in a timely manner. Where parents succeed in overcoming significant difficulties to care for a new baby, services are often withdrawn abruptly, without robust arrangements for future lower-level help being made. There is insufficient acknowledgement that other parents, with entrenched problems, may be, at least temporarily, unreachable, or need long-term, comprehensive and well-coordinated packages of services if their children are to be adequately safeguarded. Case management tends to be more active and effective for children who are supervised or placed under court orders than for those who are not. When compared with those who are reunited with their birth families, the majority of maltreated children do better in care or accommodation. These are difficult messages to act on in times of economic austerity. However, they do indicate that cutting back on early intervention and Section 17 family support services could increase the levels of maltreatment and its consequences, especially if this is accompanied by attempts to reduce the numbers of children looked after away from home.

Key messages for all who work together to safeguard children

- There is a need for proactive, not passive, practice.

- Greater attention should be given to ensuring that interventions for maltreated children and their families are informed by evidence-based assessments of need.

- Decisive and timely interventions are of vital importance. The evidence of how quickly harm occurs, and how difficult it is to reverse, makes this an imperative.

- There is a need to rebalance decision-making so it is driven by the paramount interests of the child, rather than a concern for protecting parents' rights, regardless of their capacity to change. Children's rights demand this.

- All involved need to be mindful that the purpose of the intervention is not to safeguard the family but the individual children within it.

- Care can be the best option for some maltreated children and should not be seen as a last resort. In the long run this may also prove to be the least costly and most effective option.

- Attention should be given to referring children and families back to targeted and universal services when children's social care interventions are completed.

- Expert knowledge of child development, attachment and the impact of abuse and neglect is fundamental to the work of all those responsible for safeguarding children. This should also form part of compulsory continuing professional development to ensure practitioners are up to date with new research evidence.

- About two thirds of maltreated children who return home from care or accommodation are subsequently readmitted; this rises to 81 per cent in the case of children whose parents are misusing drugs. Rates of readmission to care or accommodation should be carefully monitored and disseminated.

- Neglected and emotionally abused children who return home tend to fare worse both on indicators of wellbeing and of stability than those who remain looked after. There is incontrovertible evidence that in the absence of intensive effective packages of family support services, provided on a long-term basis, and tailored to both their and their parents' needs, these children benefit from being placed away from home.

Key messages for policymakers, strategic managers, commissioners of services and lead members for children's services and the judiciary

- Both parents and practitioners need clear guidance on what constitutes societally acceptable and unacceptable standards of parenting; initiating a properly moderated public and professional conversation about this topic should be a priority.

- There should be some formal agreement between chief executives of local authorities, directors of children's services and heads of legal services departments and the courts concerning appropriate thresholds for taking action when children are experiencing severe and chronic neglect. This should lead to protocols for intervention that have been approved by these senior managers.

- Sixty-two per cent of care plans made by the courts are either never implemented or not fully carried out; 62 per cent of supervision orders fail as the situation at home deteriorates; 87 per cent of placements with own parents break down. Some discussion needs to be held by senior managers at a strategic level concerning ways in which children can be better protected through court involvement.

Key messages for operational managers and practitioners in children's social care

- Practitioners must find out about and analyse historical information about the child and family including evidence about past family functioning, particularly in cases of neglect.

- Attention should be given to ensuring proactive case management for older as well as younger children suffering, or likely to suffer, significant harm. At present the evidence suggests that this may start to diminish for children as young as *six*.

- Repeated attempts at reunification with birth parents should be avoided. These are damaging to children's wellbeing and jeopardize their chances of achieving permanence through alternative routes.

- Written agreements between parents and local authorities need to be developed and made into more robust arrangements, with explicit plans and timescales, and clearly spelled-out consequences for non-compliance.

- It is unrealistic to expect parents who have previously experienced the removal of a child to re-refer themselves to children's social care if they run into difficulties after a case has been closed.

- Practitioners need to be aware of children's timeframes: if children need to be permanently separated then it is important to do this as quickly as possible. Those who are permanently placed by their first birthday are more likely to become securely attached to adoptive parents than those who are older when placed.

- Parents who have not succeeded in overcoming complex problems involving substance and alcohol misuse, mental ill health and intimate partner violence by the time a baby is six months old are unlikely to do so within an appropriate timeframe for that child, although they may later make sufficient progress to parent subsequent children.

Key messages for health professionals

- Health professionals need to be aware of delay and drift and their consequences for children.

- GP evidence is well regarded and might be of critical importance if brought before the courts.

Key messages for all those involved in the family justice system

- The impact of delayed decisions on children's subsequent life chances should be widely disseminated, and timescales be formally discussed.

- Consideration should be given to the use of expert assessments of parenting capacity. Assessments should be required to cover issues such as how parenting problems are impacting on children's health and development. Validated instruments such as the Crittenden CARE Index should be used to assess parent–infant interaction.

- Consideration should be given to developing guidance for repeated assessments: if there has been insufficient time for change to occur, then further assessments introduce unnecessary delays, to the detriment of children's welfare.

- Feedback arrangements should be made to ensure that courts are aware of the outcomes of their decisions. This should include the frequency with which supervision orders or returns home to birth parents break down and the impact of delays on children's welfare.

Specific Interventions for Children and Families with Additional or Complex Needs

- This chapter draws largely on the evidence from the *Physical Abuse Intervention Review*[222] and the *Emotional Abuse Intervention Review*.[223]

- This chapter has important messages for all those who have responsibility for safeguarding and promoting the welfare of children.

- It also has specific messages for the following professional groups:

  ○ policymakers (all sections)

  ○ Local Safeguarding Children Boards (all sections)

  ○ strategic managers and commissioners of services in health and children's social care (all sections)

  ○ practitioners and operational managers in health and children's social care (this chapter could be used as a resource when trying to assess whether those specific interventions that are available are likely to be appropriate or successful)

  ○ practitioners and operational managers in education (the section on child-focused interventions includes details of two school/preschool-based interventions that are aimed at helping children overcome the consequences of physical abuse and neglect).

Introduction

What focused, specific programmes can be used to complement broader interventions with children and families to help prevent further maltreatment and mitigate its effects? What do we know about 'what works' and what should be taken into account when considering the evidence?

In the last chapter we focused on broad interventions to safeguard children including out-of-home placement and social work casework. This chapter considers more focused specific interventions, often designed to complement the above. These interventions are usually rigorously time limited. They are offered by professionals such as mental health workers and therapists or by trained social workers, nurses or health visitors. In this context we use the term 'intervention' to refer to specific therapeutic programmes that involve direct work with parents, children and families. In many cases these do not stand in isolation, but might be delivered as part of a planned inter-agency intervention with a child and family.

Most of the following evidence about 'what works' comes from two rigorously conducted systematic reviews within the Research Initiative. The *Physical Abuse Intervention Review* and the *Emotional Abuse Intervention Review* each focus on a different form of maltreatment and its consequences. Where available, we have supplemented the evidence with data from complementary sources; for instance, the results of additional trials published since these studies were undertaken and other major reviews[224] which provide additional information about some of the examples we have selected.

Chapter 3 introduced our adapted version of a conceptual map that has been frequently used to illustrate the different stages of intervention. In this chapter we will continue to use this framework to discuss what the evidence says about 'what works' in terms of intervention programmes designed to be delivered in families where there is a high risk of abuse or neglect, or after children have been exposed to it. Specifically we look at what the studies say about evaluated interventions designed to:

- prevent the occurrence or recurrence of maltreatment in families where the likelihood of abuse or neglect is high

- address the consequences of maltreatment (i.e. mitigate impairment).

Although we have categorized the various interventions in this way in order to help commissioners and practitioners understand and make sense of the wide variety that is available, in the real world it is not always so easy to make clear-cut distinctions. For instance, it will often be necessary to try and prevent recurrence of maltreatment, while at the same time attempting to mitigate the impairment to a child's health and development that has already resulted from the harm suffered.

Similarly, although programmes fall into groups according to the main ways of achieving change (via parent, parent–child relationship, or whole family) as indicated below, some are not so easily categorized. The focus of interventions may be both on the parent and on the parent–child relationship or indeed the whole family in parallel.

This chapter focuses on those specific interventions which have been shown to produce the best results for children and families who encounter the types of adversity discussed in earlier chapters. Before considering them individually, there are some key issues that need to be borne in mind.

Issues for commissioners and practitioners to consider in choosing and utilizing a specific intervention

Evidence of effectiveness

In choosing a specific intervention, commissioners and practitioners first need to be sure that it is effective in addressing the issues for which it was designed. Only interventions that have been rigorously evaluated should be selected. The methodology used in the evaluation determines the weight given to the evidence of effectiveness according to an established hierarchy, as shown in Table 5.1.

Table 5.1: Hierarchy of levels of evidence[225]

Design	Advantages	Disadvantages
Level A		
Randomized Controlled Trials	No systematic differences between conditions; therefore any changes are due to treatment effects	Can be impractical or unethical to implement
Level B		
Two-Group Non-Randomized Comparative Trials	Groups can be matched to minimize known differences Practical for pre-existing groups	Groups may differ on factors for which the groups were not matched, potentially confounding the results
Level C		
Single-Group Pre-Post Studies	Measures change over time Often the only practical option	Impossible to know whether changes are due to the intervention or other factors
Level D		
Retrospective Quantitative Studies	Data may already be available and may provide some useful indications for more rigorous evaluation at a later date	Data may not have been collected specifically to evaluate this intervention and may therefore be incomplete or inadequate
Level E		
Case Studies	Data may provide useful indications for more rigorous evaluation at a later stage Qualitative data may indicate potential areas for further explorations and analysis – suggesting why rather than what is happening	Data from a small number of examples may not be generalizable

The table ranks the evidence related to five different types of evaluation. At the top of this hierarchy (Level A) are randomized controlled trials (RCTs). When rigorously implemented they produce the strongest evidence. Random allocation minimizes the potential bias that might occur if participants are selected or self-selected to treatment conditions. Including a randomly allocated control group in a study also allows the effects of an intervention to be compared with that of no intervention or 'treatment as usual'.

Because it is sometimes unethical or impractical to withhold an intervention in order to obtain a control group, other ways have been developed of measuring one treatment group against another. One common method is to compare two active treatment groups (Level B). These evaluations offer information about the relative effectiveness of two (or more) interventions but do not provide data about the absolute effects of either. It could be the case that there is little difference between the two options but we cannot determine whether either is particularly useful.

In cases where it is not possible to offer an alternative programme (for instance, where therapists are only trained to provide one service), a single-group study can be used (Level C), measuring changes over time. These studies can be useful in gaining information about the suitability and acceptability of an intervention for a population, but should be considered in the light of the possibility that any observed changes may be due to factors other than the treatment itself. Retrospective quantitative studies (Level D) and case studies (Level E) are useful in indicating factors to be taken into account in later studies, but are not evaluations in themselves.

All the interventions introduced in this chapter have been shown to be effective in addressing the issues for which they were designed. We have indicated the place in this hierarchy for each of those discussed by showing the evidence level of the evaluation. Those who are considering commissioning services may find this a useful indicator of the strength of the current evidence of effectiveness.

In addition to considering the evidence level of any evaluation, commissioners will also need to take into account the size of the sample participating and the drop-out rate (which can be high, indicating that the intervention may have little capacity to deliver change) as well as the data on outcomes. A sound evaluation will have applied sensitive outcome measures before and after the intervention and collected follow-up data to assess sustainability. However, there are also other considerations to be borne in mind.

Transferability

First, many specific interventions have been developed and evaluated outside the UK. Services for children in other countries may be different and the context in which they are delivered may have few similarities for all sorts of reasons. Thresholds may also be set at varying levels so that the population who access services may have very different needs. Thus we cannot be confident that services will produce the same level of benefit in a UK context. Nor can we automatically assume that those interventions found to be effective in another country will necessarily work in the same way in the UK. However, as we shall see, there are grounds for thinking that some interventions are transferable from one country to another. Some of the behavioural parenting interventions originally developed in Australia and the US, and discussed later in this chapter, have now been successfully trialled in the UK, with positive results.

Many specific interventions have been standardized and documented in such a way that they can be translated and used elsewhere by other service providers. These manualized programmes are often available under a licence which usually requires users to follow the guidance closely to ensure that the integrity of the intervention is maintained. The process of adhering to the design as set down in the manual is known as 'programme fidelity'. Training and supervision are frequently offered, and are often a requirement. However, there is usually scope for some adaptation to local circumstances, as few programmes translate from one context to another without the need for some change and modification.

Second, some promising interventions have been developed for 'troubled', but not specifically for maltreating or maltreated, populations. Again this raises questions about transferability. There are some grounds for optimism. There is a reasonable amount of evidence from randomized trials for the effectiveness of child-focused cognitive behavioural therapy in improving child outcomes, including depression, anxiety and trauma, that are relevant to maltreatment.[226,227,228] Well-structured parenting interventions, such as parent training, have also been shown to be effective with troubled but non-maltreating families; this should strengthen our confidence in their likely effectiveness for maltreated children because they have been shown to improve parenting *per se.*[229,230,231] On the other hand, there is ample evidence from studies in this Overview that parents with the most complex and entrenched problems appear not to respond to routine services. They may well not respond to these programmes either. Until such programmes have been rigorously evaluated in families where children are suffering, or likely to suffer, significant harm, their effectiveness remains unproven.

Implementation

Studies have consistently shown disappointingly high rates for re-abuse and poor outcomes for those who receive specific interventions.[232,233] Risks to the child are likely to remain high and things may start to go wrong if stresses within the family build up. Taking account of the risk of further maltreatment and the need for sustainability makes sense both in terms of the interests of the child and family but also in terms of the return on social investment. Specific programmes are costly and it is crucial to ensure improvement gains are sustained over time.

In a UK context, specific intervention models may most usefully be applied to families with complex needs as one of a range of Sure Start children's centre-based interventions or alongside social casework or other services from a team working with the child and family.[234] Those commissioning specific interventions should ensure that ongoing support from the network of safeguarding services is in place, bearing in mind that the follow-up is likely to be multi-disciplinary. As a programme comes to an end, a health visitor, school, social worker or a combination of all three may need to provide preventive services to ensure there is no relapse.

The remainder of this chapter first provides examples of ten specific interventions that have been shown to be effective in preventing maltreatment and/or its consequences. They have been selected using the criteria indicated above, and because of their appropriateness to the issues raised by other studies in this Overview; examples of other validated interventions may be found in the original reviews. We then conclude by introducing the reader to proposals for an innovative 'common elements' approach, which has yet to be piloted, but which could, potentially, provide more effective interventions for complex cases.

Parent-focused interventions to prevent the occurrence or recurrence of maltreatment

> Parent-focused interventions are designed to work on improving parental skills and some aspect of the parent's wellbeing or their parenting that is thought to contribute to abusive interactions with the child.

As we have already seen in earlier chapters, it is now well established that children growing up in families affected by parental substance misuse, domestic violence and mental ill health are at an increased risk of being maltreated.[235] The *Significant Harm of Infants Study* demonstrates that many parents will be unlikely to benefit from specific interventions to improve their parenting skills unless some of these and/or other underlying issues have also been addressed. The study shows that even parents who have previously had several children placed for adoption can change sufficiently to provide a nurturing, non-abusive home for a subsequent child. However, those who manage to do so will have reached a point at which they realize they will need to make radical changes to their lifestyles if they are to succeed. In order to engender sufficient change, such parents will need support to overcome adversities that increase the likelihood of children being maltreated. They may also need practical help, for instance to move away from a drug-abusing network or to deal with debts that are adding to stresses that make it difficult for them to maintain change.

Substance-misusing families

A number of innovative methods of working with families with multiple problems, including substance misuse, have been developed in recent years. One example is *Parents Under Pressure (PUP)*,[236,a] a home-visiting programme designed principally for substance-misusing parents that has since been extended to address wider needs such as mental health problems. It has been evaluated with older children in Australia in a randomized controlled trial,[237] and is currently being piloted with younger children in England.[238]

PUP targets multiple domains of family functioning, including the psychological functioning of individuals in the family, parent–child relationships and social contextual factors. Its purpose is to help parents understand their own emotional responses and the extent to which they may be influenced by substance misuse, with the objective of improving affect regulation. Key features are a focus on parental strengths and parental risk factors and on the introduction of 'mindfulness-based techniques' (i.e. techniques for 'refocusing the mind on the present moment and letting go of negative thoughts in order to shift from a severely negative mood state or feeling of anxiety, to one that is less overwhelming') in terms of improving parental affect.

This programme has been shown to be more successful in the treatment of substance-misusing mothers than standard care by a substance abuse clinic or a traditional parent-training intervention (Evidence Level A). Parents receiving the PUP programme have shown significant reductions in stress, methadone dose, and in indicators of the likelihood of child abuse. Their children have shown significant reductions in child behaviour problems and improvements in pro-social scores. It seems likely that theoretically based interventions of this nature, which address multiple domains in families' lives, may be more effective than those that adopt a single issue approach.

Parents involved in domestic violence

The *Significant Harm of Infants Study* found that in most cases the practice solution to domestic violence is to exclude the (male) perpetrator rather than to address the issues that engender it, with the result that many men are likely to go on to abuse other women and children. Further research is needed into the effectiveness of interventions for perpetrators,[239] such as anger management programmes, designed to reduce the risk of domestic violence. The systematic reviews found few interventions for this population that were both relevant and had been sufficiently evaluated. One promising intervention, the *South Tyneside*

---

a   See Example 1 in Appendix 2 for more details

Domestic Abuse Perpetrator Programme, has so far only been evaluated as a case study (Evidence Level E) with a very small sample.[240]

There may still be continuing issues for women who have been exposed to domestic violence even after the perpetrator has been excluded. There is considerable evidence that such women suffer a loss of confidence, depression and feelings of degradation; this can result in their moving on to another abusive relationship, as well as in difficulties in organizing day-to-day living and responding to the needs of children.[241] Some interventions have been developed to address these issues. The *Post-Shelter Advocacy Programme*[242,243] has been shown significantly to reduce repeat violence and improve women's quality of life at two-year follow-up, although the effect was not sustained (Evidence Level A). However, further trials are necessary to ascertain whether this intervention is effective in safeguarding children.

Parenting problems amongst abusing parents

A parent's own experience of maltreatment in childhood is known to be associated with recurrent child abuse.[244,245] We know that parents who have been physically abused or neglected in childhood are more likely to maltreat their own children in the same ways.[246] Numerous studies have also demonstrated that parents who maltreat tend to hold distorted beliefs and unrealistic expectations regarding the developmental capabilities of children, the age-appropriateness of child behaviours and their own behaviour when interacting with them. This can result in misreading children's intentions and behaviour and attributing hostile intent, which in turn has been linked with over-reactive and coercive parenting, angry feelings in parents, child behaviour problems, and the use of harsh punishment.[247] Thus programmes which are designed to address adults' own experiences of poor parenting and/or the psychological consequences of abuse can make a valuable contribution.

The *Enhanced Triple P-Positive Parenting Programme*[248,b] is one such specific intervention that has been rigorously evaluated (Evidence Level A).[249,250] Implementation of the core elements of Triple P as a targeted preventive intervention has been discussed in Chapter 3. However, these core elements can be complemented by an enhanced programme that includes elements designed to reduce anger and misattribution in parents reported for, or at self-reported risk of, emotionally abusing their children. A randomized controlled trial[251] compared the effectiveness of the standard family intervention with the enhanced version of Triple P; both are geared towards families in difficulties. While at the six-month follow-up both interventions showed similarly positive outcomes on all measures of child abuse risk, parent practices, parental adjustment, and child behaviour and adjustment, only those receiving the 'enhanced' version continued

---

b   See Example 2 in Appendix 2 for more details

to show greater change in negative parental attributions. The results point to the benefits of delivering a less intensive intervention in the first instance, followed by reassessment to gauge whether there have been changes in the risk factors for maltreatment, and then offering customized adjunctive interventions based on this assessment.

This intervention has been comprehensively evaluated in different countries and therefore demonstrated to be transferable to different national settings.[252] It is currently being implemented in the UK. In the absence of long-term effectiveness studies, and in view of the evidence of recurrence of maltreatment noted above, there still needs to be a continuing evaluation of those who have successfully completed the programme to ascertain if their children are less likely to be re-abused.

Cognitive behavioural approaches

Cognitive behavioural approaches aim to change the parents' thoughts, beliefs and behaviour in the present, rather than analysing the role of past influences. They commonly focus on helping parents to change the way in which they perceive children and supporting them to identify, confront and change their thinking and develop better child management skills. Cognitive behavioural therapy (CBT) can be provided in the home on a one-to-one basis or on a group basis away from home.

The *Emotional Abuse Intervention Review* describes a study which compared *CBT-based home-delivered parent training* with *an enhanced programme* involving additional group-based parent-training sessions.[253,c] The study showed the benefits of appropriately delivered CBT with added components specifically aimed at addressing factors known to be associated with abusive parenting such as anger and stress management. Participants showed significant reductions in stress and anxiety levels and in emotionally abusive behaviour. The study also showed that

---

Summary: Parent interventions

A number of parent-focused interventions seem to hold promise for reducing recurrence of abuse and improving outcomes for children, including child mental health and parent–child relationships. It seems likely that theoretically based interventions, which address multiple domains of families' lives, may be more effective than those that adopt a single issue approach. It is also clear that unless continuing support services are offered after a specific, time-limited programme has been completed, many parents will have difficulties in maintaining the progress they have made.

---

c   See Example 3 in Appendix 2 for more details

the most effective results are achieved when home and group interventions are combined.

> Parents Under Pressure has been shown to be more successful in the treatment of substance-abusing mothers than standard care by a substance abuse clinic or additional parent training.
>
> Few interventions for parents involved in domestic violence are specifically aimed at safeguarding children and/or have been sufficiently evaluated.
>
> The evaluation of the Enhanced Triple P-Positive Parenting Programme points to the potential benefits of providing CBT-based interventions to maltreating families. The results showed reliable improvements in child behaviour and in the management of problematic behaviours by parents, though it should be noted that some of the parents participating were at the less severe end of the spectrum.
>
> When a one-to-one home-based CBT programme is compared with an enhanced programme involving the addition of group-based sessions, the benefits of appropriately delivered CBT with added components specifically aimed at addressing factors known to be associated with abusive parenting such as anger and stress management are evident.
>
> Combining one-to-one with group-based interventions appears to achieve the most effective results.
>
> Limitations of the evaluations were that some were conducted outside the UK and were based on small samples.

Parent and child-focused interventions to prevent the occurrence or recurrence of maltreatment in families where children are suffering, or likely to suffer, significant harm

Parent and child-focused interventions are intended to focus on the parent and the parent–child relationship. They may work on aspects of parental functioning and mental health at the same time as helping to reduce parent–child conflict or child problem behaviour, which in some cases may precipitate abuse.

Parent and child-focused interventions are intended to focus on the parent and the parent–child relationship, targeting both parent and child with the aim of changing some aspect of parental functioning such as their attitudes, beliefs or behaviour. At the same time the interventions may also seek to improve parental wellbeing by working on mental health issues, such as anxiety, depression and anger. A number of theoretical constructs underpin parent and child-focused approaches; these include cognitive behavioural, psychoanalytic and attachment-based approaches. Evaluated examples of all three types of intervention are given below.

Parent–child psychotherapy to address emotional abuse

There is a growing body of evidence pointing to the effectiveness of parent–child psychotherapy in addressing emotional abuse. Interventions are underpinned by attachment theory, which argues that mother–child attachment relationships are central to positive child outcomes; the aim is therefore to tackle aspects of parenting representation but also to work simultaneously with both the parent and infant. *Preschooler–Parent Psychotherapy*[254,d] is a specific, clinic-based programme, provided to mothers and preschoolers where there is a known history of abuse in the family. Therapy focuses on helping the mother recognize how her past history is re-enacted in the present and enabling her to change her representations. Other, similar programmes have also produced positive outcomes.[255,256] A randomized controlled trial has shown this model of intervention to be more effective at improving representations of self and of caregivers than a CBT-based model directed at parenting skills.[257] However, some evaluations have only focused on factors likely to be changed by the therapy such as maternal and child representations; further evaluations that explore a wider range of outcomes are needed.

Attachment-based programmes for families where there is a likelihood of abuse or neglect

Video feedback interventions show statistically significant positive effects on parenting behaviour, attitude of parents and the development of the child.[258] *Interaction Guidance*[259,e] is a promising example of an attachment-based programme using this methodology, developed primarily for families where there is a likelihood of abuse or neglect. It is designed specifically for children with faltering growth, and consists of videotaped interaction between mother and infant, followed by discussion, education and feedback, geared towards promoting improved communication. A two-group, non-randomized trial (Evidence Level B)[260] has shown this intervention to be more effective than a behavioural feeding programme. However, the outcome measures were limited, and this should be regarded as preliminary evidence. Further trials are being undertaken, including one with maltreated infants and toddlers in foster care.[261]

---

d   See Example 4 in Appendix 2 for more details
e   See Example 5 in Appendix 2 for more details

A cognitive behavioural approach to address physical abuse

Parent–Child Interaction Therapy[262,263,f] is based on a cognitive behavioural model and shows promise as a parent–child intervention that may be effective in reducing physical abuse. The aim is to increase parental motivation and enhance skills and to improve parent–child interaction through use of direct coaching and practice of skills in didactic parent–child sessions in which parents are treated alongside children. This behavioural management intervention has a strong evidence base for helping child conduct problems, and is based on the Webster-Stratton Incredible Years programme, which has translated successfully to the UK.

A rigorous evaluation (Evidence Level A)[264] with a sample of physically abused children and their parents found that this intervention was more effective than a standard community-based parenting group in improving parent–child interactions and reducing the recurrence of physical abuse and the risks of further maltreatment. It may therefore reduce referrals to children's social care. However, it does not appear to have a significant effect on child behaviour.

Summary: Parent–child interventions

We examined three interventions representing the three different approaches to parent–child therapy, namely a psychotherapeutic approach: Preschooler–Parent Psychotherapy (PPP); an attachment-based approach: Interaction Guidance; and a cognitive behavioural model: Parent–Child Interaction Therapy (PCIT). The first two interventions are aimed at preschool children, the first being focused on parents diagnosed as emotionally abusing and the second focused on infants with faltering growth. The third intervention is directed at parents after physical abuse has been confirmed.

The strengths of the available evidence on the effectiveness of parent–child-focused interventions are reflected in the innovative nature of many of the methods of working and the clear theoretical approaches upon which they are based.

The evidence from the two evaluations of programmes to address emotional abuse is limited by the absence of adequate child outcome measures. Furthermore, both studies used measures that were directly related to the intervention (and thus likely to show improvement).

The third intervention, Parent–Child Interaction Therapy, has been shown to be associated with reduced referrals to children's social care. The evaluation used a well-validated methodology and found medium effects in both reduced negative behaviour towards the child and increased parental positive behaviours. However, it did not show a significant impact on child behaviour.

---

f   See Example 6 in Appendix 2 for more details

Family-focused interventions to prevent the occurrence or recurrence of maltreatment in families where children are suffering, or likely to suffer, significant harm

Family-focused interventions may aim both to prevent the occurrence or recurrence of abuse and neglect to ensure better outcomes for the child, because they concentrate on the interactions between all family members as well as the mental health of each individual.

Although much of the attention on the causes and origins of maltreatment focuses on the mother–child relationship, the problems may reside in the wider family group. For example, we know that inter-parent conflict, especially when it results in domestic violence, significantly increases the likelihood of maltreatment. In some families one child may be singled out and treated differently from other siblings. There may also be maladaptive relationships within and beyond the immediate family, including with foster parents.[265,266]

Family-focused interventions are intended to work with the wider family group. The family may be considered to include not just the members of a household, but also the child's larger family network, such as the biological parents, step-parents, siblings and step-siblings, and foster or respite carers. Family therapy may be most effective in situations in which multiple problems are present, because it takes into account the needs of the whole family at once; it may also be useful for situations in which multiple services are involved, because of its ability to incorporate people from outside the family into treatment.[267]

Family-focused interventions aim both to prevent recurrence of abuse and to ensure better outcomes for the child because they concentrate on the interactions between all family members as well as the mental health of each individual. Such interventions seek to change maladaptive interactions between numerous family members, rather than the behaviour of one or more individuals.

The term 'family therapy' is used to cover a wide range of methods for working with families with various psycho-biological difficulties. Indeed, there are several major schools of family therapy and therapists often incorporate elements of more than one method in practice. Nevertheless, the different schools of family therapy all have some core features in common. All models prioritize interactions, notably communication patterns, between family members in considering problems and solutions in treatment. They also always take the whole family into account, rather than prioritizing dyadic parent–child interactions.[268] All members of at least the immediate family are typically invited to treatment sessions, although some sessions may be individual and others may include people from outside the family, such as teachers or social workers.

Family therapy is difficult to evaluate using rigorous trial-type designs. The *Emotional Abuse Intervention Review* includes some interventions for children who are being emotionally abused that have been evaluated using a case study design (Evidence Level E), which indicates that the therapies are helpful. However, these findings are based on the lowest level of evidence. While it is therefore not possible to conclude that family therapy has a positive impact on emotional abuse, reviews have found strong evidence for its effectiveness in a range of relevant conditions. These include conduct disorders in children and adolescents, eating disorders, substance misuse and as a second-line treatment for depression.[269] There is also an extensive literature on the impact of family therapy in cases of child sexual abuse and, to a lesser extent, parental violence,[270] and examples of successful short-term, intensive family therapy with families in which psychological maltreatment is recognized as compounding other forms of abuse.[271]

The *Physical Abuse Intervention Review* was relatively sceptical of the value of family therapy in treating child physical abuse. Their search only yielded two randomized controlled trials, one of which compared it with CBT and found it to be less effective for some outcomes and no different for others;[272] the other compared individual family therapy with multi-family group therapy and found the latter to be more effective in reducing child abuse potential; however, there was no control condition.[273] They argued that the effectiveness of family therapy is unclear and needs to be investigated further.

Multi-Systemic Therapy for Child Abuse and Neglect

However, since then, a randomized controlled trial of *Multi-Systemic Therapy for Child Abuse and Neglect* (MST-CAN)[274,g] for physically abused young people has been completed[275] and shows promising results. A less rigorous (Evidence Level E) study indicates that it may also be of value in families where neglect is an issue.[276] This form of therapy builds on three inter-related elements. First, it adopts an ecological approach,[277] which links the physical abuse of young people with modifiable factors within the individual young people, their parents and family systems. Second, it builds on encouraging evidence from other family-based interventions for child abuse and neglect, some of which have been discussed above.[278] Third, it is an adaptation of multi-systemic therapy, a rigorously evaluated, evidence-based programme for young people displaying serious anti-social and/or offending behaviour, developed over 30 years and now being implemented or trialled across the world, including England.[279]

MST-CAN provides a social-ecological therapeutic framework to address the multiple needs of families experiencing child abuse and neglect. It consists of an

---

g   See Example 7 in Appendix 2 for more details

ongoing and extensive assessment process to conceptualize the case and establish and prioritize target behaviours, followed by implementation of evidence-based interventions.[280] Interventions are tailored to meet the family's clinical needs, and may include, for instance, CBT for deficits in anger management; a CBT protocol for families with low problem-solving skills or difficulties in communicating without conflict; and prolonged exposure therapy for parents experiencing post traumatic stress disorder symptoms. When compared with enhanced outpatient treatment for physically abused youths and their parents in the US, MST-CAN has shown promising results in reducing young people's mental health symptoms, parent psychiatric distress and parenting behaviours associated with maltreatment, and improving natural social support for parents.[281] This form of therapy is addressed to older children and would be relevant to those in the *Home or Care?* and the *Neglected Children Reunification Studies*.

Summary: Family-focused interventions

Family-focused interventions may prove valuable both because they have the potential to address multiple problems in a structured way, and because the sustainability of treatment gains is highly contingent on the ecological context. There have been few rigorous evaluations, and more research is needed in this area. However, recent evidence suggests that an adapted form of multi-systemic therapy may prove effective for families where physical abuse or neglect of older children occurs.

Child-focused interventions to mitigate impairment

Child-focused interventions predominantly aim to help children cope with the adverse effects of maltreatment such as stress, anxiety and low self-esteem, and address their immediate and long-term adjustment needs.

Child-focused interventions are designed to work specifically on children's needs and to help them cope with the adverse effects of maltreatment such as stress, anxiety, low self-esteem, aggressive or non-compliant behaviour and social isolation. Therapy can be provided at different stages in life, from infancy to teenage years. However, opportunities to intervene early are sometimes missed. Both the *Neglected Children Reunification* and the *Significant Harm of Infants Studies* found that a high proportion of children in their samples showed difficulties that could be attributed to long-standing neglect. These included children who had very delayed development or poor speech, did not put on weight, had missed a great deal of school, and had decayed teeth or untreated medical conditions.

Child-focused interventions aim to work on both immediate and long-term adjustment needs. The *Physical Abuse Intervention Review* found that there have been surprisingly few previous reviews of child-focused interventions to mitigate impairment from physical abuse or neglect.[282] However, a number of effective programmes have been identified, including therapeutic day care, peer training and treatment foster care. These examples have been selected to demonstrate effective interventions for children at different ages.

Therapeutic Preschool[283,h] provides medical, developmental, psychological and educational services to promote healthy growth and development for infants aged 1–24 months who have been, or are at risk of being, maltreated. Interventions are also offered to parents on a voluntary basis and include parenting education, concrete services, support groups, counselling and referrals to other services.

A randomized controlled trial[284] showed that this therapeutic preschool intervention had a sustained and significant impact on parenting and child behaviour. When compared with those offered routine services, children who received the therapeutic preschool intervention showed less evidence of aggression, delinquency and fewer serious offences; these results were maintained over a 12-year follow-up. The trial used multiple sources for outcome measures, which strengthens the reliability of these conclusions, although it should be noted that only half the children were traced for the final follow-up.

Peer-Led Social Skills Training[285,i] is aimed at slightly older children of three to five years with mixed maltreatment histories who are socially withdrawn. The children are paired for play sessions with resilient peers who display high levels of positive play, supported by a parent volunteer. A rigorous (Evidence Level A) evaluation[286] showed that the intervention had a positive impact on social skills in socially withdrawn children, including those who have experienced maltreatment, maintained at two-month follow-up. However, further investigation of the impact on other aspects of the children's mental health is needed to determine whether this intervention might improve other outcomes, particularly in the longer term.

Peer training has been used in UK health promotion programmes in schools to tackle substance abuse and promote healthy living.[287] Therefore, although this programme was developed in the US, there is relevant experience amongst public health professionals which could inform its translation into a UK setting.

Multidimensional Treatment Foster Care

The *Neglected Children Reunification*, the *Home or Care?* and the *Significant Harm of Infants Studies* all provided ample evidence that abused children placed with foster parents may bring with them emotional, behavioural and developmental

---

h   See Example 8 in Appendix 2 for more details
i   See Example 9 in Appendix 2 for more details

problems. The latter study concluded that prolonged exposure to maltreatment and delayed decision-making may jeopardize the life chances of about 60 per cent of very young children who are eventually permanently placed apart from their birth families. *Multidimensional Treatment Foster Care (MTFC)* is designed to deliver intensive support to such children, their foster carers and birth or adoptive parents. This therapeutic foster care programme is based on social learning theory and incorporates parent training and consultation for foster parents, parent training for birth parents and individual therapy for children who have experienced maltreatment. Rigorous evaluations conducted in the US consistently show positive outcomes, including improvements in children's attachment to caregivers, participation in school, foster parent stress levels, and likelihood of achieving permanency (particularly marked for children who have had multiple prior foster placement failures). They also show reductions in older children's delinquency and anti-social behaviour and subsequent time incarcerated.[288] Further details of one of the MTFC programmes (MTFC-P) identified by the *Physical Abuse Intervention Review* and the results of a high-quality (Evidence Level A) evaluation that provides evidence of its effectiveness when compared with regular foster care are given in Appendix 2 (Example 10).[289]

There are currently three MTFC programmes being piloted or implemented in the UK: MTFC-Adolescents; MTFC-Children of school age; and MTFC-Prevention for young children aged three to six years. At the time of writing, the MTFC-Adolescents programme is relatively well established. A pre and post (Evidence Level C) evaluation undertaken by the project team showed significant reductions in adolescent offending, self-harm, sexual behaviour problems, absconding and fire setting and in foster carers' stress levels. There were also improvements in young people's SDQ and IQ scores.[290] The results of a randomized controlled trial by independent evaluators are currently awaited.

The MTFC programmes for younger children are currently being piloted in a number of sites in England. A related programme, KEEP (Keeping Foster and Kinship Parents Supported and Trained), is also being introduced. This utilizes the same principles as MTFC, and has been developed as a means of skilling up mainstream foster carers, providing increased support to kinship carers, improving placement stability and transferring the learning from the more specialist programmes to a wider group of carers.[291]

This wide-ranging suite of programmes may prove cost-effective in the long term if they promote better outcomes for children and prevent placement disruptions. However, the many additional services that are provided to foster families may initially appear to be expensive, and studies that measure costs would clarify this issue. An exploration of the costs of one of the English pilots showed that the monthly costs of maintaining MTFC placements were on a par with placements in independent foster agencies outside the authority area, and less costly when stability and length of stay are taken into account. Social care costs incurred by children in the first six months of MTFC were about 15 per cent less than those they had incurred in the six months prior to entry to the programme.[292]

Future studies comparing MTFC with other treatments would provide more information about its effectiveness. If the results of the English pilots prove positive, this would be a useful approach to consider implementing.

Summary: Child-focused interventions

In this section we have looked at three child-focused interventions: a therapeutic day treatment programme aimed at babies between one and two years, a proportion of whom had documented histories of abuse; a peer-led programme aimed at children of 3–5 years with mixed maltreatment histories who were identified as being socially withdrawn; and a treatment foster care programme with a number of different modules, covering all age ranges.

The evaluation of the therapeutic preschool programme showed promising results in reducing anti-social behaviour in the long term and was found to be more effective than standard child protection services. The trial of the peer-led social skills training programme found the treatment group exhibited more interactive play and less solitary play than a control group but did not measure other aspects of child mental health or behaviour.

Rigorous evaluations have found that Multidimensional Treatment Foster Care shows promising effects on the stability of foster placement, children's attachment and on cortisol levels, indicating that providing both foster parents and children with extensive, specialist support and a structured programme of intervention can help to improve child outcomes.

The way forward? The 'common elements' approach

As we have noted, many maltreating families suffer a multiplicity of problems and may require a range of forms of help at the same time. It may be necessary for a care plan to address a number of elements such as parental domestic violence and/or drug and alcohol problems, as well as emotional and behavioural difficulties displayed by the child. Some of the interventions presented above address this issue by adopting a comprehensive, multi-level approach.

However, diversity of goals has led to difficulties in implementing evidence-based interventions in the real world. Although practitioners claim to be using evidence-based interventions, audit and research into actual practice in the field have shown that, despite their stated intentions, this is generally not the case. Practitioners tend not to use evidence-based practices and instead fall back on their existing familiar patterns. Furthermore, attempts to change practice, in mental health settings for instance, have met with mixed success.[293]

Appreciation of these obstacles to successful change has led to an innovative 'common elements' approach that takes on board concerns voiced by practitioners about the diversity and complexity of their real-world cases.[294] In this approach, common elements are distilled from existing evidenced-based interventions for a common problem, within four areas: treatment content, techniques, working alliance, and treatment parameters.[295] These common elements of intervention or treatment are then agreed with the authors of individual evidence-based therapies. The intention is that the common elements approach will be tried out in practice as an innovative means of addressing these very diverse and complex cases. While this holds promise for the field of maltreated children and their families, it has not yet been developed or trialled. Issues concerning programme fidelity, appropriate training and the unlooked-for consequences of mixing elements that may come from different theoretical backgrounds all need to be explored.[296]

So what can be suggested, based on the evidence reviewed above, for commissioners and practitioners seeking the best interventions for maltreated children and their families?

- Identify agreed principles and approaches to interventions, including ethical and legal considerations. This has been done in the US, and consensus reached between authors who had developed interventions with evidence for effectiveness.[297,298]

- Use evidence-based interventions which are sufficiently flexible to accept adaptation or the introduction of additional modules to allow for case diversity and complexity. For example, the Triple P Programme or Parents Under Pressure, which do allow for such variation.

- Choose interventions which can be practised by a range of professionals, and are not restricted to those from one profession.

- Use the above approach to agree the main intervention(s) that will be supported in a geographical area, and only use other interventions, with a less good evidence base, where the initial approach has proved unsuccessful, and/or where a convincing case can be made for adopting an intervention with less compelling evidence to support its use.

Conclusion

This chapter has reviewed a range of effective interventions and found that there are several which are likely to provide real benefit for children and their families where abuse and neglect has occurred. We have described ten specific interventions that have been proved to be effective in addressing the needs of maltreated children and their families (and given further details in Appendix 2), in the expectation that all who consider using them will wish to have information that will help them identify 'what works'.

At the same time, however, there is a need for caution because the programmes have limited success, and because there are significant rates of recurrence of maltreatment and poor outcomes in the follow-up studies. Moreover, not all interventions have been shown to be effective in addressing the multiplicity of adversities faced by such families.

Key messages for all who work together to safeguard children

- Reviews of evidence have identified a number of specific interventions that have been proved to be effective in addressing the needs of maltreated children and their families. Those highlighted in this chapter are examples of what is available.

- Effective programmes for parents address alcohol and drug problems, parenting problems arising from their own childhood experiences and poor parenting practices. Better evidenced programmes for addressing intimate partner violence in families where children are suffering, or likely to suffer, significant harm are required.

- Effective programmes for parents and children address parent–child relationships, conflict and parent–child interaction.

- Effective programmes for children address behavioural and emotional issues arising from the consequences of abuse. They can be tailored to different age groups and circumstances.

- There is a need for caution because the programmes only address aspects of the multiple problems faced by families, and because all the interventions have limited effectiveness and do not offer solutions for all families. For example, there are significant rates of recurrence of maltreatment and in some cases poor outcomes for children in the follow-up studies.

Key messages for strategic managers, commissioners of services and operational managers in health, education and children's social care

- Those who commission specific interventions should first ask: whether an evaluation has been undertaken and to what evidence level; whether there is evidence of sustainability; whether there is evidence that the findings can be translated into a UK context; whether the intervention is sufficiently flexible to allow for extra modules to be added to accommodate case diversity or complexity.

- Most specific interventions are of short duration. Commissioners and operational managers should be aware that maltreating parents and their children will often need continuing support from social workers, health visitors or other professionals after completing a programme in order to maintain improvements and prevent relapse.

- Proposals to identify common elements of effective interventions in this field may offer a valuable way forward, but have not yet been trialled. In the meantime the following programmes are examples of what has been proven to be effective.

Programmes for parents

- Parents Under Pressure (PUP) is an effective intervention for substance-misusing parents and holds promise to parents who have other problems too.

- The Enhanced Triple P-Positive Parenting Programme is effective in addressing adults' own experiences of poor parenting and the psychological consequences of abuse.

- Cognitive Behavioural Therapy (CBT) can be effective in reducing emotionally abusive parenting, particularly when individual sessions are combined with group-based sessions.

Programmes for parents and children

- Preschooler–Parent Psychotherapy is effective in improving maternal and child representations where there is a known history of abuse in the family.

- Interaction Guidance may be an effective intervention in improving parent–child relationships in infants with faltering growth, but further evaluation would be valuable.

- Parent–Child Interaction Therapy is a cognitive behavioural model that has been shown to be effective in reducing physical abuse.

Programmes for families

- Multi-Systemic Therapy for Child Abuse and Neglect has been shown to be effective in reducing the likelihood and mitigating the consequences of the physical abuse of adolescents.

Programmes for children

- o Therapeutic Preschool is an effective intervention for children aged 1–24 months who have been maltreated or are at risk of maltreatment. It has a significant and lasting impact on parenting and child behaviour.

- o Peer-Led Social Skills Training is an effective intervention for 3–5-year-olds with a history of maltreatment who are socially withdrawn.

- o Multidimensional Treatment Foster Care is an effective intervention for maltreated children in care or accommodation. Trials in the US have produced promising results. A range of programmes have been designed for adolescents, older children and preschoolers.

Providing a Context for Effective Inter-Agency Practice

- This chapter draws largely on the evidence from the *Local Safeguarding Children Boards Study*,[299] the *Inter-Agency Training Evaluation Study*,[300] the *Information Needs of Parents at Early Recognition Study*[301] and the *General Practitioner Tensions in Safeguarding Study*.[302]

- The chapter has important messages for all those who have responsibility for safeguarding and promoting the welfare of children.

- The chapter has specific messages for the following professional groups:

  ○ policymakers, chairs and members of Local Safeguarding Children Boards (all sections)

  ○ strategic managers and commissioners of services in health and children's social care (sections on inter-agency training; how existing structures support both inter-agency and inter-disciplinary working)

  ○ practitioners and operational managers in adult health, including GPs, psychiatrists, psychologists and substance and alcohol misuse teams, probation, police, education and children's social care (sections on what the studies tell us about inter-professional working in day-to-day practice; improving co-operation through inter-agency training).

Introduction: Why is inter-disciplinary/inter-agency work needed?

Protecting children from harm requires alertness and effective interventions from practitioners across a range of disciplines. How is this managed in an inter-agency context? How is it supported at a local level and how effective are mechanisms designed to promote joint working?

Evidence from high-profile reports into child deaths, including those of Victoria Climbié and Peter Connelly,[303] provide compelling evidence about the need for services to work together to protect children from harm. Findings from the biennial *Analyses of Serious Case Reviews* further highlight and reinforce this.

Inquiries and serious case reviews focus on what happens when things go wrong. However, evidence from other studies covered in the Research Initiative also demonstrates the importance of inter-disciplinary working in routine practice because of the multi-faceted nature of problems which beset families for whom neglect and abuse is a concern. In Chapter 2 we saw the importance of an integrated approach to referral and recognition. In Chapters 3, 4 and 5 we saw the need for inter-agency working in the assessment of need and supply of services.

Thus, inter-professional work is needed at all stages of the child protection system. The studies demonstrate ways in which this works well, as well as times when it appears to go wrong. In the first part of this chapter we explore what the studies tell us about how inter-disciplinary working operates in routine practice. In the second part, we consider the evidence about the effectiveness of arrangements designed to promote good practice in an inter-agency context. However, we first need to consider the likely impact of recent developments in policy on the effectiveness of inter-agency working.

Recent developments in policy: the context for effective inter-agency working

Lord Laming's Inquiry into the tragic death of Victoria Climbié[304] found serious problems in inter-agency and inter-disciplinary practice at a local level, which needed urgent attention. These difficulties involved poor working across organizational boundaries and manifested themselves in a variety of ways. Senior managers in relevant agencies did not see themselves as accountable for the protection and welfare of children and appeared to refuse to take responsibility. The quality of information exchanged between agencies was poor, in particular between health and children's social care, and there was reluctance amongst some professionals to share it. The use of eligibility criteria by local authorities to restrict access to social services was applied inappropriately, without proper assessment of children's needs or the likelihood of significant harm.

The challenge of developing new ways of working to promote a more integrated approach across services lies at the heart of reforms since the Victoria Climbié Inquiry. A number of new structures were set up at a local level as part of reforms introduced by the Children Act 2004.[305] These include Children's Trusts and Sure Start children's centres as well as Local Safeguarding Children Boards (LSCBs). Whereas the Children's Trust arrangements have a wider role in planning and delivery of services, the LSCB objectives are about co-ordinating and ensuring effectiveness of their member organizations both individually and together.[306]

As Chapter 1 has shown, since the election of the Coalition Government in May 2010, there has been a series of major policy developments which will have a significant impact on the manner in which children are safeguarded from harm. One particular reason for their anticipated impact is that they will change the context in which inter-disciplinary practice takes place, and this will alter approaches to inter-agency working. Reforms such as the reshaping of responsibilities for partnership arrangements through relaxation of Children's Trust requirements;[307] policies designed to encourage more schools to take academy or free school status;[308] the introduction of greater diversity of services and service providers; the reduction of joint targets and performance indicators as drivers of quality; and the introduction of numerous incentives to increase local autonomy[309] may all provide opportunities for creative, positive change. On the other hand, greater autonomy and increased diversity may make inter-agency collaboration more problematic. It may prove particularly difficult to ensure that responsibilities for safeguarding are genuinely shared, particularly when this brings a financial cost at a time when budgets are being cut. As the evidence from the studies shows, successful inter-agency working already poses considerable challenges.

What do the studies tell us about inter-agency working in day-to-day practice on the ground?

Inter-agency and inter-disciplinary working are difficult to achieve for a variety of reasons. Service sectors such as health, the police and education have different structures, policies and priorities. There is evidence of distrust between some professional groups and this can result in poor information sharing, insufficient communication and reluctance to refer between services.

In the following sections we trace the process from recognition and referral through different stages to intervention. However, it is important to note that, rather than focusing specifically on the recognized processes, the studies in the Research Initiative give an insight into some of the challenges and dilemmas faced by practitioners when engaging in them.

Recognition and referral: dilemmas facing some front-line workers

The *General Practitioner Tensions in Safeguarding Study* examines the stresses faced by general medical practitioners (GPs) in relation to child protection work. GPs clearly face a dilemma about what action to take if they have concerns but are unsure that this amounts to a likelihood of a child suffering significant harm. Whilst they are familiar with the formal process of referral and understand what to do when a case is clear cut, they are reluctant to approach children's social care when they have less immediate concerns. Their reluctance is based on a number of factors. First, they are concerned about the high threshold for services which means that a case referral can lead to no service being provided. Second, there is the potential impact that referral to children's social care might have on their own relationship with the parents with whom they have a long-standing and continuing relationship.

In clear-cut cases many GPs see their role primarily as referral agents, passing on their concerns as they would for other issues which need a specialist view. This is consistent with other aspects of the GP role, which involves referral to a wide range of agencies. But it suggests a lesser engagement with child protection services than is expected by other players or is recommended in statutory child protection guidance.[310,311] GPs are often frustrated because they are unable to speak directly to a social work practitioner. Lack of feedback about progress and actions following a referral are further causes of friction. Provided there is not a very high level of concern, many GPs therefore prefer to keep the problem within the health system by consulting a health visitor or another member of the health team. However, both the *Recognition of Neglect Review* and the *Significant Harm of Infants Study* found that health visitors also see themselves largely as referral agents, and are equally frustrated when children's social care does not routinely provide feedback.

Slow responses by children's social care to referrals arise for a number of reasons. National statistics show a steady increase in numbers of referrals in recent years, which social workers are finding problematic to manage.[312,313] In addition, some practitioners argue that the reluctance of other agencies to share safeguarding responsibility clogs the system up with inappropriate referrals.[314] Other explanations for slow responses may lie in the way in which children's social care services are organized: the Munro report offers examples of good practice in multi-disciplinary arrangements for dealing with enquiries and referrals.[315] The *Local Safeguarding Children Boards Study* also found that the responsiveness of the referral process is better in some areas than others. This study found that specialized contact centres for referral may help improve accessibility for other professionals, but there were some concerns about whether the staff who work in them are adequately qualified to respond appropriately. In one area the police have a clear system for recording the details and times of feedback and this has served to strengthen their working relationship with children's social care.

Other evidence from the two *Analyses of Serious Case Reviews* and the two studies of children returned home from care or accommodation indicate that the way in which cases are seen by practitioners affects their response. Slow or inappropriate action may arise because each incident is viewed in isolation; the threshold for action is set too high; the 'rule of optimism' is being applied especially with parents with whom workers are already engaged; the allegations are denied by parents; or there are delays or staffing problems within children's social care. Referrals from neighbours or relatives may also be ignored. However, when concerns are not adequately followed up, children are often left unprotected.

Over and above the shortcomings in response from children's social care, there are also concerns about sharing responsibility. Referrals should be about continuing to work in a multi-disciplinary way;[316] after a referral has been accepted by children's social care, inter-agency working remains important in assessment, planning and intervention. For example, the assessment of neglect requires attention from a range of agencies, as each may hold separate pieces of information or knowledge that together show the whole picture.[317,318] However, referrals are sometimes seen as a means of handing over responsibility for the child and family. The *Significant Harm of Infants Study* found little evidence that responsibilities are equitably shared:

> 'It's frustrating when they won't, they don't recognize that they've got as much responsibility as what you have…they've got as much of a duty to protect, and support and nurture, as what you have, so you know again that's frustrating. And there are times when…they'll phone you up and make all these complaints and then you'll get them into a meeting and they'll backtrack and they won't say what they've said to you, as if, you know, they're scared to say it in front of a parent.' (Social worker)[319]

The amount of time spent by health teams agonizing about whether a referral should take place or not is also a cause for concern. Health professionals are often frozen by the decision 'to refer or not to refer' and do not appear to consider alternatives such as arranging access for children and families to therapeutic and support services. Nevertheless, there are important opportunities for GPs and health visitors to arrange for families to be assessed and be encouraged to participate in preventive programmes, such as some of the parenting initiatives described in Chapter 3. When health professionals are reluctant to refer, some maltreated children inevitably fall through the net and do not receive the help and protection they need. The *Significant Harm of Infants Study* confirms that this happens in the case of very young children.

Different perspectives between providers of adult and children's services

Chapter 2 explored how some practitioners were reluctant to recognize or act on concerns about maltreatment. The studies say more about how these issues impact on effective inter-agency working.

General medical practitioners are reluctant to refer for a number of reasons, including the fact that they treat the whole family. When there are concerns about maltreatment there is sometimes confusion as to whether their loyalties lie with the parents or the child,[320] an issue that was noted in the *General Practitioner Tensions in Safeguarding Study*. Providers of adult services, such as adult psychiatrists, other mental health professionals and substance abuse workers, can be reluctant to refer because they focus on adults and often do not appreciate how, for example, parents' mental health problems are impacting on their children. They often see progress in terms of improvements in adult functioning and do not question whether this is sufficient to meet the child's timeframe. Parents may receive false reassurances that all is going well, and then be surprised and angry when social workers argue that children remain at risk of suffering significant harm.

As Chapter 2 has shown, practitioners in adult mental health services should be particularly alert to the possibility that those of their patients who are parents may maltreat their children, especially where mental ill health is linked with other problems. However, adult services currently pay very little attention to the needs of these children, and often fail to recognize the potential risks to their welfare.

There appears to be some reluctance on the part of substance misuse workers to refer the children of their service users to social care; these practitioners often give parents false reassurance that all is going well because they focus on parental progress rather than on children's needs. They:

> '...have a different perspective to social workers for children, in that they will regard themselves as working for the adults and sometimes they will struggle with the role that social workers have, in that they will want to remain positive and supportive to parents'. (Team leader, children's social care)[321]

None of the studies were designed to address the question of how far those who work with substance-misusing and/or violent adults recognize the risk of harm to children or the actions they need to take in response. Nevertheless, it is clear that opportunities for recognition of abuse or neglect are missed by practitioners working with adults. Assessment of the impact of parents' problems on child welfare should be a routine part of normal practice in adult as well as children's services. These are important issues, indicating that further attempts need to be made to better integrate adult and children's services.

As we shall see below, the *Inter-Agency Training Evaluation Study* found that drug and alcohol workers generally do not participate in inter-agency training provided by Local Safeguarding Children Boards. An important opportunity to develop greater understanding of children's services is therefore being missed. Without involvement in such opportunities for joint training these workers will continue to have a poor understanding of the impact of parental substance and alcohol misuse on children and the importance of sharing relevant information.

Lord Laming[322] recommended strengthening channels between adult and children's services in social care and health. He also advised that feedback be provided to those who make referrals, as a matter of course. The findings of studies in this Research Initiative would strongly endorse these recommendations, while recognizing that, given high rates of referral, heavy caseloads and insufficient staffing, the capacity to do so may be limited.[323]

How are thresholds applied on the ground?

The role given to LSCBs in developing local policy on thresholds demonstrates the importance attributed to gaining agreements between agencies about what these should be. The studies in this Research Initiative further emphasize this issue, highlighting problems, particularly in relation to neglect and emotional abuse. The *Neglected Children Reunification Study*, for example, found that, whilst many social workers are able to comment on its impact on the child, they have difficulty in defining neglect. They consider that the concept is difficult to grasp, particularly as there is no one clear indicator which signals that children are being neglected. They find that neglect is less tangible than physical or sexual abuse, but emotional abuse is an even more slippery concept than neglect.

The difficulties in defining neglect and its chronic rather than acute nature also feed into difficulties of formulating protocols for agreeing thresholds. Social workers interviewed in the *Neglected Children Reunification Study* commented on this issue as follows:

> 'To put together a threshold document based on neglect type issues is incredibly difficult.'

> 'Neglect is something which is very hard to determine the point at which [it becomes] significant harm…when does it become a risk to their children?' (Social workers)[324]

Similarly, neglect tends to be cumulative over a period of time, with the result that it is not always easy to be aware when the threshold for significant harm has been reached. Thus, 'It's easy I think for things to deteriorate gradually without you noticing.'[325]

Moreover, the *Local Safeguarding Children Boards Study* shows that agencies do not always perceive the likelihood of significant harm in the same way, so that they hold different interpretations of thresholds:

> 'It's difficult because thresholds tend to differ and they're different for different agencies and different areas; it's very inconsistent. There are issues around how children's services prioritise referrals but this often comes down to perceptions of urgency. Often social care and mental health have different views in terms of how anxious they are about a certain case.' (Safeguarding nurse)[326]

'There are different views about how a case should be dealt with and as a school nurse I don't always agree with the level of priority given to some cases. I feel that sometimes we are all on a different page.' (Health practitioner)[327]

Not only are there differences between agencies but also differences between teams within them. For example, an assessment team can operate a threshold which is 'much higher' than that held by a looked after children's team, with consequent confusion about who is eligible to receive services. In the current economic climate, agencies will need to be increasingly transparent about their thresholds, both between themselves and with the general public. Greater clarification about how thresholds are understood would be of benefit to all.

Further issues concerning the difficulty of setting appropriate thresholds for court involvement in cases of neglect have been discussed in Chapter 4.

What do the studies say about the response after children's social care has received a referral?

Evidence from the three empirical studies – the *Home or Care? Study*, the *Neglected Children Reunification Study* and the *Significant Harm of Infants Study* – suggests there may be some justification for the concerns expressed by health and other professionals that children's social care may be too slow to act, or offer too little support in response to referrals.

For example, where children have been returned home after being looked after by the local authority, one might expect re-referrals from other professionals, neighbours or relatives to be followed up more fully than first referrals because these families are already known to children's social care. However, the *Neglected Children Reunification Study* found that insufficient action is taken in response to more than half the re-referrals; either no action or a minimal response is made, which does not appear to reflect the seriousness of the risks of harm to children, and cases are sometimes closed shortly afterwards. The *Significant Harm of Infants Study* also found that very small children who remain with their birth parents but appear insufficiently safeguarded frequently have their cases closed and then are re-referred shortly afterwards. Both studies identified cases where social work staff had been so concerned about premature case closure that they had re-referred children themselves. It appears to be relatively common for concerns not to be adequately followed up or appropriate action taken following a referral to children's social care.

The result is that children are often not sufficiently protected from harm. Some go on to experience further maltreatment, which might have been prevented if different actions had been taken. Other children and families do not access the intensive services they need to help them address the consequences of maltreatment: in the case of older children this may result in deterioration in behavioural patterns or in becoming increasingly involved in offending or substance misuse. There is also substantial evidence that maltreated and neglected children frequently return home from being looked after to situations that were unchanged from those that existed when they were first placed away. The *Analysis of Serious Case Reviews 2005–7* also found evidence of some children and families 'bumping along the bottom' with no services being offered at all.

Professionals from all agencies have to have confidence that referrals to children's social care will lead to suitable action. The *Local Safeguarding Children Boards Study* found widespread sympathy amongst other professionals for the work pressures on social workers. However, some give their uncertainty as to whether a referral will lead to suitable action and the poor level of feedback about the response as a reason for not referring cases.

Inter-agency working to supply support services both prior to and after removal from home

Once referrals have been accepted, there is encouraging evidence of good inter-disciplinary practice to support children and families, especially in the early stages. For example, the *Home or Care? Study* found that there is clear evidence of the provision of comprehensive support services for around two thirds of children who return home from being looked after.

The *Neglected Children Reunification Study* found that, in the period from the first referral until five years after reunification, about 80 per cent of families receive some kind of additional service. Interventions may be aimed at the parent or the child or can focus on the whole family. Such services include support for parental mental health problems, help with parental substance misuse, parenting programmes, help from a family centre, respite care, assistance from family support workers, counselling, life story work, support from Child and Adolescent Mental Health Services (CAMHS), play therapy, mentors and befrienders, play schemes, keep safe work and help from the youth offending team. However, in about one third of the cases in the *Home or Care? Study* sample, it was unclear what support services (if any) had been offered.

Social workers refer many parents to specialist services dealing with substance misuse or domestic violence and sometimes assist in negotiating alternative accommodation with housing providers. The *Significant Harm of Infants Study* found, as have other studies in this area,[328] that housing is an important issue for many families attempting to overcome problems such as substance misuse or domestic violence, because it is easier to extract oneself from a drugs culture or from an abusive relationship if one can change address. There is scope for closer relationships and improved inter-agency working between housing agencies and children's social care.

The *Sure Start Local Programmes Safeguarding Study* noted that co-location of health, social work and other practitioners facilitates improved inter-disciplinary and inter-agency working and leads to better communication and delivery of services to families at the front line. The benefits of co-location and/or embedded health professionals for multi-disciplinary working have also been demonstrated in related areas such as in work with disabled children and those with special educational needs. More recently, the contribution and importance of embedding health visitors and a range of practitioners in Sure Start children's centres, particularly in the protection and support of vulnerable families, has been recognized by the Coalition Government.[329] However, there is a danger that some of this innovative work will be lost under new NHS arrangements if clinical commissioning groups decide to opt out of commissioning such structures.

Whilst inter-agency working is shown to be strong in the provision of support services, this does not mean they are always sufficient or fully meet all the families' needs. Neither does it mean that families take up the services offered.

The *Neglected Children Reunification Study* explored the reasons why outcomes for neglected children who return home from being looked after are so poor. In many cases the level of support offered is limited and insufficient for the high level of need amongst children and families. There are particular shortages of services for parental alcohol misuse, the provision of direct help with children's behavioural problems and advice on behavioural management for their parents. Other services that are insufficient to meet the needs of children and families where the likelihood of maltreatment is high include: services for parental substance misuse; work on parenting; services to address young people's offending behaviour and their drug and alcohol problems; psychotherapeutic support for children and young people; respite care; material support; and help with children's education. In some cases support negotiated on an inter-agency basis, as part of a child protection plan, is not forthcoming. However, caution should be exercised in noting these findings, because they are based on case records which have been shown in the past not to be consistent in recording specialist interventions.

Even when support is readily available, families are not always willing to engage with services. The following example is typical:

> Mrs Jennings did not take up offers of therapeutic help for her three children when they returned home to her, despite these being strongly recommended. Mrs Jennings felt that the input would unsettle the children and they themselves did not want to attend.[330]

The *Home or Care? Study* found that, in nearly one in ten cases, parents' unwillingness to engage with professionals, and with the services offered, contributed to the decision to place children away from home.

Although engagement with services is sometimes regarded as a positive indicator of parents' attempts to overcome their difficulties, it does not necessarily distinguish between those families which will be successful in doing so, and those which will not. Some parents interviewed in the *Significant Harm of Infants Study* made it clear that they were aware that they had to appear to comply with plans by keeping appointments, but had little intention of using the services offered to address their problems. This issue has also been raised by both the *Analyses of Serious Case Reviews* and needs to be taken into account in social work training and supervision.

Even when interventions are acceptable and available, they may be too short to facilitate lasting change. Specific interventions are inevitably more focused than those of children's social care, and are often strictly time limited. This can be problematic. For example, maltreating parents who receive time-limited substance and alcohol misuse programmes may require support for much longer periods than they are offered. Some specific interventions achieve their greatest impact within the first few weeks or months, and there may be little value in extending them; however, many families will still require more general ongoing support after completing the programme.

The *Home or Care? Study* notes that in some cases social care interventions are, at most, only limited, or short-lived, and the failure to change parenting behaviour may result in a decision that the child's needs will be best met through placement away from home. However, the *Significant Harm of Infants Study* found no children who were unnecessarily or prematurely removed from their birth parents.

Improving co-operation through inter-agency training

The new Local Safeguarding Children Boards should be required to ensure training on an inter-agency basis is provided. Staff working in relevant agencies should be required to demonstrate that their practice in inter-agency working is up to date by completing appropriate training courses.[331]

There is some evidence that inter-agency and inter-disciplinary working has improved since the *Victoria Climbié Inquiry Report* in 2003.[332] However, we have also seen that many challenges remain and are manifest in working relationships between different practitioner and professional groups that are characterized by a lack of trust and reciprocity. One way to tackle the many cultural and practical barriers which can act as obstacles to effective joint working is through inter-agency training, which LSCBs are mandated to arrange.

The Guidance on inter-agency working to safeguard children cites the *Inter-Agency Training Evaluation Study*, stating that:

> Inter-agency training is highly effective in helping professionals understand their respective roles and responsibilities, the procedures of each agency

involved in safeguarding children and in developing a shared understanding of assessment and decision-making practices.[333]

Training for inter- and multi-agency work is defined as:

> ...training and education that equips people to work effectively with those from other agencies to safeguard and promote the welfare of children.[334]

Introductory courses on identifying and responding to child protection concerns are offered to a wide range of people in regular contact with children, including nurses, teachers, librarians, fire officers and social workers. Some of these courses are offered as e-learning programmes. More advanced courses are provided for professionals working regularly with children and those who may be required to contribute to assessments. These focus on effective, collaborative inter-agency working, and on understanding roles and responsibilities. These courses, typically over two days, include a focus on child protection conferences. Specialist courses address a range of topics including safeguarding disabled children, safeguarding children and domestic abuse, and safeguarding in the context of parental mental illness and drug and alcohol misuse. Other specialist courses concern working with young people with sexually harmful behaviours and female genital mutilation.

The *Inter-Agency Training Evaluation Study* investigated inter-agency training in eight case study local authorities. The high-quality, time-series design incorporated a pre-course baseline and a follow-up at three months. It was much more rigorous than the standard "happy sheet" assessments that are routinely provided.

The project aimed to establish a substantial evidence base for inter-agency training and set out to collect a large amount of data from a wide range of courses. Training outcomes were measured using specially developed, validated scales across a range of domains that included: attitudes to inter-professional learning; knowledge of the topic (e.g. the effects of parental substance misuse on children) and how to work together to safeguard children (i.e. inter-agency policies and procedures); and attitudes to children and families in safeguarding situations and to inter-professional working and self-efficacy (i.e. beliefs that you *can* work well and effectively). There is substantial accumulated empirical evidence that self-efficacy is a powerful predictor of behaviour.[335] An evaluation toolkit containing all the materials is available on the Research Initiative website.[336] The evidence discussed below comes from this evaluation.[337]

Participation

The introductory courses are attracting much of the target audience of people in contact with children, including support workers as well as nurses and social workers. Social workers, teachers and nurses are well represented on at least some of the advanced programmes. However, some groups including housing workers, librarians and leisure staff are barely represented on any courses. There are also three areas of particular concern:

- Alcohol and substance misuse workers do not generally attend inter-agency training. Their attendance might do much to resolve the differences in perspective and thresholds for action noted in earlier chapters.

- Hospital doctors and GPs are poorly represented on the advanced courses on inter-professional working to safeguard children. Only 54 of the 96 GPs who responded to questionnaires in the *General Practitioner Tensions in Safeguarding Study* had received any training in this field in the previous three years and only half of these had taken part in multi-agency events.[338] This is both surprising and disappointing in the light of inter-collegiate guidance which emphasizes flexible training and attendance for attainment of competencies (including safeguarding) in the portfolio for revalidation.[339] This is also a major concern in the context of evidence from government reports, serious case reviews and the other studies in this Research Initiative that suggests a continuing problem of trust and communication between doctors and other practitioners in the child protection field. Much training of doctors is undertaken within the health system; in the absence of their participation in LSCB courses, it is critically important that training should deal effectively with child protection matters and the essential role of inter-agency working in protecting children.[340]

- Most of those who attend the advanced courses do so on a voluntary basis, and the great majority are relatively inexperienced staff. Professionals with more than five years' experience are generally not using these courses. It is unclear whether they are not being put forward, or are given lower priority by their employing agencies. Alternatively they may simply not be taking opportunities to update their knowledge and skills. There was disturbing evidence in the *Significant Harm of Infants Study* that some social workers did not regard ongoing professional development as necessary once they were qualified.

Outcomes

The courses appear to be of a consistently high quality and they address the learning needs of participants. Outcomes are remarkably consistent both across different types of course and between LSCBs. They are encouraging. Attendance brings substantial gains in knowledge of the topic (i.e. domestic violence and child abuse; sexually abusing adolescents), and in self-confidence regarding safeguarding policies and procedures. These positive outcomes are found irrespective of the participants' gender, age, ethnicity, service experience and the compulsory or voluntary nature of their attendance.

The opportunity to learn and work together is also very highly valued, and clearly promotes effective inter-agency working. Participants show very substantial improvements in self-reported understanding of the roles of different professionals who engage in work to safeguard and promote the welfare of children and in confidence and comfort in working collaboratively. This has an important impact on the self-confidence of social workers, and other professionals' understanding of their roles and responsibilities. Three months after the course these gains appear to be maintained, although modest response rates at follow-up mean that this evidence is relatively weak.

Inter-agency training courses, as provided by LSCBs, are therefore making an important contribution to promoting better inter-disciplinary practice amongst practitioners at local level. They are also cost-effective in that these one or two-day intensive courses produce significantly positive, lasting outcomes. However, while this type of partnership working is mandated by central government, it does not receive ring-fenced funding. Training relies very significantly on the good will of partner agencies and the professional and personal relationships developed locally. It is therefore particularly vulnerable to cuts, especially within a context where changed responsibilities, greater diversity of service provision and economic stringency may all re-ignite old tensions. It would be regrettable if the strong platform of inter-agency training created in recent years were now allowed to disintegrate and fall away.

How do existing structures support both inter-agency and inter-disciplinary working?

This section focuses largely on findings from the *Local Safeguarding Children Boards Study*, the only one in the Research Initiative to focus on the structural context of inter-agency working. The study involved a national mapping exercise and a series of case studies of six Boards. Data from the mapping exercise were used to inform Lord Laming's Progress Report on *The Protection of Children in England*.[341]

Local Safeguarding Children Boards (LSCBs) were set up in 2006. They are currently the key local strategic body responsible for co-ordinating and ensuring the effectiveness of child protection and safeguarding services. The core objectives of LSCBs, set out in the Children Act 2004, are as follows:

(a) To co-ordinate what is done by each person or body represented on the Board for the purposes of safeguarding and promoting the welfare of children in the area of the authority; and

(b) To ensure the effectiveness of what is done by each person or body for that purpose.[342]

The scope of the LSCB role falls into three categories:

First, activity that affects all children and aims to identify and prevent maltreatment, or impairment of health or development, and ensure children are growing up in circumstances consistent with safe and effective care…

Second, proactive work that aims to target particular groups…

Third, responsive work to protect children who are suffering, or likely to suffer, significant harm…[343]

LSCBs were set up to address a number of weaknesses that had been identified in their predecessors, the Area Child Protection Committee (ACPC). These included insufficient authority to deliver effective agreement on policies across a range of service sectors; variations in levels of representation and membership, structure and practice; poor leadership; and insufficient resources.[344,345] The Boards also have a wider role that is not only framed in terms of child protection but in safeguarding and promoting the welfare of children.

The Munro Review[346] recognizes that LSCBs are uniquely positioned to monitor how professionals and services are working together to safeguard and promote the welfare of children. Recommendations to LSCBs to include an assessment of effectiveness in their annual reports, and to ensure that these are submitted to the most senior local leaders are designed both to strengthen their role and to ensure that multi-agency accountability and partnership in safeguarding children is not lost at a time of rapid change in public services.

Size matters

There are two ways in which the size of the strategic body matters: in the breadth of its remit and in the representation of different professional groups.

Breadth of remit

It is not possible to separate the protection of children from wider support to families. Indeed often the best protection for a child is achieved by timely intervention of family support services.[347]

LSCBs currently have wide responsibilities, ranging from prevention of occurrence of maltreatment to responsive work to protect children. While all Boards actively seek to address the wider agenda and are signed up to its principles, those that concentrate on the 'core business' of child protection and only expand into prevention activities when resources permit are most successful.[348] To be effective, Boards need to set appropriate boundaries and determine what is feasible within a given planning year, making allowances for resource-intensive activities such as serious case reviews.

Board members from key sectors need to be involved to ensure their commitment to plans. The role of Chair, as strategic lead, is central in ensuring this takes place and in assisting the Board to determine and maintain its focus as work programmes get under way.

Size, representation and shared responsibility

> The future lies with those managers who can demonstrate the capacity to work effectively across organizational boundaries.[349]

The *Victoria Climbié Inquiry Report*[350] criticized senior managers and professionals working in different agencies for refusing to share responsibility. Findings from the *Analyses of Serious Case Reviews* also demonstrate that the problem of joint responsibility has not yet been fully resolved. For example, the 'silo' working mentality continues to be a repeated feature of cases which go seriously wrong. Achieving cultural change and getting agencies to work together is extremely challenging and requires cross-sector commitment.

As the key strategic bodies responsible for local co-ordination, LSCBs need to have the appropriate composition, structure and leadership to gain shared commitment across agencies. Active membership and participation by representatives of partner agencies is of fundamental importance. However, whilst all the core statutory agencies are meeting their membership obligations, there are a number of practical issues that can hinder effective working. Many of these reflect the sheer number of agencies with responsibilities for safeguarding children, and the complexity of the task of ensuring their involvement in decision-making. Securing the appropriate involvement of agencies within large structures such as health and children's services poses an ongoing challenge to Boards, both in terms of identifying appropriate people to represent organizations and professional groups and in getting consistent attendance. Levels of participation in meetings may fluctuate; non-attendance by key partners impacts negatively on the work programme of the LSCB and is very detrimental to progress. Membership of the LSCB takes time, so some agencies, notably health and the police, operate a system of member substitution which can impact on continuity, undermine the collective identity of the Board, and lead to delays in the decision-making process.

These problems are likely to intensify with the fragmentation of responsibility for provision of local health and education services under new arrangements for local GP-led commissioning and foundation trusts and free schools, independent of the local authority. The Coalition Government has emphasized the continuing importance of inter-sector co-operation in the interests of vulnerable children, but it is yet to be seen how successful this will be at local level under new arrangements.[351]

Managing communication within a complex structure

Poor inter-agency communication is a major feature of child protection tragedies. The Victoria Climbié Inquiry was highly critical of the narrow sectorial approach adopted by front-line practitioners and their managers. The report found that professionals construed their roles in compartmentalized terms and were too focused on the narrow perspective of their own disciplinary interest to see whether the wider welfare needs of the child were being met.

At a strategic level, leadership is needed to improve inter-agency communication. There is some evidence that protocols aimed at facilitating information sharing, developed by LSCBs, are clearer than they used to be and have increased trust, thus promoting information exchange. However, concerns are still raised about the speed of responses to requests for information and the unwillingness of certain groups, particularly GPs, to share it.

Another way of improving inter-agency communication is through membership of the Board. However, achieving appropriate involvement from professionals is not without its difficulties and has proved challenging. For example, while general practitioners and head teachers do not necessarily need to sit on the LSCB, mechanisms do need to be in place to input their views and to ensure that they are fulfilling their safeguarding responsibilities. The 'quasi autonomous' status of these professionals can also raise challenges. It is difficult to find representatives to become members of Board structures to gain effective involvement of these professional groups. Some of these issues are being addressed for GPs in the Health and Social Care Bill (2011) before Parliament at the time of writing, which will make GP-led clinical commissioning groups statutory members of LSCBs.

One way to tackle insufficient involvement is through specialist subgroups. The *Local Safeguarding Children Boards Study* showed that all Boards have developed specialist subgroups to increase active participation and gain wider involvement of professionals and relevant practitioners. The scale and focus of subgroups on each Board varies considerably; there is an average of 6, but a range from 2 to 20.

An 'inclusive model' that engages as broad a membership of the LSCB as possible, with a large number of subgroups, has the advantage of greater numbers to promote greater awareness amongst professionals and direct links into practice. However, it is unwieldy to manage and the contribution of subgroups to planning and development is limited. Another problem is a relative lack of clarity amongst subgroups about their role. By contrast an 'exclusive' model that restricts membership of the Board and controls the composition of subgroups ensures that all contribute directly to development and planning and engage in good joint communications. However, in such a model there are no direct routes (apart from representatives on the Board) into professional practice and information is not always widely disseminated.

Leadership issues

The sheer size and complexity of the strategic partnership that forms the LSCB means that strong leadership is required if it is to fulfil its functions.[352] Moreover, the two Laming Reports[353,354] highlight the continuing significant issues of accountability and challenge. Accountability requires managers in different agencies to embrace their responsibilities and provide leadership to those at more junior levels. A significant role of the LSCB is both to promote this style of leadership amongst partner agencies and to encourage a culture of challenge, without blame, between agencies and disciplines. A further important task is to challenge agency managers about the quality of their service delivery when concerns are identified.

Leadership of the LSCB is therefore a very demanding role. LSCB Chairs need to provide a sense of direction to ensure that the Board has an independent voice and operates effectively. They also need to be of sufficient standing and expertise to gain both respect and authority from Board members not only to manage meetings and provide effective leadership, but also to act as a core representative for the LSCB in external meetings with partners and other bodies.[355]

In the wake of the serious case review into the death of Peter Connelly[356] and the subsequent Progress Report,[357] Boards were instructed to work towards appointing independent Chairs. The *Local Safeguarding Children Boards Study* found that there were strengths and weaknesses to this arrangement. The advantages of an independent Chair are to be found in the enhancement of the Board's independence and hence its capacity to challenge agency decision-making. However, there are also attendant problems. For example, it is difficult for independent Chairs to establish effective links to local networks and structures because they are not routinely part of these.

In terms of accountability, there are also challenges since Chairs usually report to the Director of Children's Services. This can cause problems for independent Chairs who may wish to challenge the operation of children's services. Similar difficulties arose in relation to accountability to the Children's Trust. The research found that this 'mutual accountability' of being both accountable and 'scrutinized' by the Trust, especially when people can be members of both organizations, was not appropriate. An alternative option, linking accountability to either (or both) the chief executive's office or political scrutiny, is recommended. This allows the independence of the LSCB to remain, while also establishing a form of public accountability.

Steps should also be taken to ensure the authority of the Chair and the LSCB is acknowledged and respected by agencies, enabling them to engender changes in policy and practice to safeguard and promote the welfare of children. Independent Chairs can have difficulty getting different partners to respond to their requirements. In this case the chief executive can be involved and mechanisms for resolving non-compliance should be agreed by agencies. It is important that mechanisms for addressing such issues are transparent and that there is a shared understanding of the actions that will be taken if agencies are perceived to have failed to respond to issues raised by the LSCB.

In addition, the implications of non-compliance with Board recommendations should be clarified and systems should be put in place to support the resolution of differences of opinion. The serious case review into the death of Peter Connelly[358] found, for instance, that, in making decisions, equal weight was given to the opinions of all members of the LSCB, regardless of their expertise in the issue under discussion. More attention might need to be given to exploring how decision-making can be better balanced.

Resource issues

To be effective the LSCB needs adequate resources to support its infrastructure and business activities. Without adequate support, independent Chairs are unable to operate effectively, independently from children's social care services. The Children Act 2004 made provision for payments to be made in connection with an LSCB to provide stronger support.[359]

Two thirds of Boards have established an executive group to progress business and separate strategic and executive matters. The majority have also appointed a full-time business manager, a role that is seen as fundamental to their effective functioning. However, staff turnover is a problem: every Board experienced a change of business manager over the course of the *Local Safeguarding Children Boards Study*.

As we have already seen, Boards have been active and successful in developing inter-agency training. However, one area of particular concern is that insufficient attention is given to the training (and career progression routes) for business managers, given their high level of turnover. Access to training is also needed for independent Chairs, but they are usually contracted for a relatively low number of days so opportunities can be limited. There is a need for clear training plans to be put in place to address these needs.

Without adequate funding and the release of staff to attend meetings and undertake activities to take forward work, LSCBs are unable to operate effectively. Yet resourcing of the independent Chair post, and, in some cases, administrative support, can be a problem. Fifty-four per cent of Chairs reported that their budget was adequate for their LSCB to function effectively, but given funding uncertainties and staff turnover, inadequate support may prove to be a continuing constraint on the effective operation of Boards.

The sharing of financial responsibility across agencies has proved to be another continuing challenge. Resource shortages and differences in funding mechanisms are known to hinder inter-agency working.[360] Key contributing agencies to the funding of LSCBs are children's services, health and the police. Bodies can contribute finance or staff, goods, services, accommodation or other resources.[361] However, the levels of funding needed for effective operation and the relative contributions of individual agencies are not prescribed. As a result, there are considerable variations in LSCB budgets and expenditure, and the contributions from agencies. The *Local Safeguarding Children Boards Study* collated data from 18 Boards and found that the local authority and children's services made the largest contribution to the operation of LSCBs, followed by health. Table 6.1 shows the range of financial contributions by agency.

Table 6.1: Financial contributions to the operation of LSCBs by agency[362]

Contributor	Smallest percentage contributed	Largest percentage contributed	Mean percentage contribution	Median percentage contribution
LA and children's services	31	77	56	56.5
Health	8	40	25	24.5
Probation	1	6	3	2
Police	0	20	9	7.5
CAFCASS	0	1	0	0
Connexions	0	10	4	2.5
Other contributors (where applicable)	1	23	11	9

Analysis of the minutes of Board meetings also reveals considerable time is spent discussing these issues. Annual negotiation of the various agencies' financial contributions to the LSCB and uncertainty concerning the budget from year to year can limit the scope for effective strategic planning. A common complaint is the absence of a funding formula to clarify the contributions from individual agencies.

In the current financial climate there is a danger that funding contributions will fall as agencies seek to reduce their budgets. This is likely to exacerbate existing tensions between agencies, further limit the scope for effective strategic planning and consequently limit the capacity of LSCBs to fulfil their responsibilities.

Conclusion

There is compelling evidence of the need for effective inter-disciplinary and inter-agency working at all stages of child protection work. Evidence comes from multiple ways of looking at service delivery including analyses of what happens when things go wrong, and research on everyday routine practice. It is also clear that joint working both at an inter-agency and front-line level is difficult and involves overcoming cultural differences as well as organizational and cross-sector boundaries. The challenge is to achieve continual improvement in the interests of children and families.

In the last 20 years or so, many reforms have addressed efforts to promote joint working at the local level. Reforms introduced by the Children Act 2004 sought to improve services to children both in terms of joint working of front-line services, and co-ordination across agency boundaries at the strategic organizational level.[363] There is evidence of some success at both front-line and strategic levels but much improvement is still needed, building on the developments of the past to deliver an effective joined-up approach to children and families.

Many new changes are now on the horizon. These take the shape of reforms to the configuration of local services which provide the context in which safeguarding and child protection services are delivered. The reforms affect three key areas: child protection service delivery; local health service delivery; and new arrangements for greater independence of schools under academy and free schools arrangements.

The impact of the *Munro Review of Child Protection*[364] is likely to result in a greater focus on promoting standards of professional practice by social workers and professional judgement in work with children and families. The recommendations are intended to improve the quality of practice, with a more confident workforce being able to develop better relationships with other professionals. Recording systems are likely to be restructured, and it will be important to ensure that the capacity for information sharing and exchange maintained. The recommendations from the Munro review are also designed to ensure that an emphasis on multi-agency accountability and partnership working are maintained throughout new challenges and changes to the structure and delivery of services. They specifically identify the need to research the impact of health reorganization on effective partnership arrangements.

The impact of NHS reforms is likely to pose challenges in terms both of strategic thinking about safeguarding and of commissioning services. New clinical commissioning may decide not to invest in multi-disciplinary services. This may have negative consequences on innovative approaches to meeting the needs of vulnerable children. The NHS White Paper, *Equity and Excellence: Liberating the NHS*,[365] and associated official announcements provide reassurances that local authorities, through Health and Wellbeing Boards, will have a duty to ensure the supply of joint services to vulnerable groups, including greater flexibilities in sharing NHS/local authority budgets. However, voluntary arrangements have proved unsatisfactory in the past and, with GP-led consortia as the major commissioners, as yet there is no evidence of how investment in these services will be assured.

The impact of schools reform on protecting vulnerable children is as yet unclear. More independent status for schools may lead to improved educational outcomes for disadvantaged children and head teachers may increase their investment in school nursing and education welfare/psychology services. However, it may prove increasingly difficult to find ways to involve head teachers in Local Safeguarding Children Boards or to achieve a strategic voice for education services in LSCB arrangements.

The studies show that, though there have been some improvements, much still needs to be done at both practitioner and organizational level to promote better inter-agency working. Forthcoming changes will need to ensure that agencies continue to work more closely together to ensure that children are properly safeguarded from harm.

Key messages for all who work together to safeguard children

- Inter-disciplinary and inter-agency working is vital at all stages of child protection work. Evidence comes from multiple ways of looking at service delivery, including analyses of what happens when things go wrong and research on everyday routine practice.

- Important advances have been made in recent years at the practice level through innovative approaches to service delivery such as mixed disciplinary teams and co-location of workers.

- There are also slow but important advances in a shared sense of responsibility between agencies and reductions in the silo mentality to working. It is important to build upon these gains.

- Local Safeguarding Children Boards have played an important part in building stronger relationships through providing high-quality inter-agency training and building networking arrangements between and across disciplinary groups.

- There are risks that these advances could be lost as a result of radical restructuring of services.

Key messages for policymakers

- Care needs to be taken to ensure that proposed reforms to the NHS and to schools do not unintentionally impact on recent advances in inter-agency and inter-disciplinary working.

- Care needs to be taken to ensure that measures to restrict public spending do not have a negative impact on initiatives to share financial responsibility for maltreated children, and specifically on the work of Local Safeguarding Children Boards.

Key messages for practitioners

Health professionals

- GPs should give much greater priority to demonstrating safeguarding children competencies as set out in the *Safeguarding Children and Young People: Roles and Competences for Health Care Staff*[366] inter-collegiate document.

- Members of the health team should take a more proactive role in cases where they are uncertain whether a child is suffering significant harm and so referral to children's social care is required. There are many suitable early interventions available which could be offered to families and children (see Chapter 3).

- Referral should not be seen as absolving the referrer from further involvement but rather as a step to protecting the child and safeguarding the welfare of children and families.

Practitioners in adult services

- Practitioners in mental health, substance abuse and intimate partner violence services need to establish better links with colleagues in children's social care to ensure that suspicions or concerns about possible risks of children being maltreated are recognized and acted upon. These could be initiated through attending inter-agency training.

Social workers

- The failure to respond with feedback to referrals is a significant difficulty in gaining co-operation and good working relationships with other professionals such as those in health and education. Specific efforts should be made to improve responses to referrals, including those from concerned members of the public, by adopting good practice methods for ensuring feedback is given a high priority.

Strategic management of services at local authority level

Directors of adult and children's services

- Urgent arrangements need to be put in place to build systematic links between adult services in mental health, substance abuse and intimate partner violence with children's social care services to ensure that suspicions or concerns about possible risks of children being maltreated are recognized and acted upon.

Clinical commissioning groups

- There are risks that as a result of the reconfiguration of commissioning arrangements some of the advances made in inter-agency practice may be lost. Strenuous efforts need to be made to avoid the loss of valuable multi-disciplinary working, including embedding practitioners in other services.

Local Safeguarding Children Boards

- Inter-agency training is effective and highly valued by participants. Courses are well run and of a high standard. Training committees should be supported and properly resourced.

- Focusing on the core task of safeguarding children from harm and keeping the number of subgroups to a manageable level may be the most effective ways of working.

Chairs of Local Safeguarding Children Boards

- The opportunities for building cross-sector arrangements and joint engagement in planning are valued and important. As well as dealing with the business aspects of the task, efforts need to be redoubled to improve networking both amongst and between disciplinary groups as provided by subgroups and specialist groups.

Overview
Principal Messages and their Implications

Introduction

This Overview draws out the messages from 15 studies conducted following the tragic deaths from abuse and neglect of Victoria Climbié in 2000 and Peter Connelly in 2007. The Inquiry which followed the death of Victoria Climbié[367] identified three areas which required further research: identification and initial responses to abuse and neglect; effective interventions after maltreatment or its likelihood had been identified; and effective inter-agency and inter-disciplinary working to safeguard children. Similar issues were also raised by Peter Connelly's death. The 15 studies focus on these issues. The full list of studies has been given in Chapter 1, Table 1.1, and short synopses are given in Appendix 3. Full research briefs, reports and information concerning related publications can be downloaded from the Safeguarding Children Research Initiative website at www. education.gov.uk/researchandstatistics/research/scri.

Why is it important to identify neglect and emotional abuse early and take action?

Many of the studies have focused specifically on neglect and emotional abuse. These were both key components in the deaths of Victoria Climbié and Peter Connelly, although both Victoria and Peter were also physically abused. Despite being the most prevalent forms of maltreatment, neglect and emotional abuse have previously received less research attention in the UK.

Chapter 2 discussed both the causes and consequences of abuse and neglect. There is compelling evidence to show that parents who maltreat their children are frequently struggling with problems such as poor mental health, substance and alcohol misuse, and domestic violence.[368] Such difficulties are particularly conducive to abuse and neglect when they occur in combination and/or are compounded by other stressors such as parental learning disability, financial or housing problems and unsupportive or inadequate social and familial networks.[369] A number of studies have explored the manner and extent to which such problems impact on parents' capacity to meet their children's needs[370] and increase the likelihood of neglect and emotional abuse as well as other forms of maltreatment.

One reason why it is so important to identify emotional abuse and neglect early and take action is because they frequently first occur in early childhood (often before birth) when their impact can be particularly severe. What happens in the first three years of life is critical to children's subsequent development, because successful completion of the early developmental tasks of infancy and toddlerhood impacts on the extent to which children are able to negotiate later developmental stages.

A growing body of research has demonstrated the extent to which neglect can impact on the neurological and endocrine development of infants, affecting those parts of the brain that are concerned with emotional life and its regulation and increasing children's vulnerability to a range of psychological, emotional and physical health problems.[371,372]

Emotional abuse is an element of all types of child abuse, although it can occur on its own. It may be the most damaging type of child maltreatment, particularly in the early years, because it represents the antithesis of a child's need for safety, love, belonging and wellbeing by the person responsible for meeting these needs – their primary caregiver. It compromises children's ability to negotiate the primary tasks of infancy: forming a secure attachment with an adult caregiver, developing trust in others to provide a stable environment and becoming confident in their own ability to solicit the care they need.

Early recognition is necessary if long-term damage is to be avoided, because the effects of emotional abuse and neglect appear to be cumulative and pervasive. Both these types of child abuse have serious adverse long-term consequences across all aspects of development, including children's social and emotional wellbeing, cognitive development, physical health, mental health and behaviour. Failure to recognize and address these forms of maltreatment may result in life-long damage to the child and high costs to society through burdens on health and other services.

While the first three years are important, the impact of maltreatment is also damaging at all stages of childhood, including the teenage years. By adolescence 'neglect and/or neglectful parenting are associated with poorer physical and mental health, risky health behaviours, risks to safety including running away, poorer conduct and achievement at school and negative behaviours such as offending and anti-social behaviour'.[373] Emotional abuse is also associated with teenage suicide.

However, although emotional abuse and neglect may be the most damaging types of maltreatment, they are also the most difficult to recognize and respond to. This is because they are long-term, corrosive conditions which rarely erupt in the type of crisis that precipitates action. There are particular difficulties in determining when these types of abuse have reached a threshold for referral to children's social care or for action by the courts.

Early intervention is of key importance. All forms of maltreatment, including emotional abuse and neglect, are most likely to be first indicated to professionals across a range of universal and targeted services: health professionals, the police, nursery nurses, teachers and educational psychologists. Primary health care professionals such as GPs, midwives and health visitors are in a unique position to recognize early signs of parental and child difficulties and to identify poor parent–infant interaction. Teachers and nursery nurses see children on a daily basis and are in the best position to identify chronic, slowly deteriorating situations.

Practitioners in adult services are likely to be well placed to consider the potential impact of parents' problems on children's welfare and it should be routine practice for them to do so. The police are often the first agency to become aware of domestic violence, often associated with community violence as well as physical and emotional abuse of children. In order to recognize and respond adequately to emotional abuse and neglect, all these practitioners, as well as those who work in children's social care, will need to be aware of:

- the growing body of research on child development which demonstrates the consequences of maltreatment for children's mental and physical health, learning and education, socialization and life chances

- key signs and symptoms to look for in children, young people and in parents that indicate the likelihood of maltreatment

- the damage that can derive through not taking action, or through delaying decisions about intervention

- what steps to take as a practitioner, whether alone or in conjunction with others.

Chapter 2 described in some detail a number of recognized signs and symptoms that should alert professionals to consider whether maltreatment is likely. These range from passivity, sudden weight loss and poor infant–parent interaction in very young children to emotional and behavioural difficulties and risk-taking behaviours in adolescents. They may also be manifest in indicators such as parents' social isolation from their local community and from health, education and children's social care services; their failure to attend appointments for routine medical services or delays in their seeking medical treatment for childhood accidents such as burns and scalds; in their lack of attention to children's education; and in poor supervision or exclusion from the household of older children and teenagers.

What can be done to prevent abuse and its recurrence?

Although maltreatment can have long-term adverse consequences for children, there is increasing evidence as to how it can be prevented or its consequences mitigated. Knowledge about 'what works' is improving; it is important to use existing evidence well, to ensure that interventions are selected on the basis of their proven effectiveness and to evaluate them rigorously.

Population-based and targeted approaches

It is clear that early interventions are of paramount importance. Programmes that prevent the occurrence of maltreatment are likely to be more effective than those that address its consequences. They also require practitioners to be proactive, rather than reactive, moving the focus from considering thresholds for intervention to exploring how parenting can be improved in the population as a whole, on a public health basis. A population approach is non-stigmatizing, more likely to reach families early and prevent escalation of abuse, and more likely to reach those children whose maltreatment tends to pass unnoticed. Such an approach may be effective in shifting normative behaviour and so influencing extreme behaviour patterns in a positive direction.

Effective population-based approaches include legislative change, mass media public education programmes and universally accessible parenting programmes. Examples include the introduction of legislation to ban physical punishment in some countries, the Healthy Child Programme[374] currently implemented across the UK and the Triple P-Positive Parenting Programme being introduced on a population-wide basis in Glasgow.[375] There is a case for using a population-based approach to address issues that are particularly pertinent to adolescents, such as exploring normative standards of parental monitoring and supervision outside school and reducing violence in early intimate partner relationships, both of which might respond to mass media public education programmes.

There is also a place for targeted programmes to prevent abuse and neglect amongst vulnerable populations. The most effective targeted programmes being introduced in the UK at present are some (though not all) home-visiting programmes such as Nurse Family Partnerships[376] and validated parenting programmes such as the Webster-Stratton Incredible Years.[377] Targeted approaches are valuable but they need to be carefully piloted, adapted, if necessary, to a UK context and thoroughly trialled before being implemented on a widespread basis.

Specialist interventions to safeguard children from harm

Where abuse has occurred or the likelihood is strong, families will need intensive support to prevent its recurrence or to mitigate its impact on children. Some parents can and do overcome extensive difficulties and succeed in providing a nurturing home for their children, sometimes after an older child has been placed for adoption. Factors that indicate that parents may have the capacity to change include the development of insight into how problems such as substance misuse have affected their children and the part that their actions may have played in previous separations; genuine rather than superficial engagement with services; and for many, a wake-up call when they have realized that they will need to take substantial action if they are to meet their children's needs. Parents who succeed in making sufficient and sustained changes appear to have been less likely to have experienced abuse in their own childhoods – an ominous indicator of the long-term, sometimes inter-generational consequences of maltreatment. We need more research, however, to test out the reliability of these indicators, to understand more about the causes and timing of positive change, and to learn more about why some parents become more motivated to change than others.

A number of specific, validated programmes are now available to support parents in making necessary changes and help them sustain them. However, parents need to be motivated to change before entering such programmes. Chapter 5 of this Overview offered ten examples of programmes that have been rigorously evaluated and shown to promote positive change on the range of issues covered by the studies.[378] Those available include programmes that focus on parents; parents and children together; wider families; and children alone. Selected examples of programmes that focus on parents include effective interventions for: substance-misusing parents;[379] and parents who have been exposed to harsh parenting and abuse in their own childhoods.[380] Those that focus on parents (and/or wider family members) and children together include interventions to improve: maternal and child representations where there is a known history of abuse in the family;[381] parent–child relationships in infants with faltering growth;[382] and interventions to reduce physical abuse and parent–child conflict.[383,384] Effective programmes that focus on mitigating the consequences of abuse for children include a therapeutic preschool for neglected infants;[385] peer-led social skills training for maltreated and socially withdrawn children;[386] and interventions for maltreated children who require placements away from home.[387] Programmes such as these form part of the increasing body of evidence about effective interventions in families where child abuse and neglect are already evident or likely to occur.

When descriptions of these interventions are juxtaposed, as in the previous paragraph, it is obvious that they address overlapping populations; most families where abuse and neglect occur will experience multi-faceted problems that impact on both parents and children. It is therefore difficult to select a specific intervention that addresses all their needs. Moreover, the interventions themselves have numerous elements in common, and again treatment content, techniques and parameters often overlap. It may be possible to develop an approach which distils the common elements from existing evidence-based interventions to address diverse and complex cases. Whether such an approach can be converted into effective practice will need to be tested on a small scale initially.[388]

Care should be taken in commissioning specific interventions as not all of those available have been successfully evaluated.[389] Commissioners should first consider whether, if developed elsewhere, an intervention has been successfully adapted for a UK context. In assessing the findings of any evaluations, they will also need to take account of the evidence level of the study design; the size of the sample and the rate of attrition; whether there is evidence of sustained change – and for how long. They will also need to consider whether the intervention is sufficiently flexible to be adapted to allow for complexity and diversity of cases; and how to make good use of locally available practitioners' expertise and resources. Some existing interventions, that have no proven effectiveness, may need to be dropped in favour of those where the evidence base is more robust.

Social work interventions to safeguard children from harm

Specific, focused interventions may be offered as part of a package of intensive support that will include more generic social work casework. Three studies in the Research Initiative collected primary data from social work case files and interviews with professionals, parents and children, to explore the impact of these interventions.[390,391,392]

Proactive social work can be very effective. Outcomes for children tend to be better where there is evidence of careful assessment, thoughtful planning and proactive case management. Children and families also receive a better quality of service if social care involvement is the compulsory result of a child protection plan or a care order than if it is offered on a less intrusive, voluntary basis. However, the quality of assessment and planning tends to vary significantly between different authorities and indeed between different teams within the same authority, suggesting that supervision, culture, training and experience have a major impact on effective case management.

Although some of these research messages are positive, there is also evidence that many children are left for too long or returned prematurely to abusive or neglectful families where their welfare is inadequately safeguarded. There are numerous reasons why this happens. First, there is evidence that many social work practitioners are insufficiently aware of the impact of abuse and, particularly, neglect on children's long-term welfare or of the need to take swift and decisive action when very young children, including those *in utero*, are suffering significant harm. Theories of child development should be a central element in social work training, but the subject is often quickly passed over and soon forgotten. Practitioners are also often insufficiently aware of the need to understand a family's previous history in order to make sense of present circumstances and to assess any evidence of change. There is also evidence that practitioners can become desensitized to evidence of neglect or so overwhelmed by parents' difficulties that they are unable to see the situation clearly and, in particular, the child's needs.

Second, almost all decisions made by the wide range of practitioners involved, from health, adult mental health, education and the family justice system as well as by professionals in children's social care, are made in the expectation that children will fare best if looked after by their birth families. This is in keeping with the Children Act 1989 and with human rights legislation, as well as with social work values and theories of empowerment. However, it means that decisions to separate children from their families go very much against the grain and are particularly difficult to make. Expert assessments ordered by the courts tend to follow this line, as do court decisions themselves, with the result that parents are given numerous chances to demonstrate their capacity to look after a child; if these efforts prove unsuccessful they delay the progress of a case to the detriment of children's welfare.

Practitioners are not always aware of the urgency of children's timeframes. Very small children are more likely to develop secure attachments to permanent carers if they are placed within their first year. If they are left too long in abusive or neglectful families pending a decision to separate them, their long-term wellbeing may be compromised both by the far-reaching consequences of maltreatment, by the later impact of rupturing secure attachments with temporary carers, and by the difficulties of finding permanent placements as they grow older. There is also evidence that, after children reach the age of six, proactive case management tends to diminish as the chances of achieving permanency recede. In fact, parents' timeframes also appear to be relatively short: there is some evidence, that needs ratification, that the birth of a baby can serve as a catalyst, and those parents who are able to make the often radical changes required to offer a nurturing home will have done so by the time the child is six months old. Many such parents will have begun the process of change before the baby is born. Those who have not succeeded in making significant changes within this timeframe may be unlikely to do so within the timescale of the child concerned, but may make sufficient changes at a later date to care for subsequent children.

While all those involved may strive to keep children out of care or accommodation or to return them swiftly to their birth families if separation becomes necessary, the evidence suggests that maltreated children, and particularly those who are neglected or emotionally abused, may benefit by being looked after away from home. Where there has been evidence of past abuse, and particularly neglect, maltreated children who remain looked after find greater stability and achieve better wellbeing than those who return home. The *Home or Care? Study* found that those who remain looked after are less likely to have misused alcohol or drugs or to have committed offences than those who return home; they have significantly better mean scores for health; they are more likely to have close adult ties; and they are more likely to have a range of special skills, interests and hobbies. They are less likely to be in pupil referral units, in alternative forms of education, without a school place or to be persistent truants than those who return home.[393]

We have quoted these findings in full because concerns about the poor outcomes of care are widespread. Yet all three empirical studies in this Research Initiative, as well as an increasing body of other research, demonstrate that the majority of children who become looked after in the UK today benefit from care.[394,395,396] This is not to say that the concerns are unfounded: unstable placements, low aspirations and insufficient support for young people as they move towards independence are all long-standing problems that have not been sufficiently addressed.[397,398,399] There is also evidence that some residential and foster homes are at best insensitive to children's needs and at worst openly abusive.[400]

Nevertheless, taken as a whole, when compared with their home circumstances, care is often a positive alternative for children and young people who have been maltreated. However, a major problem is that, though it may offer a safer and more nurturing environment, care can, as yet, rarely compensate for past disadvantages. We have seen how children and young people who have experienced maltreatment may require intensive, specific interventions to help mitigate the consequences of abuse and neglect. Although, as previously indicated, the evidence about effective interventions is growing, and some that have been validated elsewhere are now being adapted and trialled in the UK, they are not widely available. Nor are many carers sufficiently trained to provide the intensive, specialist support required. There is also a paucity of interventions that are tailored to the needs of neglected adolescents. Moreover, there is often a loss of continuity: when children move placement or return home from care or accommodation they may cease to access a programme of support that was previously available.[401] There is clearly a need to develop this area further so that care becomes a more specialist service, offered as one element in a package of specific interventions aimed both at safeguarding children and young people and helping them to overcome the consequences of abuse and neglect.

One feature of both the generic interventions of social workers and the more specific interventions from psychologists, psychiatrists and other specially trained professionals is that they may be offered for too short a period or withdrawn too abruptly. Many of the parents and children who access such interventions have entrenched and deep-seated problems that are unlikely to be overcome within a few weeks or months. Most specific interventions are strictly time-limited; if the impact is to be sustained, ongoing, less intensive support and relapse prevention needs to be offered for a longer period. However, more generic social work family support is often also of very short duration. Half the child protection plans for the babies in the *Significant Harm of Infants Study* were for 32 weeks or less, and almost all for less than a year. Similarly, wherever possible the least intrusive intervention is chosen, so that children who are placed on care orders tend to be placed with their parents at the first opportunity and, in fact, many of them never leave home. Cases are also quickly closed; when parents have overcome substantial adversities, there is little formal monitoring to check that change has been sustained. Expectations that abusive parents will re-refer themselves if they run into further difficulties are unrealistic.

This tendency for specialist, tertiary, interventions to be offered on a short-term basis and then prematurely withdrawn can be counter-productive and, in the long term, costly.[402,403] About two thirds of looked after children who return home are subsequently readmitted, and those who experience repeated, failed, attempts at reunification have the worst outcomes. Nevertheless pressures to close cases will be exacerbated as services are reduced in response to the current economic situation. If children are to be adequately safeguarded in such circumstances there is a greater need for inter-agency co-operation. Where there is a risk of maltreatment or its recurrence, children and families will continue to need transitional, and in some cases long-term, multi-disciplinary support from cross-sector services such as health, mental health, social work and education.

How can we ensure that inter-agency working works well?

The reports following the deaths of Victoria Climbié and Peter Connelly both stressed the importance of improving inter-agency and inter-disciplinary working to ensure that maltreatment is recognized and responded to early and that the multi-faceted needs of children and family members are addressed in a co-ordinated way. The consequences of not doing this are high, both to children individually and to society. The studies in the Research Initiative found that there have been improvements, but there are many issues that still need to be addressed.

Inter-agency working at practitioner level

At a practitioner level there are concerns about high thresholds for referrals to children's social care and about the lack of feedback when they are made. There are also concerns about the limits of responsibility: at present there can be a hiatus at the point of referral to children's social care and at the point of case closure, where children may be left in limbo, without adequate support. If specialist services are unavailable or reduced then targeted services need to be made more accessible to ensure that children are adequately safeguarded.

There are also concerns about different perceptions of risk of harm between professionals. Where the role of professionals is to focus on parents, as is the case with substance abuse workers, or both parents and children, as is the case with GPs, there may also be divided loyalties. Better networking and communication at practitioner level can help to dispel some of the misperceptions about the roles of other professionals and resolve some of these difficulties.

Developing multi-disciplinary teams and embedding practitioners in other services is a valuable way of improving inter-agency working. Attendance at LSCB inter-agency training events has also been shown to be an effective means of forging links and fostering better understanding of shared roles and responsibilities. However, at present those practitioners who are least engaged in inter-agency working are also the least likely to attend. This is an issue that might be addressed as part of continued professional development for GPs and professionals in adult services.

Inter-agency working at local and national level

LSCBs should note that the inter-agency training they provide is highly valued and effective in terms of both impact and costs. The opportunities LSCBs offer for building cross-sector arrangements and joint engagement in planning are also important and have done much to break down silo mentalities. However, LSCBs require adequate resources to support their infrastructure and business activities if they are to be effective. LSCBs might restrict their role, and indeed there is evidence that focusing on the core task of safeguarding children from harm and keeping the numbers of subgroups to a manageable level may be the most effective ways of working. However, for them to function properly, training subcommittees should be supported and properly resourced, as should the post of the business manager. At present LSCBs are jointly funded by the various agencies which share responsibilities for safeguarding children, but there is no funding formula to clarify their proportionate contributions. In the current financial climate these may fall as agencies seek to reduce their budgets. There is a danger that this will exacerbate tensions between agencies and limit the capacity of LSCBs to fulfil their responsibilities for safeguarding children.

At a national level, there are concerns that proposed reforms to the NHS and schools might unintentionally impact on recent advances in inter-agency and inter-disciplinary working. The links that bind agencies together into partnerships are fragile and easily destroyed; many are dependent on hard-won trust that can swiftly be lost. New arrangements such as the proposed Health and Wellbeing Boards need to be sufficiently robust to ensure that greater diversity of provision and increased freedom to innovate do not inadvertently lessen collaboration.

Conclusion

The purpose of this Overview is to distil the messages from a research programme developed to strengthen the evidence base for the development of policies and practice to improve the protection of children in England. Each chapter ends with a resumé of the key messages from the research on the topic covered.

Many of these messages are not new: failure to attend to early warning signs, lack of understanding of child development, delays in responding to children's timeframes, and unresolved professional tensions have all been identified before as key issues to address in improving the way that children are safeguarded. One of the key questions for policymakers is how to ensure that these messages are better implemented in the drive to improve services, and why it is so difficult to do so.

In our view, the most important messages to be drawn from the Research Initiative as a whole are as follows:

1. Efforts should be made to facilitate a closer alignment between targeted services and GP as well as specialist services, so that families considered to be at risk of harming their children are better supported when they fall below the threshold for social care intervention, both prior to referral and following case closure.

2. Social workers and social care agencies should ensure that feedback to referrals is given a higher priority.

3. Better systematic links are needed between adult services in mental health, substance misuse and intimate partner violence and GPs and children's services to ensure that risk factors for abuse and neglect are identified and concerns about children being maltreated are acted upon.

4. There is a strong case for developing public education campaigns aimed at promoting good parenting supervision, reducing adolescent neglect and reducing intimate partner violence in early adolescence.

5. The neglect of adolescents is too often unnoticed. Anti-social behaviour, risky behaviour such as experimenting with drugs, and very poor performance in school should be seen as possible signs of parental neglect of older children. Targeted programmes to reduce risky behaviour amongst adolescents and to promote positive models of parental supervision need to be developed and tested in the UK.

6. Thresholds for referral to children's social care and the family courts need to be clearly articulated and agreed at the most senior managerial level. There should be formal discussions between local authority senior managers, legal departments and the judiciary concerning appropriate thresholds for taking legal action. Post-order reviews of children's progress would provide useful feedback.

7. Child development should be given a very high priority in social work training and continuing education. There is abundant evidence in the studies of insufficient appreciation of fundamental child development knowledge. Gaps in knowledge about the importance of simple chronologies; understanding histories by reading case files; the risk factors related to parental problems; avoiding 'start again' syndrome; and becoming desensitized to poor parenting standards need to be urgently addressed in training and continuing professional development.

8. Key to effective intervention are interpersonal skills. All practitioners and professionals who intervene with children and families need these skills. Priority should be given to developing and consolidating interpersonal

skills in all forms of training, supervision and professional development. This should encompass work with non-compliant parents, and scepticism about apparent compliance.

9. High-quality specific interventions exist to address the multi-faceted needs of both parents and children. These should be commissioned alongside casework interventions by multi-disciplinary teams including social workers.

10. Commissioners of services need to evaluate the cost of premature case closure or rigidly time-limited therapeutic interventions versus that of ignoring long-term therapeutic and welfare needs.

11. All professionals with safeguarding responsibilities should be aware that the majority of maltreated children who are looked after by local authorities do better in terms of wellbeing and stability than those who remain at home. Care works for these children, though there is an urgent need for more specialist provision to help them overcome past adversities.

12. More services need to be developed, in particular for alcohol and substance abuse, but also to improve aspects of parenting and addressing the needs of children, after they have experienced maltreatment. Such interventions may be home grown or adopted from tested versions from overseas but should be subject to rigorous evaluation in the UK. Research funding bodies should prioritize such evaluation.

13. There is a particular need for evidence-based services to address intimate partner violence: for adult victims, affected children and for perpetrators.

14. Urgent action is needed at government level to ensure that advances in inter-agency and inter-disciplinary working are not lost. Care needs to be taken to ensure that proposed reforms to the NHS and schools do not unintentionally impact on recent advances in inter-agency and inter-disciplinary working. Measures to restrict public spending must not have a negative impact on initiatives to share financial responsibility for maltreated children, and specifically on the work of Local Safeguarding Children Boards. Funds should be ring-fenced for inter-agency training, which has been shown to provide good value for money.

15. Further research is needed on particular support or access issues for adolescents, fathers and families of diverse ethnicity.

Implementation and Advisory Group

- Rosalyn Proops: Child Protection Coordinator, RCPCH, Norfolk and Norwich NHS Trust

- Colin Green: Director of Children, Learning and Young People's Directorate, Coventry City Council

- Martin Pratt: Corporate Director for Children and Learning, Luton Council

- Fiona Smith: Children and Young People's Adviser, Royal College of Nursing

- Janice Allister: RCGP Child Safeguarding Lead

- Richard Stowe: Independent Chair, Dorset Safeguarding Children Board

- Malcolm Ward: Chair of Southwark LSCB

- Enid Hendry: NSPCC Head of Training, NSPCC National Training

- Jenny Gray (Chair): Professional Adviser, Department for Education

- Zoltan Bozoky: Head of Child Health Research, Policy Research Programme, Department of Health

- Isabella Craig: Statistician, Department for Education

- Julie Wilkinson: Senior Research Officer, Department for Education

- Christine Humphrey: Safeguarding Adviser, Department of Health

- Jane Barlow: Professor of Public Health in the Early Years, University of Warwick

- Jan Horwath: Professor of Child Welfare, University of Sheffield

- Daryl Dougdale: Teaching Fellow in Social Work, University of Bristol

- Heather Brown: Divisional Manager, OFSTED

- Sue Eardley: Senior Policy Lead, NHS Review, Care Quality Commission

- Jane Lewis: Director, Research in Practice

- Harriet Ward: Director, Centre for Child and Family Research, University of Loughborough

- Carolyn Davies: Scientific Coordinator, Safeguarding Children Research Initiative, Thomas Coram Research Unit, IOE

- His Honour Judge Tony Mitchell: Nottingham Crown and County Courts

- Richard Bartholomew: Chief Research Officer, Department for Education

Details of Evaluations of Specific Interventions Discussed in Chapter 5

Example 1: Parents Under Pressure[404]

This programme has been rigorously evaluated (Evidence Level A).[405]

What is the programme?

Parents Under Pressure (PUP) comprises an intensive, manualized, home-based intervention of ten modules conducted in the family home over 10–12 weeks, with each session lasting between one and two hours. Modules include issues such as: challenging the notion of an ideal parent; parenting under pressure; encouraging good behaviour; mindful child management; coping with lapse and relapse; extending social networks; and life skills and relationships. The programme is delivered by an accredited trained therapist; training can be undertaken by anyone with a commitment to working with multi-problem families.[406]

What has been evaluated?

This programme has been evaluated in an RCT[407] comprising 64 methadone-dependent primary carers, 86 per cent of whom were mothers with at least one child aged between two and eight years in their full-time care. The Parents Under Pressure (PUP) programme was compared with a brief (two-session) traditional parent-training intervention and standard care (i.e. routine care by methadone clinic staff involving three-monthly meetings with the prescribing doctor and access to a caseworker to assist in housing, employment and benefits).

Results

Participants receiving the PUP programme showed significant reductions in parental stress and in methadone dose. There was also a significant reduction in the risk of child abuse as measured by the Child Abuse Potential Inventory (CAPI). Children of parents in the brief intervention showed a modest reduction in the risk of child abuse but no other changes. There was a significant increase in the risk of child abuse in parents receiving standard care. Children of parents who received PUP showed significant improvements in child behaviour problems and an increase in child pro-social scores. There were no improvements in the children of parents who received the brief intervention or standard care.

Issues for implementation

This programme was developed in Australia where it has been evaluated with positive results: elements are now being used in the UK[408] as part of the Helping Families Programme.[409] Information about training and supervision plus further information about the programme is available on the PUP website: www.pupprogramme.net.au.

Example 2: Enhanced Triple P-Positive Parenting Programme[410]

This programme has been rigorously evaluated (Evidence Level A).[411,412]

What is the programme?

The enhanced Triple P-Positive Parenting Programme is based on a cognitive behavioural approach involving a combination of social learning theory and cognitive theory. The theoretical framework derives from evidence that children are emotionally abused because parents have learned dysfunctional child-management practices.[413]

The Triple P-Positive Parenting Programme is 'a multi-level, parenting and family support strategy that aims to prevent severe behavioural, emotional and developmental problems in children by enhancing the knowledge, skills and confidence of parents'. It comprises a manualized programme that is provided by fully trained practitioners who receive ongoing support and supervision during its delivery. It incorporates succeeding levels of intervention of increasing strength for children from birth to the age of 12.

The 'standard' family intervention (Triple P, Level Four) requires parents to attend group sessions of parent training followed by individual telephone consultations; they also receive a copy of *Every Parent's Group Workbook*.[414] Parents are taught 17 core child-management strategies designed to promote children's competence and development; and help them manage misbehaviour. They are also taught a planned activities routine to enhance the generalization and maintenance of parenting skills.

The 'enhanced' version of the Triple P Programme (Level Five) comprises an additional four sessions that are aimed explicitly at addressing cognitive (attributional retraining) and affective (anger management) factors that have been shown to differentiate between maltreating and other parents.[415] In these additional sessions, parents are taught 'a variety of skills aiming to challenge the beliefs they hold regarding their own behaviour and the behaviour of their child, and to change any negative practices they currently use in line with these beliefs'. Parents are also taught 'a variety of physical, cognitive, and planning strategies to manage their anger' including the use of advanced planning for high-risk situations.

What has been evaluated?

The study targeted 98 parents of children aged two to seven years, who had been referred by child protection services for emotional abuse, or had self-referred primarily because of concerns about their anger. The mean age of participating parents was 34 years and that of their children 4.4 years. The level of disadvantage of the parents was unspecified, as were factors such as their ethnicity.

Results

Parents in both groups had improved levels of anxiety and depression following the intervention. There was also a significant decrease in both groups in parental distress and parental conflict, for both versions of the programme. At the six-month follow-up, parents who had taken part in the enhanced programme continued to improve at a greater rate in terms of anger management than those who had taken part in the standard programme. The study also found reliable improvements in child behaviour. Parents in both groups reported a significant decrease in the number of parenting and childcare situations in which they experienced problem behaviour both in the home and in the community. Significant improvements were found in the management of problematic situations by parents in both groups, with no differences between them at follow-up.

Issues for implementation

The programme is currently implemented in the UK under the auspices of the NHS in at least two locations: first, in North Staffordshire NHS Combined Healthcare, where it is offered in a number of Sure Start children's centres and primary school locations; and second, in Glasgow under the Greater Glasgow NHS Board Starting Well project, where it is the subject of a qualitative evaluation.

Example 3: Individual compared with enhanced individual plus group-based cognitive behavioural therapy (CBT)[416]

This intervention has been evaluated to Evidence Level B.[417]

What is the programme?

The individual parent training comprises ten weekly sessions of two hours' duration and involves the development of a collaborative partnership with parents in terms of the arrangement and agreements made regarding the process and content of weekly sessions. Topics covered include developmental counselling, improving parent–child interactions and relationships through the exploration of parental attitudes and feelings about the child, and putting them into interactional contexts, and managing children's and parents' problematic behaviours. Frequent telephone calls are made between sessions to support parents in the learning of new skills, to provide advice, rehearse difficult tasks, and encourage and reinforce their efforts. The enhanced programme provides additional ten weekly two-hour sessions of group-based parent training including a play group for the children and the transport of clients to sessions where appropriate. The programme focuses on training in stress-management skills; self-control training; problem-solving abilities; and the provision of a forum for mutual support, encouragement and exchange of ideas.

What has been evaluated?

The evaluation was undertaken with 34 emotionally abusive and neglectful parents with a median age of 25 years, referred by a paediatric assessment centre, outpatient clinics, and local authority senior social workers. One sixth of the sample were black and a similar proportion were single parents. Most families were of a low socio-economic status.

Results

The results show significant reductions in the stress and anxiety levels of parents receiving both home and combined home and group-based interventions. Parents' perceptions of the parent–child relationship before and after were stronger in the combined group. Direct observations of parent–child behaviours were undertaken by social workers to assess 22 forms of emotionally abusive behaviour. These showed greater improvements in parents' perceptions of the parent–child relationship and statistically significant reductions in emotionally abusive behaviours, with both changes more significant in the combined group.

Implications

Overall, the moderately rigorous evaluation of this programme suggests that both formats produce a range of improvements in emotionally abusive parenting, but that the additional group-based intervention results in significant improvements in areas other than childcare.

Issues for implementation

This evaluation offers evidence that an appropriately delivered CBT programme can have an impact in reducing emotionally abusive parenting. It could be provided in the UK by appropriately trained therapists.

Example 4: Preschooler–Parent Psychotherapy (PPP)[418]

This intervention has been evaluated to Evidence Level A.[419]

What is the programme?

Preschooler–Parent Psychotherapy is a specific programme, provided to mothers and preschoolers who attend a clinic for weekly, hour-long sessions. Therapy focuses on helping the mother recognize how her past history is re-enacted in the present and enabling her to change her representations.

What has been evaluated?

This intervention has been compared with a CBT-based psycho-educational home-visiting programme focused on parenting skills training (HVP), and a standard community services programme (CS) for maltreated preschoolers and their mothers, as well as with no treatment controls.

This high-quality evaluation explored the impact on parents, a large proportion of whom were from minority ethnic groups. Eighty-seven mothers and their infants took part. All the children had experienced a number of combinations of different types of abuse. One third had been identified as suffering emotional abuse only or emotional abuse and neglect and 38 per cent had experienced physical abuse.

Results: Parent outcomes

Parents were found to demonstrate significant improvement in their parental representations post treatment in the PPP group compared with the other two groups. The study also found a significant post-intervention difference in the positive self-representations of children.

Issues for implementation

In terms of implementation, this form of therapy works well; regular supervision is core to its delivery. Key groups of professionals, including social workers and health visitors, could be appropriately trained to deliver this intervention.

Example 5: Interaction Guidance[420]

This intervention has been evaluated to Evidence Level B.[421]

What is the programme?

Interaction Guidance consists of videotaped interaction between mother and infant followed by a lengthy session of discussion, education and feedback. It includes an individually tailored information component on specific problems exhibited by the infant. The intervention is delivered in five, weekly 90-minute sessions in a clinical setting by therapists including one dietician trained in the use of behavioural therapy, supervised by a clinical psychologist.

What has been evaluated?

This intervention has been evaluated using a two-group, non-randomized model in which Interaction Guidance was compared with a behavioural feeding programme. Twenty-eight infants diagnosed with faltering growth and their mothers were included in each group. The median age of the mothers was 32 years and that of the infants was 18 months. Just under half of the sample was from disadvantaged social groups. Ethnicity was not specified.

Results: Parent outcomes

A significant decrease in disrupted communication was found between mothers and infants in the Interaction Guidance group, in contrast with the feeding-focused group, which remained stable. Those in the Interaction Guidance group were significantly more likely to attain a classification of 'non-disrupted' by the end of the intervention than those in the feeding-focused group.

Example 6: Parent–Child Interaction Therapy (PCIT)[422]

This intervention has been evaluated to Evidence Level A.[423]

What is the programme?

The intervention is delivered over three modules: a six-session orientation group aimed at increasing motivation by fostering understanding of negative consequences of severe physical discipline, building confidence and self-efficacy expectations; 12–14 sessions of clinic-based PCIT designed to enhance parent–child relationship skills through clinic-based individual parent–child dyad sessions aimed at developing discipline skills, following a protocol designed to promote child compliance; and a four-session follow-up group programme with parents to address any implementation problems, while the children attend a concurrent social skills programme.

What has been evaluated?

PCIT was compared with PCIT plus individualized enhanced services and a standard community-based parenting group in a randomized controlled trial. The 110 parents in the sample had been repeatedly referred to child protection services, had displayed severe parent to child violence, had low household income and had significant levels of depression, substance abuse and anti-social behaviour.

Results

The evaluation looked at recurrence of abuse and found a significant difference between those given Parent-Child Interaction Therapy and those placed in the standard community-based parenting group. The trial showed a significant result favouring the PCIT group on reduced recurrence of physical abuse and on improved parent–child interaction. There was also a small non-significant difference favouring the PCIT group on a standardized measure of child abuse risk (Child Abuse Potential Inventory (CAPI)).

Issues for implementation

The therapy can be delivered by trained therapists with Master-level qualifications in psychology, social work or a related field. Further information, including training and treatment guidelines, is available on the PCIT websites.[424,425,426]

Example 7: Multi-Systemic Therapy for Child Abuse and Neglect (MST-CAN)[427]

This programme has been evaluated to Evidence Level A.[428]

What is the programme?

Multi-Systemic Therapy for Child Abuse and Neglect (MST-CAN) includes the core components of standard multi-systemic therapy, as well as several adaptations for treating maltreated young people and their families.

MST-CAN uses a recursive analytical process to identify, develop and prioritize interventions. Stakeholders are interviewed to attain their views of desired outcomes, and these become the over-arching goals of treatment. Following a comprehensive assessment of the strengths and needs of individuals and systems in the family's social ecology, each target behaviour is assessed to determine its *fit* or drivers (e.g. harsh discipline is associated with parental anxiety, youth non-compliance, and low parenting skills). The fit factors that are the strongest drivers to the target behaviours are prioritized for intervention. Evidence-based interventions (e.g. CBT for deficits in anger management) are implemented with the support of the family's social ecology, and outcomes are assessed. Fit factors and interventions are re-examined and modified in a recursive process until desired outcomes are achieved.

Adaptations to address serious child safety concerns include: the development of a safety plan agreed by all family members; close working with child protection agencies to promote positive relations and ensure that CPS decision-making is based on clinical need or progress; and a clarification process on completion, to help the parent address cognitions about the abuse incident, accept responsibility and apologize to the child and family. In the trial, interventions, tailored to the family's needs, included CBT for deficits in anger management; a CBT protocol with families who had low problem-solving skills or difficulties communicating without conflict; and prolonged exposure therapy for parents experiencing PTSD symptoms.

What has been evaluated?

MST-CAN has been evaluated in an RCT comprising 86 physically abused young people and their parents. MST-CAN was compared with standard services (individual therapy, family therapy and parent and child sessions; referral to outside agencies; and medication where deemed appropriate) and Enhanced Outpatient Treatment (EOT) (standard services plus enhanced engagement and parent-training interventions).

Results: Young people's outcomes

Young people in all three programmes showed improvements in self-reported PTSD and depressive symptoms and parent-reported social skills. However, the improvement in self-reported PTSD symptoms was significantly greater for those in MST-CAN. MST-CAN, but not EOT young people, showed significant decreases in parent-reported internalizing, PTSD, total symptoms and self-reported dissociative symptoms.

Parent outcomes

Parents across all three programmes reported significant decreases in global psychiatric distress and a number of positive symptoms. Those who received MST-CAN, however, reported significantly greater decreases in psychiatric distress than did counterparts in the EOT condition. MST-CAN was significantly more effective than EOT at reducing neglect (youth and parent report), psychological aggression (youth report), minor assault (youth report) and severe assault (parent and youth report). Although use of non-violent discipline decreased significantly for both groups over time, this decline was significantly less for MST-CAN. MST-CAN parents also reported significant increases in total perceived support, appraisal support (perceived ability of someone to talk about one's problems) and belonging support (perceived availability of people with whom to do things), whereas EOT counterparts did not. The numbers for re-abuse were very small, and group differences were not significant. Improvements were maintained at 16 months' follow-up.

Example 8: Therapeutic Preschool (Childhaven)[429]

This intervention has been evaluated to Evidence Level A.[430]

What is the programme?

Childhaven is a therapeutic day treatment programme for infants aged 1–24 months who have been maltreated or are at risk of maltreatment. The treatment programme is primarily directed towards the child, providing medical, developmental, psychological and educational services to promote healthy growth and development. Children are transported to and from the programme by staff. Parent interventions are also offered on a voluntary basis and include parenting education, concrete services, support groups, counselling and referrals to other services as necessary.

What has been evaluated?

Participants in the trial were randomly allocated to Childhaven or standard child protection services. Twelve years after the original intervention, 35 of the participants were located and agreed to follow-up measures. These comprised home observation and examinations of records including juvenile court files; parent, child and teacher reports were also obtained.

Results

While only about half the children were traced in the long-term follow-up, multiple sources were used to inform the findings. Results showed significant improvements in terms of more than one type of outcome measure. At home, there was a significantly more positive emotional climate and more responsiveness to children on the part of Childhaven parents than the 'treatment as usual' families. Juvenile court files showed that participants from the 'treatment as usual' group were first arrested at an earlier age and were arrested for serious or violent crimes (i.e. assault, arson, child abuse and robbery) significantly more often than those in the Childhaven group. Children in the 'treatment as usual' group were also reported by parents to show more aggressive behaviour on the Child Behavior Checklist.

Issues for implementation

Implementation could be undertaken in the UK, supplied by appropriately trained therapists in a preschool setting.

Example 9: Peer-led social skills training[431]

This programme has been evaluated to Evidence Level A.[432]

What is the programme?

Peer-led social skills training involves identifying children in the Head Start[433] classrooms who display high levels of positive play and an ability to encourage play in socially withdrawn children. A parent volunteer arranges an area in the classroom in which pairs of resilient peers and socially withdrawn children may play, and provides support. Play sessions occur three times per week for five weeks.

What has been evaluated?

The participants were 46 children in Head Start programmes who were rated by teachers and classroom observers as socially withdrawn. All of the children were African-American. Seven had documented histories of physical abuse, 11 had experienced physical neglect, and four had experienced both forms of maltreatment. The remaining 24 children in the sample did not have documented histories of maltreatment. The children were randomly assigned to receive peer-led social skills training or to control conditions.

Results

The results are from blind observations of children's social interactions post treatment. Before treatment, maltreated children were significantly more isolated and less interactive in peer play than non-maltreated children. The results show a significant difference in children's levels of interactive play between the treatment group of children and the control group, with the treatment group exhibiting more interactive play and less solitary play than the control group. These improvements were evident in both maltreated and non-maltreated socially withdrawn children. Treatment gains in social interactions were sustained at two months' follow-up. Observed teacher-rated skills were also more improved in the treatment group than the control group, as were teacher-rated behavioural problems.

Example 10: Multi-Treatment Foster Care for Preschoolers (MTFC-P) (Multidimensional Treatment Foster Care – Prevention (MTFC-P) in UK)[434]

This intervention has been evaluated to Evidence Level A.[435,436]

What is the programme?

Multi-Treatment Foster Care for Preschoolers (MTFC-P) is a therapeutic foster care programme for younger children that incorporates parent training and consultation for foster parents, parent training for birth or adoptive parents and individual therapy for children who have experienced maltreatment. The programme consists of training for the foster parents before receiving the child and daily telephone support and supervision, weekly group meetings and 24-hour on-call crisis interventions when the child is in placement. In addition, the children receive a behavioural treatment intervention in the foster home and attend weekly therapeutic play groups. When children move from the foster placement to a permanent placement, the new caregivers are trained in the same techniques that the foster parents have been utilizing with the child. Most of the intervention team have Bachelor's or Master's degrees and are supervised by a licensed psychologist and supported by a psychiatrist for any medication needed by the children.

What has been evaluated?

In one North American city all preschool children aged between three and six years old entering new foster placements and expected to remain there for at least three months were randomly assigned to MTFC-P or regular foster care. Recruitment occurred continuously over three years. The two evaluations discussed here covered one sample of 90 children (47 MTFC-P and 43 regular foster care) and one of 117 (57 MTFC-P and 60 regular foster care).

Results

The first evaluation[437] explored whether the children were able to remain successfully in adoptive placements or with their birth parents after treatment. The results showed that there were permanent placement failures for 36 per cent of children in the regular foster care group as opposed to 10 per cent of children in the MTFC-P group ($p<.05$).[438] The second evaluation showed that, at 12-month follow-up, the morning–evening cortisol levels of children in the MTFC-P group were significantly better than those of the regular foster care group, and were more closely comparable to those of a non-maltreated community sample.[439] This is important because raised cortisol levels are related to stress in children who have experienced maltreatment or loss of a parent; they are associated with anxiety and poor control of emotions. A further evaluation showed that children in the MTFC-P group also displayed significantly more secure attachment behaviours and significantly fewer avoidant attachment behaviours than children in the regular foster care group.[440] The intervention appears to increase fostered toddlers' ability to rely on their foster carers for comfort and to reduce their insecure proximity-seeking behaviours.

Project Summaries

Full details of all these studies, including unpublished reports, research briefs and information about published papers and books, can be downloaded from the Safeguarding Children Research Initiative website: www.education.gov.uk/researchandstatistics/research/scri.

Safeguarding Children from Emotional Abuse: What Works?; published as Safeguarding Children from Emotional Maltreatment – What Works (The Emotional Abuse Intervention Review)

Jane Barlow and Anita Schrader McMillan

Introduction

Emotional maltreatment is an inadequately researched and poorly understood concept, despite increasing awareness about the harm it can cause to children's lives. This review of the literature summarizes the evidence about what works to prevent child emotional maltreatment *before it occurs* and also to *prevent its recurrence* once it has taken place.

Aims

To identify studies that evaluate the effectiveness of interventions in the secondary prevention and treatment of child emotional abuse involving the parents or primary carers of children aged 0–19 years.

Methodology

A broad search strategy was developed to identify as many relevant studies as possible. Studies were included if they involved any intervention directed at emotionally abusive parenting, and that measured change in (i) emotional unavailability; (ii) negative attributions; (iii) developmentally inappropriate interactions; (iv) recognition of children's boundaries; (v) inconsistency in the parenting role; and (vi) mis-socialization or consistent failure to promote the child's social adaptation. The primary outcomes thus evaluated proxy measures of a range of parent, family and child outcomes.

Key findings

- A 'one-approach-fits-all' to the complex issues underlying emotional abuse is unlikely to lead to sustained change.

- There is currently no research evaluating the use of population strategies in reducing emotional abuse, although recent evidence suggests that the use of population-level Triple P may be effective in reducing child abuse more generally.

- A number of attachment-based interventions (including video-interaction guidance and parent–infant psychotherapy) improved maternal sensitivity and infant attachment security.

- The limited evidence suggests that some forms of emotionally abusive parenting may respond to cognitive behavioural therapy. Parent–infant/child psychotherapy also appears to hold promise.

- The Family Nurse Partnership programme is effective in reducing child physical abuse, and is underpinned by a theoretical model which targets parent–child attachment and parental sensitivity. Such an approach may also reduce emotional abuse.

- Similarly, interventions underpinned by models of working that target *aspects* of emotionally abusive parenting (e.g. misattributions and excessive anger) may prove effective in treating emotional abuse.

- The evidence points to the value of implementing both population-based and targeted interventions to *prevent the occurrence of child emotional maltreatment*, alongside therapeutic-based interventions aimed at preventing *its recurrence*.

- Absence of evidence does not equal absence of efficacy. Practitioners and commissioners of services should acknowledge the importance of research to practice.

- There is a need for multi-level interventions that target not only parenting practices but also aetiological factors affecting the parent.

- The effective reduction of child emotional maltreatment requires that staff working at all service levels have the necessary skills to work more 'therapeutically' with families.

Analysing Child Deaths and Serious Injury through Abuse and Neglect: What can we Learn? A Biennial Analysis of Serious Case Reviews 2003–2005 (The Analysis of Serious Case Reviews 2003–5)

Marian Brandon, Pippa Belderson, Catherine Warren, David Howe, Ruth Gardner, Jane Dodsworth and Jane Black

Introduction

Serious case reviews are carried out when abuse or neglect are known or suspected factors when a child dies (or is seriously injured or harmed). An overview analysis of serious case reviews in England is conducted biennially so that lessons learnt from these cases as a whole can inform both policy and practice. This is the third such analysis.

Aims

1. To use the learning from serious case reviews to improve multi-agency practice at all levels of intervention.

2. To analyse the ecological-transactional factors for children who became the subject of serious case reviews.

Methodology

The study analysed a near total sample of serious case reviews undertaken during the two-year period from April 2003 to March 2005. The 'full sample' of 161 cases included all of the available incidents of child fatality or serious injury through abuse or neglect which were the subject of a serious case review. The 'intensive sample' is a subsample of 47 reviews drawn from the full sample where fuller, more detailed information is available.

Key findings

- Two thirds of the 161 children died and a third were seriously injured.

- A total of 47 per cent were aged under one, but 25 per cent were over 11 years, including 9 per cent who were over 16. Many older children were 'hard to help' and failed by agencies.

- Twelve per cent of children were named on the child protection register, and 55 per cent were known to children's social care at the time of the incident.

- The families of very young children who were physically assaulted tended to be in contact with universal or adult services rather than children's social care.

- In families where children suffered long-term neglect, children's social care often ignored past history and adopted the 'start again syndrome'.

- Practitioners should be encouraged to think critically and systematically. Being aware of the way in which separate factors can interact to protect or cause increased risks of harm is a vital step in this process.

- A key test of the effectiveness of Local Safeguarding Children Boards will be the extent to which they are able to rectify long-standing problems with thresholds.

- Although domestic violence, parental mental ill health and substance misuse were common, there were no clear causal relationships between these potentially problematic parental behaviours and child death or serious injury.

- More consistently reported minimum information would help build a more rigorous knowledge base to provide better pointers to prevention of injury or death where abuse or neglect is a factor.

Understanding Serious Case Reviews and their Impact: A Biennial Analysis of Serious Case Reviews 2005–07 (The Analysis of Serious Case Reviews 2005–7)

Marian Brandon, Sue Bailey, Pippa Belderson, Ruth Gardner, Peter Sidebotham, Jane Dodsworth, Catherine Warren and Jane Black

Introduction

Serious case reviews are local enquiries into the death or serious injury of a child, where abuse or neglect are known or suspected. They are carried out under the auspices of Local Safeguarding Children Boards so that lessons can be learnt locally. An overview analysis of these reviews throughout England is undertaken biennially so that the lessons learnt can inform both policy and practice. This is the fourth such analysis.

Aims

1. To learn from the analysis of interacting risk factors present in the cases under review.

2. To transfer this learning to everyday practice and to the process of serious case reviews.

Methodology

The study analysed a sample of 189 reviews undertaken in 2005–7. It utilized the same transactional ecological approach to make sense of interacting risk factors as that employed in the previous biennial analysis of reviews. Results from both studies (350 cases over four years) were compared and contrasted, and key themes and trends and their implications for policy and practice were identified. The study also explored the way reviews are commissioned and scoped; how they are published; and how key messages are disseminated and implemented locally.

Key findings

-   The two studies show similarities in: age profiles of children; proportions known to children's social care; proportions subject to a child protection plan; proportions of deaths and serious injuries; and high levels of current or past domestic violence and/or parental mental ill health and/or parental substance misuse, often in combination.

-   The chaotic behaviour in families was often mirrored in professionals' thinking and actions. Many families and professionals were overwhelmed by having too many problems to face and too much to achieve, circumstances which contributed to children becoming unseen. Good support, supervision and a fully staffed workforce are crucially important for these practitioners.

- Reluctant parental co-operation and multiple moves meant that many children went off the radar of professionals. However, good parental engagement sometimes masked risks of harm to the child.

- Information about men and about the child was very often missing.

- Interviews with practitioners showed the profound impact of being involved with such cases. None of those interviewed felt adequately involved in the serious case review process or its subsequent learning.

- Many children not known to children's social care are living with high levels of vulnerability which can quickly tip into high risks of harm. Recognizing these factors is an important step in helping and protecting children at all levels of intervention.

Organisation, Outcomes and Costs of Inter-Agency Training for Safeguarding and Promoting the Welfare of Children (The Inter-Agency Training Evaluation Study)

John Carpenter, Simon Hackett, Demi Patsios and Eszter Szilassy

Introduction

It is the responsibility of Local Safeguarding Children Boards (LSCBs) to ensure that single-agency and inter-agency (or multi-agency) training in safeguarding and promoting welfare is provided in order to meet local needs.[441] This study investigated the training provided by eight LSCBs in England.

Aims

To develop an evidence base for inter-agency training to safeguard and promote the welfare of children by asking how it is organized, what training is provided and by whom, whether it is effective and how much it costs.

Methodology

The project was carried out collaboratively with the training co-ordinators in eight LSCBs in four parts of England and with the support of an advisory group. The research team observed meetings of LSCB training subgroups and carried out 60 interviews with LSCB representatives to investigate the means by which inter-agency training is planned and delivered. Specific questionnaire measures were developed to assess the outcomes of both generic and specialist courses, and completed at course registration, the start and end of the course, and three months later. Mean total scale ratings were compared at each time point. The costs to LSCB partners of providing and participating in training were calculated, based on staff time and use of resources.

Key findings

- LSCB training subgroups generally offered good examples of effective partnership working.

- The opportunity to learn together was very highly valued. However, doctors, adult services staff and more experienced staff across agencies were under-represented on specialist courses designed to update their knowledge and skills. Professional bodies, especially in medicine, should review the reasons for low participation. Consideration should be given to building LSCB inter-agency courses into the post-qualifying professional development frameworks for different groups of staff.

- Outcomes were remarkably consistent across types of course and LSCBs. There were significant gains in knowledge of the substantive topic and in self-confidence regarding safeguarding policies and procedures and promoting the welfare of children.

- Some partner agencies were making substantial in-kind contributions to the provision of training in addition to their 'annual subscription' to the Board. The only explanation for the considerable variations in proportional contributions between LSCBs was historical precedent.

- Inter-agency training is vulnerable to cuts in partner agencies' financial contributions and to changes in personnel.

- The costs were seen as very good value for money and compared favourably to the fees charged by commercial organizations.

- Training co-ordinators and their support staff are critical in ensuring the effective operation of the training programme.

- More generic and specialist trainers are needed. An expanded 'training for trainers' should include standards and accreditation.

Noticing and Helping the Neglected Child: Literature Review; published as Recognizing and Helping the Neglected Child – Evidence-Based Practice for Assessment and Intervention (The Recognition of Neglect Review)

Brigid Daniel, Julie Taylor and Jane Scott

Introduction

Despite increased awareness of its impact on development, recognition of neglect is inconsistent and referrals to services are often triggered by other events or concerns about vulnerable children. This systematic review of the literature examined the evidence on the extent to which practitioners are equipped to recognize and respond to the indications that a child's needs are likely to be, or are being, neglected, whatever the cause.

Aims

The primary aim was to contribute to the evidence base that equips practitioners and organizations with the information they need to consider themselves to be part of a protective network around children, and to be able and willing to recognize that a child's needs are not being met, or are in danger of being unmet. The study explored the following questions:

1. What is known about the ways in which children and families directly and indirectly signal their need for help?

2. To what extent are practitioners equipped to recognize and respond to the indications that a child's needs are likely to be, or are being, neglected, whatever the cause?

3. Does the evidence suggest that professional response could be swifter?

Methodology

The method was based on systematic review guidelines. The search strategy yielded 20,480 possible items of which 63 were of sufficient quality for inclusion.

Key findings

- There is considerable evidence to assist identifying how parents and children indirectly signal their needs for help, but less on how they do this directly. There is only limited evidence on whether parents try and fail to seek help from professionals or whether they tend not to do so.

- The overwhelming effect of poverty is strongly associated with neglect, as is the corrosive power of an accumulation of adverse factors. Neglect affects children's development to an extent that signs should be apparent to professionals. Indirect signs can be identified in a range of settings.

- Professionals' views of neglect differ from those of the general public, with the latter setting higher standards for children's care. Operational definitions can affect the number of children receiving a service, with variations potentially contributing to concerns over different thresholds.

- The concerns of health staff were more about the most appropriate response and access to resources than about their capacity to recognize neglect. Studies of social workers tend to focus on responses to referrals.

- Some overseas studies suggest that earlier detection could be possible with appropriate training, protocols for communication and provision of support and guidance for practitioners.

- There is little research about children's and parents' views about how they would seek help, what kind of support would be most helpful and what factors hamper access to support services.

Case Management and Outcomes for Neglected Children Returned to their Parents: A Five Year Follow-Up Study; published as Working Effectively with Neglected Children and their Families – Understanding their Experiences and Long-Term Outcomes (The Neglected Children Reunification Study)

Elaine Farmer and Eleanor Lutman

Introduction

Practitioners have very little research to inform them about which kinds of case management or combinations of services keep neglected children safe and contribute to improved outcomes.

Aims

1. To examine the case management, interventions and outcomes of a consecutive sample of neglected children, from the point of first referral until five years after they had returned home from care/accommodation.

2. To investigate which factors are related to outcomes for children five years after return.

3. To explore how far parents and children engage with professional interventions and whether there are particular issues in cases of neglect.

Methodology

The sample consisted of 138 children who had been neglected from seven local authorities. All had been looked after and returned to their parents during a one-year period. The study followed the children up for five years from this return; data were collected from case files and interviews with social workers, team managers, leaving care workers and some parents and children.

Key findings

- Three fifths of referrals about harm did not lead to sufficient action. Decisive action often awaited a trigger incident of physical/sexual abuse or severe domestic violence. Over time abuse and neglect were sometimes minimized.

- Outcomes were much better for younger children. The cut-off age was six at the time of reunification, after which action to safeguard children and plan for their future reduced and permanence outside the birth family was more rarely achieved.

- Two fifths of children who were the subject of child protection plans were not adequately safeguarded. Plans made during care proceedings did not work out in three fifths of cases.

- Patterns of case management varied by local authority, with four patterns evident: proactive throughout, initially proactive and later passive, initially passive and later more proactive, and passive throughout.

- After five years, 43 per cent of the children were stably at home, 29 per cent had achieved permanence away from home, whilst 28 per cent had had unstable experiences in care or at home. Those living stably away from home were more likely to have good overall wellbeing (58%); wellbeing was poor for 70 per cent of those with unstable outcomes, and for a third of those at home. Children with the most returns had the poorest wellbeing: 38 per cent experienced two or more failed returns.

- Two years after return, 59 per cent of the children had been maltreated. Returning to a changed or different household increased return stability.

- Children with poor wellbeing at follow-up and those subjected to the most severe neglect were especially likely to have been living with parents with alcohol misuse problems. There were significant gaps in services for these parents as there were also for drug-misusing parents.

Effectiveness of the New Local Safeguarding Children Boards in England (The Local Safeguarding Children Boards Study)

Alan France, Emily R. Munro and Amanda Waring

Introduction

Local Safeguarding Children Boards (LSCBs) were intended to address the weaknesses found in the Area Child Protection Committees that they superseded. They were identified as a potentially important means of ensuring an integrated approach to service provision and enabling children to achieve their potential.

Aims

To examine whether the new structures and processes established by LSCBs had overcome identified weaknesses of ACPCs and promoted inter-agency co-operation.

Methodology

A mixed method approach was adopted, including a national survey and mapping exercise of all LSCBs in England and in-depth case study work in six areas. Data were collected from face-to-face interviews with six LSCB Chairs and business managers and five interviews with the directors of children's services in each area; 49 telephone interviews with board members; 132 telephone interviews with front-line professionals (holding both managerial and non-managerial responsibilities); content and thematic analysis of the minutes of board meetings; examination of the relationships between individuals and groups within the LSCB structure in two case study areas, utilizing social network analysis; and a detailed analysis of costing of LSCB meetings in two case study areas.

Key findings

- Across a range of conditions, LSCBs in case study areas were performing at 65 per cent effectiveness.

- LSCBs that have been able to determine their main priorities, that have been realistic about what is feasible and that have maintained focus have been more effective than those that have been overly ambitious.

- Professionals at the strategic and operational levels are embracing the notion that safeguarding children is a shared responsibility. However, there were different perspectives as to whether LSCBs should be embracing the wider safeguarding agenda or concentrating their efforts more narrowly on protecting children from harm.

- Local authorities have struggled to establish accountability mechanisms, especially for Chairs. Governance arrangements generally remain weak.

- LSCB Chairs have provided strong leadership. Independent Chairs have struggled to be active in the wide strategic framework within local areas.

- Demarcation of roles and responsibilities between the board and Children's Trust has not always been clear.

- Securing appropriate levels of participation by board members in LSCB meetings remains a challenge.

- The most effective size for a LSCB appears to be between 20 and 25 members.

- LSCBs have struggled to fulfil all their functions. The time and resources required to undertake serious case reviews, in particular, has inhibited capacity to fulfil other responsibilities.

- Effective communication channels between the LSCB and partner agencies are relatively weak.

- Although LSCBs are helping progress inter-agency work, developments have also been influenced by wider changes. There has been progress in inter-agency communication and the development of a shared language, although a number of challenges remain.

Does Training and Consultation in a Systematic Approach to Emotional Abuse (FRAMEA) Improve the Quality of Children's Services? (The Emotional Abuse Recognition Training Evaluation Study)

Danya Glaser, Vivien Prior, Katherine Auty and Susan Tilki

Introduction

Emotional abuse continues to pose difficulties for professionals in its definition, recognition, thresholds and effective interventions. A conceptual framework has been developed for the recognition, assessment and management of emotional abuse (FRAMEA). It organizes factors pertinent to overall child maltreatment, including specifically emotional abuse and emotional neglect, into four tiers: environmental and social circumstances; parental risk factors or attributes; ill-treatment; domains of child functioning. Emotional abuse and neglect is defined as persistent, harmful parent–child interactions; five categories are distinguished and defined. The framework also incorporates the necessary notion of a trial of the family's capacity to change.

Aims

To address some of the difficulties encountered by professionals in dealing with emotional abuse by exploring whether training and follow-up consultation in FRAMEA would improve professional activity in terms of clarity of conceptualization of concerns, recognition of emotional abuse and the nature of professional response and intervention.

Methodology

Sixteen professional teams comprising health visitors, children's social care (referral and assessment and children in need) and child and adolescent mental health services (CAMHS) in four ethnically diverse geographical areas participated. Data were collected through specifically designed questionnaires and semi-structured interviews.

Professional practice concerning five cohorts of children aged under 11 and their families was tracked over time. Training was randomly distributed between teams over four time points and followed by up to three consultations to each team, during which FRAMEA was applied to actual cases brought by the professionals. Finally, inter-agency meetings were held in each of the four geographical areas.

Key findings

- Fifty per cent of referrals to CAMHS and 69 per cent of referrals to social care children in need teams included emotional abuse.

- Health visitors were unable to refer 21 per cent, and social workers 13 per cent, of emotionally abusive or neglectful families for further intervention because services were unavailable. Lack of clarity about the respective roles and responsibilities in service provision in relation to emotional abuse across the three agencies and the absence of a shared threshold were major issues raised by professionals.

- Eighty-nine per cent of participants rated the FRAMEA training as excellent or very good, but some effects were not sustained in post-consultation cohorts.

- There was significantly more recognition of emotional abuse following training.

- *Health visitors* showed a significant *increase*, and *social workers* a very significant *decrease*, in separation of tiers following training. *CAMHS teams* showed a significant *increase* in separation of tiers post-training with consultation.

- Following training, all professional groups reported significantly more harmful parent–child interactions when certain parental risk factors were present.

- All professional groups showed significant improvements in some areas of service provision following training.

Understanding Parents' Information Needs and Experiences where Professional Concerns Regarding Non-Accidental Injury were not Substantiated (The Information Needs of Parents at Early Recognition Study)

Sirkka Komulainen and Linda Haines

Introduction

Determining whether or not a presenting sign is a non-accidental injury (NAI) is a difficult area for health professionals; poor communication triggers complaints from parents.

Aims

1. To explore parents' experiences of situations where concerns of non-accidental injury were raised, with a particular focus on communication processes.

2. To generate data on parents' experiences and set these in context.

3. To identify what information participants wished to receive and describe how they remembered and reflected on their experiences.

4. To increase the awareness of health professionals of what parents perceive as helpful and less helpful practice.

5. To make suggestions for paediatric training to improve communication.

Methodology

Ten pilot and 12 formal interviews were conducted with consenting parents/carers. Participants were recruited through parents' support groups and NHS Trusts. A narrative interview method was adopted for this sensitive topic to allow participants to express themselves in their own words, with additional probing to address particular paediatric training in communication and public information needs. Interviews were recorded, transcribed, anonymized and analysed with a specialist software package designed to manage qualitative data (NVIVO).

Key findings

- Concerns were usually articulated to parents/carers by consultant paediatricians.

- Most parents had sought help because they were worried about their child's health; they needed to be kept informed about their child's medical care and progress throughout the investigation.

- Many reported feeling they had been treated less courteously once concerns of NAI were raised. Participants were dissatisfied when their concerns and explanations were not listened to or when not enough time was allowed for communication. Participants were particularly dissatisfied where concerns of NAI were raised in a public place.

- Parents understand the professional duty to investigate further if there are concerns. They prefer honest, clear and early face-to-face communication on what a child protection enquiry means; what referral to social services or the police means; who else (including schools and other family members) will be involved; whether emergency proceedings are taking place; what the child protection medical examination involves; how long the child has to stay in hospital; what different tests involve; whether further tests are needed; and how long it will take to receive results. Written information leaflets were of uncertain value.

- Participants expected clear, written communication that their case was closed. Years later some were uncertain whether they were 'still being monitored'.

- Being subject to child protection investigations – however briefly – left many parents distressed and had a long-lasting effect on the whole family. Disappointment with the 'system' and anxieties about future contacts with health professionals were expressed.

- Awareness of media reports where child protection cases had 'gone wrong' contributed to parents' anxieties.

Systematic Reviews of Interventions Following Physical Abuse: Helping Practitioners and Expert Witnesses Improve the Outcomes of Child Abuse (The Physical Abuse Intervention Review)

Paul Montgomery, Frances Gardner, Paul Ramchandani and Gretchen Bjornstad

Introduction

Physical abuse is highly prevalent across the world and is frequently a component of broader maltreatment. The focus of this study is on secondary prevention of adverse child outcomes and recurrence of abuse in children who have experienced maltreatment.

Aims

1. To conduct three reviews that synthesize the published grey literature for interventions for children who have experienced physical abuse, in order to present a complete picture of all the available evidence.

2. To draw out the implications of this evidence for policy, practice and future research.

Methodology

Three separate electronic search strategies were conducted for each of three categories of child-focused, parent-focused or family-focused intervention. These searches aimed to identify all studies investigating interventions for children who have experienced physical abuse. The search included efforts to find studies in the grey literature and contacts with experts in the field. All evidence was reviewed so as to capture a complete picture; methodological quality is indicated in discussion of the results, as research shortcomings may produce a biased picture.

Key findings

-   There is evidence to support well-structured, manualized parenting and treatment foster care interventions. Training and supervision for practitioners to be able to deliver such interventions would have positive benefits for many children and families where a child has experienced physical abuse.

-   However, family preservation services, home visiting, psychodrama, therapeutic day treatment, individual child psychotherapy and art therapy do not yet have sufficient evidence to support their effectiveness. Residential treatment and play therapy were not found to be effective, with comparison treatments showing better outcomes.

- However, fidelity to treatment protocols would be crucial for practitioners who wish to replicate results in their own practices. Systems need to be in place for ongoing supervision and quality control. Few of the reviewed studies provided details about the settings in which they delivered treatment. Practitioners will have to consider the effects that compulsory or non-compulsory interventions might have on participant retention and motivation, and to know about the types of children or families for whom interventions are effective.

- In general, the evidence pointed to the value of parenting and cognitive behavioural approaches as having a stronger evidence base than other interventions and thus worthy of further investigation.

- Funding for research that includes measures of recurrence of abuse as a primary outcome is needed to determine the effects of parent and family-focused interventions.

- There is insufficient information about the costs of interventions, although we need to know whether these are justified by their benefits.

Neglected Adolescents: A Literature Review; published as Adolescent Neglect – Research, Policy and Practice, with Rees as first author (The Recognition of Adolescent Neglect Review)

Mike Stein, Gwyther Rees, Leslie Hicks and Sarah Gorin

Introduction

'Neglect' as it applies to adolescents is a significant under-explored area in the UK. This literature review considers the research, policy and practice implications of international research in this area. It has also informed: a multi-agency guide for teams who work with young people and a guide for young people about neglect.

Aims

1. To provide an accessible summary of relevant literature on adolescent neglect and to draw out the implications for further developments on this topic.

2. To inform the preparation of guides for multi-agency teams and for young people.

Methodology

The method was based on systematic review guidelines. The searches covered the years 1997–2006 and initially yielded 450 potentially relevant items. Focus groups were carried out with young people and members of two LSCBs to inform the guides for young people and multi-agency workers.

Key findings

- There is a need for more age-sensitive definitions of neglect for both research and practice purposes. These should reflect differences in the way neglect is conceptualized as children grow older.

- Neglect is the most common form of maltreatment across all age groups, including adolescence. Relatively little is known about the distinctive background factors associated with adolescent neglect. However, experiences of neglect in adolescence are associated with a range of negative outcomes.

- No effective interventions aimed specifically at adolescent neglect were identified; however, some more generic approaches, based on an ecological or multi-systemic approach, may be of relevance.

- There is a need to raise awareness among young people about the meaning and potential consequences of neglect, so that they may feel able to seek appropriate support. Similarly, there is a need to raise professional awareness of definitional issues and of the scale and outcomes of adolescent neglect, in order to promote more effective responses to the needs of these young people. The guide for young people and the multi-agency guide for professionals, produced as part of this project, will contribute to these objectives.

- At a management and policy level, the review suggests a need for additional documentation to support age-specific assessments in cases of potential neglect; potential improvements to official definitions and measurement of maltreatment; and the need for more dedicated funding to undertake further research and to pilot new interventions in this area.

- The findings present a major challenge to the research community to pay more attention to neglect and to issues affecting adolescents within the field of maltreatment research.

The Child, the Family and the GP: Tensions and Conflicts of Interest in Safeguarding Children (The General Practitioner Tensions in Safeguarding Study)

Hilary Tompsett, Mark Ashworth, Christine Atkins, Lorna Bell, Ann Gallagher, Maggie Morgan and Paul Wainwright

Introduction

The role of GPs in safeguarding children is vital to inter-agency collaboration in child protection processes and to promoting early intervention in families. However, potential conflicts of interest may constrain their engagement.

Aims

1. To explore the nature and consequences of tensions and conflicts of interest for GPs in safeguarding children.

2. To evaluate how these are seen and responded to from a range of professional, parent and child perspectives.

3. To consider ways of managing these issues to promote best practice.

4. To explore the complexity of relationships between GPs, parents and children and other professionals (added in response to initial piloting).

Methodology

This exploratory mixed methods study focused particularly on GPs in two contrasting Primary Care Trusts (PCTs) and groups of GPs accessed through training events. It included interviews with Local Safeguarding Children Board (LSCB) key stakeholders and drew on a panel of 25 independent experts, who used the Delphi structured communication technique to guide their discussions, and three focus groups of parents, young people and a minority ethnic group. It was supported by a literature and policy review and demographic and child protection statistics in the PCTs. Data were collected through 96 questionnaire responses and 14 interviews with GPs.

Key findings

- GPs saw their role as referring patients/families on, while key stakeholders expected fuller engagement in all stages of child protection processes.

- GPs see supporting parents as the best way to support children and families.

- Although GPs are clear about 'what to do' when the situation clearly warrants referral to children's social care services, they would first seek advice and support from a paediatrician or a health visitor in more complex cases.

- Not being able to speak directly to social workers in children's services, over or under-response to concerns, lack of feedback when referrals were made and potential impact on families of intervention were reasons for hesitance in referral and dilemmas in confidentiality.

- Most GPs (and key stakeholders) did not refer to the views and wishes of children.

- The health visitor's important role in safeguarding children, both for parents and as a key fellow professional for the GP, was confirmed.

- GPs perceived that child protection work is not as valued as other activities rewarded under the Quality and Outcomes Framework.

- GPs reported low attendance at child protection conferences, though provision of reports was higher than expected. Conferences may be better informed by other/health professionals who may hold more relevant information.

- Changing policies, structures and guidance emerging since this study was initiated will provide a new framework in which these tensions can be addressed.

Understanding the Contribution of Sure Start Local Programmes to the Task of Safeguarding Children's Welfare. Report of the National Evaluation (The Sure Start Local Programmes Safeguarding Study)

Jane Tunstill and Debra Allnock

Introduction

The initial 524 community-based Sure Start Local Programmes (SSLPs, now Sure Start children's centres) were rolled out from 2000; each supported an average population of between 400 and 800 children under four years old. This study formed part of the *Implementation Module* of the National Evaluation of Sure Start (NESS).

Aims

1. To explore ways in which SSLPs and children's social care can work in collaboration.

2. To ascertain if, and how, SSLPs are represented in local structures such as LSCBs.

3. To explore the nature of concerns likely to trigger referrals between children's social care and SSLPs and *vice versa*.

4. To identify the range of supports requested and provided.

5. To explore the SSLP contribution to positive outcomes for children.

6. To identify and describe examples of good practice.

Methodology

The study comprised: (a) an exploration of the safeguarding policy and practice of eight local programmes, identified as exemplifying 'relatively good practice'; (b) an in-depth study of four local authorities, to enable the fuller exploration of wider partnerships and networking activity across a 'whole local authority'. A conceptual framework was developed for studying existing arrangements and identifying key challenges. Data were collected through: an analysis of documentation; interviews with key stakeholders; and a study of referrals from SSLPs to children's social care.

Key findings

- Collaboration reflected ongoing tensions between services designed to *support families* and those designed to *protect children*.

- Inter-professional and inter-agency collaboration requires a shared understanding/acceptance of thresholds; confidence in information-sharing; and systematic recording systems.

- Staff reluctance to collaborate in safeguarding activity was minimized by establishing operational linkages between child protection and family support and having managers who helped staff see support in terms of *packages* rather than *isolated services*.

- Regular contact and access to informal advice from other professionals can improve service provision and lead to more appropriate referrals between organizations. Having social workers co-located within the centre develops confidence and competence around child protection for other staff members.

- The Common Assessment Framework (CAF) can provide a bridge for communication about individual children between members of the workforce and underpin the provision of a seamless service at Tiers Two and Three (targeted and specialist levels).

- Co-location of multi-disciplinary teams has both strengths and limitations – the consequences for different groups of families should be carefully thought through, so practitioners can offer a choice of routes to services for parents in different circumstances.

- The ongoing debate around the balance to be struck between the targeted and universal provision within children's services ensures the continuing relevance of study findings for policy and practice in and around children's centres.

Maltreated Children in the Looked After System: A Comparison of Outcomes for Those Who Go Home and Those Who Do Not; published as Caring for Abused and Neglected Children – Making the Right Decisions for Reunification or Long-Term Care (The Home or Care? Study)

Jim Wade, Nina Biehal, Nicola Farrelly and Ian Sinclair

Introduction

Around six in ten children enter the looked after system for reasons of abuse or neglect. Many subsequently return home. This study set out to strengthen the evidence base about the long-term consequences of decisions to reunify or not reunify maltreated children.

Aims

1. To compare the care pathways of maltreated children with those of children looked after for other reasons and account for any differences identified.

2. To investigate which maltreated children are more, or less, likely to go home and why this may be the case.

3. To examine how the decision concerning return was made; to identify the main factors that were taken into account and how this decision was supported over the next six months.

4. To compare the progress of children in relation to their safety, stability and psychosocial wellbeing up to four years (on average) after this 'effective decision' was made.

Methodology

The research design comprised:

1. A *census study* of all 3872 children who were looked after by seven local authorities at some point in 2003–04. Information primarily from administrative systems was used to track their pathways for up to three years and to compare those for maltreated and other looked after children.

2. A *survey* of 149 of these children, all of whom had been maltreated and of whom 68 returned home and 81 remained continuously looked after. Data were collected from case records, interviews with a small number of birth parents and children, and survey responses from current social workers and teachers who assessed progress and outcomes at final follow-up.

Key findings

- Maltreated children were less likely than children looked after for other reasons to leave the care system within the study timeframe. Placement with parents was an important pathway, although breakdowns were higher for this group.

- Outcomes for maltreated children who remained looked after were better than for those who went home, with respect to stability and wellbeing. Even those whose home placements had endured had lower wellbeing than those who had not gone home.

- Careful assessment of risks, evidence of parenting change, slow and well-managed returns and provision of services to support them were associated with home placements that endured.

- Although services helped placements to last, they were not sufficient to help improve children's overall wellbeing at home. Intensive, long-term provision of services will be needed to support home placements.

- Where reunification failed, there were often early signs. Over one third of children (35%) had returned to care within six months.

Infants Suffering, or Likely to Suffer, Significant Harm: A Prospective Longitudinal Study; published as Safeguarding Babies and Very Young Children from Abuse and Neglect (The Significant Harm of Infants Study)

Harriet Ward, Rebecca Brown, David Westlake and Emily R. Munro

Introduction

Decisions made by practitioners to protect and promote the welfare of infants suffering, or likely to suffer, significant harm will have long-term consequences for their life chances. It is therefore important to know how such decisions are made and whether they can be improved.

Aims

To trace the decision-making process influencing the life pathways of a sample of very young children who had been identified as suffering, or being likely to suffer, significant harm in order to: improve understanding about how such decisions are reached and their consequences; the weight given to risk and protective factors; and the role participants, including birth parents, play in the decision-making process.

Methodology

This mixed methods study took place in ten local authorities and focused on a sample of 57 children who were the subject of a core assessment, Section 47 enquiry or became looked after before their first birthdays; 43 were followed until they were three. Quantitative data concerning children's life experiences, evidence of need, reasons for referral and changes of circumstances were collected from case files; qualitative data came from interviews with birth parents, carers, social workers, team leaders, children's guardians, senior managers, judges, magistrates and local authority solicitors, and focus groups with health visitors.

Key findings

- Parents showed a high prevalence of factors known to be associated with an increased risk of children suffering significant harm.

- About a third of the mothers had already been separated from at least one older child before the birth of the index child. Nearly two thirds of the infants were identified before birth.

- About a third of the children were maltreated *in utero*. However, at age three 44 per cent of the sample had apparently never been maltreated.

- The long-term wellbeing of over half of the children who were permanently separated had been doubly jeopardized – by late separation from an abusive birth family followed by the disruption of a close attachment with an interim carer on entering a permanent placement. There is no evidence that any child was unnecessarily separated.

- At age three, 43 per cent of those children remaining with their birth parents were considered to be at continuing risk of significant harm.

- All but one of the 16 (37%) parents who made sufficient changes to provide good enough care did so before the baby was six months old.

- By their third birthdays over half the children were displaying developmental problems or significant behavioural difficulties. These were more evident amongst children who had experienced maltreatment, often whilst professionals waited fruitlessly for parents to change.

- Decisions to separate children permanently from birth parents go against the grain for all those involved. However, if such children are to be adequately safeguarded within their birth families, then much greater consideration needs to be given to the development of effective policies and practices to engage potentially abusive parents and to support them in reducing those factors that place their children at risk of being maltreated.

Endnotes

Chapter 1

1   Mahony, Cardinal R. (1998) *Creating a Culture of Life* (unpublished letter).

2   Laming, Lord (Cm 5730) (2003) *The Victoria Climbié Inquiry: Report of an Inquiry by Lord Laming*. London: The Stationery Office.

3   Laming, Lord (HC 330) (2009) *The Protection of Children in England: A Progress Report*. London: The Stationery Office.

4   See www.education.gov.uk/researchandstatistics/research/scri.

5   Laming, Lord (HC 330) (2009) *op. cit.*

6   Munro, E. (2011b) *The Munro Review of Child Protection: Final Report. A Child-Centred System*. London: Department for Education.

7   Laming, Lord (Cm 5730) (2003) *op. cit.*

8   See for instance Chief Inspector of Social Services, Commission for Health Improvement, HM Chief Inspector of Constabulary, HM Chief Inspector of the Crown Prosecution Service, HM Chief Inspector of Schools and HM Chief Inspector of Prisons (2002) *Safeguarding Children: A Joint Chief Inspectors' Report on Arrangements to Safeguard Children*. London: Department of Health.

9   Department for Education (Cm 5860) (2003) *Every Child Matters*. London: The Stationery Office.

10 Ward, H. and Jones, H. (2009) 'Le système de protection en Angleterre.' *Santé, Societé et Solidarité 1*, 181–192.

11 Children Act (2004) London: HMSO.

12 Department of Health, Department for Education and Skills and Home Office (2000) *Framework for the Assessment of Children in Need and their Families*. London: The Stationery Office.

13 See Department for Children, Schools and Families (2011) *Common Assessment Framework*. Accessed on 15 April 2011 at: www.education.gov.uk/childrenandyoungpeople/strategy/integratedworking/caf.

14 HM Government (2010) *Working Together to Safeguard Children: A Guide to Inter-Agency Working to Safeguard and Promote the Welfare of Children*. London: Department for Children, Schools and Families.

15 Cleaver, H., Walker, S., Scott, J., Cleaver, D., Rose, W., Ward, H. and Pithouse, A. (2008) *The Integrated Children's System: Enhancing Social Work and Inter-Agency Practice*. London: Jessica Kingsley Publishers.

16 Department of Health and Department for Education and Skills (2004) *National Service Framework for Children, Young People and Maternity Services*. London: Department for Education and Skills and Department of Health.

17 Laming, Lord (HC 330) (2009) *op. cit.*

18 Field, F. (2010) *The Foundation Years: Preventing Poor Children from Becoming Poor Adults*. London: HM Government.

19 Allen, G. (2011) *Early Intervention: The Next Steps*. An Independent Report to Her Majesty's Government. London: HM Government.

20 Social Work Reform Board (2010) *Building a Safe and Confident Future: One Year On*. London: HM Government.

21 HM Treasury (Cm 7942) (2010) *Spending Review*. London: The Stationery Office.

22 Department for Education (2010a) *Reform of Children's Trusts Safeguarding and Social Work Reform*. News release: 22 July 2010. Accessed on 26 January 2011 at: www.education.gov.uk/children and young people/.

23 Department for Education (2010b) *More Freedom and Flexibility: A New Approach for Children's Trust Boards, Children and Young People's Plans, and the 'Duty to Cooperate'*. News release, 3 November 2010. London: Department for Education.

24 Department for Education (2010c) *Secretary of State for Education's Letter to Local Authorities: 4 November 2010*. London: Department for Education.

25 Department for Education (2010b) *op. cit.*

26 Department of Health (2010) (cm 7881) *Equity and Excellence: Liberating the NHS*. London: The Stationery Office.

27 Munro, E. (2011a) *The Munro Review of Child Protection: Interim Report. A Child's Journey*. London: Department for Education, p.14. See also Munro, E. (2010) *The Munro Review of Child Protection. Part One: A Systems Analysis*. London: Department for Education.

28 Department for Education (2011) *A Child-Centred System: The Government's Response to the Munro Review of Child Protection*. London: Department for Education

29 Department for Children, Schools and Families (2009a) *Building a Safe, Confident Future: The Final Report of the Social Work Taskforce*. London: Department for Children, Schools and Families.

30 HM Government (2010) *op. cit.*

31 Department for Education (2010d) *Children in Need in England, including their Characteristics and Further Information on Children who were the Subject of a Child Protection Plan (2009–2010 Children in Need Census, Final)*. London: Department for Education.

32 Department for Children, Schools and Families (2009b) *Referrals, Assessment and Children and Young People who are the Subject of a Child Protection Plan, England – Year Ending March 31 2009*. Accessed 3 August 2011 at: www.data.gov.uk/dataset/referrals.

33 See Gilbert, R.E., Widom, C., Browne, K., Fergusson, D., Webb, E. and Janson, S. (2009) 'Child maltreatment 1: Burden and consequence of child maltreatment in high income countries.' *The Lancet 373*, 68–81.

34 Radford, L., Corral, S., Bradley, C., Fisher, H., Bassett, C., Howat, N. with Collishaw, S. (2011) *The Maltreatment and Victimisation of Children in the UK: NSPCC Report on a National Survey of Young People's, Young Adults' and Caregivers' Experiences*. London: NSPCC.

35 See Finkelhor, D. (2008) *Childhood Victimization: Violence, Crime, and Abuse in the Lives of Young People*. Oxford: Oxford University Press, Chapter 7, pp.122–147.

36 See Radford *et al.* (2011) *op. cit.*

37 Stevenson, O. (2007) *Neglected Children and their Families (Second Edition)*. Oxford: Blackwell Publishing.

38 For an overview of the evidence see for instance Jones, D.P.H. (2008) 'Child Maltreatment.' In M. Rutter, D. Bishop, D. Pine, S. Scott, J. Stevenson, E.Taylor and A.Thapar (eds) *Rutter's Child and Adolescent Psychiatry (Fifth Edition)*. Oxford: Blackwell Publishing, pp.421–439; Cleaver, H., Unell, I. and Aldgate, J. (2011) *Children's Needs – Parenting Capacity. The Impact of Parental Mental Illness, Learning Disability, Problem Alcohol and Drug Use and Domestic Violence on Children's Safety (2nd Edition)*. London: The Stationery Office, pp. 95–193.

39 Munro, E.R., Brown, R., Sempik, J. and Ward, H. with Owen, C. (2011) *Scoping Review to Draw Together Data on Child Injury and Safeguarding and to Compare the Position of England with that in Other Countries*. Research Report DfE-RR083. London: Department for Education.

40 Daniel, B., Taylor, J. and Scott, J. (2011) *Recognizing and Helping the Neglected Child: Evidence-Based Practice for Assessment and Intervention*. London: Jessica Kingsley Publishers.

41 Rees, G., Stein, M., Hicks, L. and Gorin, S. (2011) *Adolescent Neglect: Research, Policy and Practice*. London: Jessica Kingsley Publishers.

42 HM Government (2010) *op. cit.* pp.38–39.

43 Haringey Local Safeguarding Children Board (2010) *Serious Case Review: Child A, March 2009*. London: Department for Education.

44 Rees, Stein, Hicks and Gorin (2011) *op. cit., passim.*

45 Brandon, M., Bailey, S. and Belderson, P. (2010) *Building on the Learning from Serious Case Reviews: A Two-Year Analysis of Child Protection Database Notifications 2007–2009*. London: Department for Education.

46 Holmes, L., Westlake, D. and Ward, H. (2009) *Calculating and Comparing the Costs of Multidimensional Treatment Foster Care, England (MTFCE)*. Report to the Department of Children, Schools and Families. Loughborough: Centre for Child and Family Research, Loughborough University.

47 See National Mental Health Development Unit. Accessed on 24 January 2011 at: www.nmhdu.org.uk/news/multi-systemic-therapy-new-therapy-brings-results-for-troubled-young-people/.

Chapter 2

48 Daniel, B., Taylor, J. and Scott, J. (2011) *Recognizing and Helping the Neglected Child: Evidence-Based Practice for Assessment and Intervention*. London: Jessica Kingsley Publishers.

49 Rees, G., Stein, M., Hicks, L. and Gorin, S. (2011) *Adolescent Neglect: Research, Policy and Practice*. Jessica Kingsley Publishers.

50 Brandon, M., Belderson, P., Warren, C., Howe, D., Gardner, R., Dodsworth, J. and Black, J. (2008) *Analysing Child Deaths and Serious Injury through Abuse and Neglect: What can we Learn? A Biennial Analysis of Serious Case Reviews 2003–2005*. DCSF-RR023. London: Department for Children, Schools and Families.

51 Brandon, M., Bailey, S., Belderson, P., Gardner, R., Sidebotham, P., Dodsworth, J., Warren, C. and Black, J. (2009) *Understanding Serious Case Reviews and their Impact. A Biennial Analysis of Serious Case Reviews 2005–07.* DCSF-RR129. London: Department for Children, Schools and Families.

52 For further information see Barlow, J. and Schrader McMillan, A. (2010) *Safeguarding Children from Emotional Maltreatment: What Works.* London: Jessica Kingsley Publishers, pp.30–34.

53 Gilbert, R., Widom, C., Browne, K., Fergusson, D., Webb, E. and Janson, S. (2009) 'Child Maltreatment 1: Burden and consequences of child maltreatment in high income countries.' *The Lancet 373,* 68–81.

54 *Ibid.* p.68.

53 Farmer, E. and Lutman, E. (forthcoming) *Working Effectively with Neglected Children and their Families – Understanding their Experiences and Long-Tern Outcomes.* London: Jessica Kingsley Publishers.

56 De Bellis, M.D. (2005) 'Psychobiology of neglect.' *Child Maltreatment 10, 2,* 150–172.

57 See Twardosz, S. and Lutzker, J.R. (2010) 'Child maltreatment and the developing brain: A review of neuroscience perspectives.' *Aggression and Violent Behavior 15,* 59–68; and McCrory, E., De Brito, S. and Viding, E. (2010) 'Research review: The neurobiology and genetics of maltreatment and adversity.' *Journal of Child Psychology and Psychiatry 51,* 1079–1095.

58 Longitudinal Studies of Child Abuse and Neglect (LONGSCAN) Accessed on 3 August 2011 at: www.iprc. unc.edu/longscan.

59 See O'Hagan, K. (2006) *Identifying Emotional and Psychological Abuse.* Maidenhead: Open University Press.

60 Rees, Stein, Hicks and Gorin (2011) *op. cit.* p.51

61 The Bridge Consultancy (1995) *Paul: Death through Neglect.* The Bridge Consultancy.

62 Brandon, M., personal communication concerning further analysis of SCR data.

63 HM Government (2010) *Working Together to Safeguard Children: A Guide to Inter-Agency Working to Safeguard and Promote the Welfare of Children.* London: Department for Children, Schools and Families.

64 See Barlow and Schrader McMillan (2010) *op. cit.* pp. 30–35.

65 Egeland, B. (2009) 'Taking stock: Child emotional maltreatment and developmental psychology.' *Child Abuse and Neglect 33,* 22–26.

66 Cleaver, H., Unell, I. and Aldgate, J. (2011) *Children's Needs – Parenting Capacity. The Impact of Parental Mental Illness, Learning Disability, Problem Alcohol and Drug Use and Domestic Violence on Children's Safety (2nd Edition).* London: The Stationery Office.

67 Egeland (2009) *op. cit.* p.23.

68 Department of Health, Department for Education and Employment and Home Office (2000) *Framework for the Assessment of Children in Need and their Families.* London: The Stationery Office.

69 Cleaver, Unell and Aldgate (2011) *op. cit.*

70 See Farmer and Lutman (2009) *op. cit.* pp. 10–14.

71 Tunnard, J. (2004) *Parental Mental Health Problems: Key Messages from Research, Policy and Practice.* Dartington: Research in Practice.

72 Cleaver, Unell and Aldgate (2011) *op. cit.*

73 Zahn-Waxler, C., Duggal, S. and Gruber, R. (2002) 'Parental Psychopathology.' In M. Bornstein (ed.) *Handbook of Parenting: Social Conditions and Applied Parenting.* New Jersey: Erlbaum, pp.295–327.

74 Advisory Council on the Misuse of Drugs (2003) *Hidden Harm: Responding to the Needs of Children of Problem Drug Users.* London: Home Office.

75 Prime Minister's Strategy Unit (2004) *Alcohol Harm Reduction Strategy for England.* London: Cabinet Office.

76 Klee, H., Jackson, M. and Lewis, S. (2002) *Drug Misuse and Motherhood.* London: Routledge.

77 Moe, V. and Slinning, K. (2001) 'Children prenatally exposed to substances: Gender-related differences in outcome from infancy to 3 years of age.' *Infant Mental Health Journal 3,* 334–350.

78 Kroll, B. and Taylor, A. (2003) *Parental Substance Misuse and Child Welfare.* London: Jessica Kingsley Publishers, p.16.

79 Barnard, M. (2007) *Drug Addiction and Families.* London: Jessica Kingsley Publishers.

80 Cleaver, H. and Nicholson, D. (2007) *Parental Learning Disability and Children's Needs: Family Experiences and Effective Practice.* London: Jessica Kingsley Publishers.

81 McConnell, D. and Llewellyn, G. (2002) 'Stereotypes, parents with intellectual disability and child protection.' *Journal of Social Welfare and Family Law 24, 3,* 297–317.

82 Kroll and Taylor, (2003) *op .cit.,* pp.163–191.

83 Freisthler, B., Merrit, D.H. and LaScala, E.A. (2006) 'Understanding the ecology of child maltreatment: A review of the literature and directions for future research.' *Child Maltreatment 11, 3,* 263–280 (see pp.272–273).

84 Rees, G. and Siakeu, J. (2004) *Thrown Away: The Experiences of Children Forced to Leave Home.* London: The Children's Society.

85 Safe on the Streets Research Team (1999) *Still Running – Children on the Streets in the UK.* London: The Children's Society.

86 Coohey, C. (1996) 'Child maltreatment: Testing the social isolation hypothesis.' *Child Abuse and Neglect 20,* 3, 241–254.

87 National Working Group on Child Protection and Disability (2003) *It Doesn't Happen to Disabled Children: Child Protection and Disabled Children.* London: NSPCC, pp.21–23.

88 Westat Inc (1993) *A Report on the Maltreatment of Children with Disabilities.* Washington DC: National Center on Child Abuse and Neglect.

89 Sidebotham, P. (2003) 'Red skies, risk factors and early indicators. Invited comments on early indicators of child abuse and neglect: A multi-professional Delphi study by Catherine Powell.' *Child Abuse Review 12,* 41–45.

90 Wooster, D. (1999) 'Assessment of nonorganic failure to thrive: Infant–toddler intervention.' *The Transdisciplinary Journal 9,* 4, 353–371.

91 Haringey Local Safeguarding Children Board (2010) *Serious Case Review: Child A, March 2009.* London: Department for Education.

92 Hultman, C.S., Priolo, D., Cairns, B.A., Grant, E.J., Peterson, H.D. and Meyer, A.A. (1998) 'Psychosocial forum. Return to jeopardy: The fate of pediatric burn patients who are victims of abuse and neglect… including commentary by Doctor M.' *Journal of Burn Care & Rehabilitation 19,* 4, 367–376.

93 Chester, D.L., Jose, R.M., Aldlyami, E., King, H. and Moiemen, N.S. (2006) 'Non-accidental burns in children: Are we neglecting neglect?' *Burns 32,* 2, 222–228.

94 Benoit, D., Madigan, S., Lecce, S., Shea, B. and Goldberg, S. (2001) 'Atypical maternal behaviour toward feeding-disordered infants before and after intervention.' *Infant Mental Health Journal 22,* 6, 611–626.

95 Main, M. and Hesse, E. (1990) 'Parents' Unresolved Traumatic Experiences are Related to Infant Disorganised Attachment Status: Is Frightened and/or Frightening Parental Behaviour the Linking Mechanism?' In M.T. Greenberg, D. Cicchetti and E.M. Cummings (eds) *Attachment in the Preschool Years.* Chicago: University of Chicago Press, pp.161–182.

96 Carpenter, M., Kennedy, M., Armstrong, A.L. and Moore, E. (1997) 'Indicators of abuse and neglect in preschool children's drawings.' *Journal of Psychosocial Nursing and Mental Health Services 35,* 40, 10–17.

97 See Thornberry, T.P., Ireland, T.O. and Smith, C.A. (2001) 'The importance of timing: The varying impact of childhood and adolescent maltreatment on multiple problem outcomes.' *Development and Psychopathology 13,* 4, 957–979.

98 Cleaver, Unell and Aldgate (2011) *op. cit.*

99 Department of Health, Department for Education and Employment and Home Office (2000) *op. cit.*

100 Brandon, Belderson, Warren, Howe, Gardner, Dodsworth and Black (2008) *op. cit.* p.67.

101 Daniel, B., Taylor, J. and Scott, J. (forthcoming) *Training Resources on Child Neglect for a Multi-Agency Audience.*

102 Hicks, L. and Stein, M. (2010) *Neglect Matters: A Multi-Agency Guide for Professionals Working Together on Behalf of Teenagers.* London: Department for Education.

103 Paavilainen, E., Astedt-Kurki, P. and Panounen, M. (2000) 'School nurses' operational modes and ways of collaborating in caring for child abusing families in Finland.' *Journal of Clinical Nursing 9,* 5, 745–746.

104 Roldan, M.C., Galera, S. and O'Brien, B. (2005) 'Women living in a drug (and violence) context: The maternal role.' *Revista Latino-Americana de Enfermagem 13,* 1118–1126.

105 Morrison, T. (2006) *Staff Supervision in Social Care: Making a Real Difference for Staff and Service Users (Third Edition).* Brighton: Pavilion.

106 Tompsett, H., Ashworth, M., Atkins, C., Bell, L., Gallagher, A., Morgan, M. and Wainwright, P. (2009) *The Child, the Family and the GP: Tensions and Conflicts of Interest in Safeguarding Children.* DCSF-RBX-09-05-ES. London: Department for Children, Schools and Families.

107 Rose, S.J. and Meezan, W. (1995) 'Child neglect: A study of the perceptions of mothers and child welfare workers.' *Children and Youth Services Review 17,* 4, 471–486.

108 Rose, S.J. and Meezan, W. (1996) 'Variations in perceptions of child neglect.' *Child Welfare Journal 75,* 2, 139–160.

109 Rose, S.J. and Selwyn, J. (2000) 'Child neglect: An English perspective.' *International Social Work 43,* 2, 179–192.

110 Boulton, S. and Hindle, D. (2000) 'Emotional abuse: The work of a multi-disciplinary consultation group in a child psychiatric service.' *Clinical Child Psychology and Psychiatry 5,* 3, 439–452, p.440.

111 Brandon, Belderson, Warren, Howe, Gardner, Dodsworth and Black (2008) *op. cit.* p.135.

112 Appleton, J.V. (1996) 'Working with vulnerable families: A health visiting perspective.' *Journal of Advanced Nursing 23*, 5, 912–918, (see p.8).

113 Ward, H., Brown, R., Westlake, D. and Munro, R. (forthcoming) *Safeguarding Babies and Very Young Children from Abuse and Neglect.* London: Jessica Kingsley Publishers.

114 See Paavilainen, Astedt-Kurki and Panounen (2000) *op. cit.*

115 Gilbert, R., Kemp, A., Thoburn, J., Sidebotham, P., Radford, L., Glaser, D. and MacMillan, H. (2009) 'Child maltreatment 2: Recognising and responding to child maltreatment.' *The Lancet 10*, 373, 167–180.

116 Angeles Cerezo, M. and Pons-Salvador, G. (2004) 'Improving child maltreatment detection systems: A large-scale case study involving health, social services, and school professionals.' *Child Abuse and Neglect 28*, 1153–1170.

117 See Cleaver, Unell and Aldgate (2011) *op. cit.*

118 Barlow and Schrader McMillan (2010) *op. cit.* p.28.

119 See Harnett, P. (2007) 'A procedure for assessing parents' capacity for change in child protection cases.' *Children and Youth Services Review 29*, 1179–1188.

120 Daniel, Taylor and Scott (2011) *op. cit.* p.45.

121 *Ibid.*

122 See also Gilbert, Kemp, Thoburn, Sidebotham, Radford, Glaser and MacMillan (2009) *op. cit.*

123 Maiter, S., Alaggia, R. and Trocme, N. (2004) 'Perceptions of maltreatment by parents from the Indian sub-continent: Challenging myths about culturally based abusive parenting practices.' *Child Maltreatment 9*, 3, 309–324.

124 Andrews, A.B. (1996) 'Public opinions about what a citizen can do to help abused and neglected children in addictive families.' *Journal of Community Practice 3*, 1, 19–33, p.25.

Chapter 3

125 Barlow, J. and Schrader McMillan, A. (2010) *Safeguarding Children from Emotional Maltreatment: What Works.* London: Jessica Kingsley Publishers.

126 Rees, G., Stein, M., Hicks, L. and Gorin, S. (2011) *Adolescent Neglect: Research, Policy and Practice.* London: Jessica Kingsley Publishers.

127 Tunstill, J., Allnock, D. and The National Evaluation of Sure Start Team (2007) *Understanding the Contribution of Sure Start Local Programmes to the Task of Safeguarding Children's Welfare.* London: HMSO.

128 After Barlow and Schrader McMillan (2010) *op. cit.* p.15

129 Gilbert, R., Widom, C.S., Browne, K., Fergusson, D., Webb, E. and Janson, S. (2009) 'Child maltreatment 1: Burden and consequences of child maltreatment in high income countries.' *The Lancet 373*, 68–81.

130 Radford, L., Corral, S., Bradley, C., Fisher, H., Bassett, C., Howat, N. and Collishaw, S. (2011) *The Maltreatment and Victimisation of Children in the UK: NSPCC Report on a National Survey of Young People's, Young Adults' and Caregivers' Experiences.* London: NSPCC.

131 Department for Education (2010d) *Children in Need in England, including their Characteristics and Further Information on Children who were the Subject of a Child Protection Plan (2009–2010 Children in Need Census, Final).* London: Department for Education; see also Munro, E. (2011a) *The Munro Review of Child Protection: Interim Report. A Child's Journey.* London: Department for Education.

132 See also Gilbert, Widom, Browne, Fergusson, Webb and Janson (2009) *op. cit.*

133 Gaudin, J.M. (1993) 'Effective intervention with neglectful families.' *Criminal Justice and Behaviour 20*, 1, 66–89.

134 Sanders, M.R. (2008) 'The Triple P-Positive Parenting Programme: A public health approach to parenting support.' *Journal of Family Psychology 22*, 506–517.

135 Prinz, R.J., Sanders, M.R., Shapiro, C.J., Whitaker, D.J. and Lutzker, J.R. (2009) 'Population-based prevention of child maltreatment: The US Triple P system population trial.' *Prevention Science 10*, 1, 1–12.

136 Department of Health (2009) *Healthy Lives, Brighter Futures: The Strategy for Children and Young People's Health.* London: Department of Health and Department for Children, Schools and Families.

137 Department of Health (2009, updated 2010a) *The Pregnancy Book.* London: Department of Health.

138 Department of Health (2009, updated 2010b) *Birth to Five.* London: Department of Health.

139 Department of Health (2009) *op. cit.*

140 Tanner, K. and Turney, D. (2006) 'Therapeutic Interventions with Children who have Experienced Neglect and their Families in the UK.' In C. McAuley, P. Pecora and W. Rose (eds) *Enhancing the Well-Being of Children through Effective Interventions: International Evidence for Practice.* London: Jessica Kingsley Publishers.

141 Department of Health (2009) *op. cit.* p.25.

142 *Ibid.*

143 Asthana, A. (Policy Editor) (2001) 'Sure Start children centres told to charge for some services.' *The Observer*, 14 November.

144 See Rees, Stein, Hicks and Gorin (2011) pp. 28-29; 61–63

145 Vazsonyi, A.T., Hibbert, J.R. and Snider, J.B. (2003) 'Exotic enterprise no more? Adolescent reports of family and parenting processes from youth in four countries.' *Journal of Research on Adolescence 13*, 2, 197–207.

146 Stanton, B., Cole, M., Galbraith, J., Li, X., Pendleton, S., Cottrel, L., Marshall, S., Wu, Y. and Kaljee, L. (2004) 'Randomized trial of a parenting intervention.' *Archives of Pediatrics and Adolescent Medicine 158*, 947–955.

147 Hicks, L. and Stein, M. in collaboration with the Children's Society and the NSPCC (2010) *Neglect Matters: A Guide for Young People about Neglect.* London: ChildLine.

148 Durrant, J.E. (1999) 'Evaluating the success of Sweden's corporal punishment ban.' *Child Abuse and Neglect 23*, 5, 435–448.

149 Triple P Programme. Accessed on 24 January 2011 at: www.triplep.net/.

150 Prinz, Sanders, Shapiro, Whitaker and Lutzker (2009) *op. cit.*

151 See Health Scotland. *Starting Well? What is Triple P?* Accessed on 24 January 2011 at: www.healthscotland. com/uploads/documents/swsection%208.pdf.

152 Morrell, C.J., Spiby, H., Stewart, P., Walters, S. and Morgan, A. (2000) 'Costs and effectiveness of community postnatal support workers: Randomised controlled trial.' *British Medical Journal 321*, 593–598.

153 Department of Health (2009) *op. cit.*

154 Hindley, N., Ramchandani, P.G. and Jones, D.P.H. (2006) 'Risk factors for recurrence of maltreatment: A systematic review.' *Archives of Disease in Childhood 91*, 9, 744–752.

155 Department for Education and Skills (2006) *Common Assessment Framework for Children and Young People: Practitioners' Guide for Service Managers and Practitioners.* London: The Stationery Office.

156 Brandon, M., Howe, A., Dagley, V., Salter, C. and Warren, C. (2006) 'What appears to be helping or hindering practitioners in implementing the Common Assessment Framework and lead professional working?' *Child Abuse Review 15*, 390–413.

157 Munro, E. (2006) 'What tools do we need to improve identification of child abuse?' *Child Abuse Review 14*, 374–388.

158 Alarm Distress Baby Scale (2004) Accessed on 1 December 2010 at: www.adbb.net/gb-intro.html.

159 Crittenden Care Index: Family Relations Institute. Accessed on 24 January 2011 at: www.patcrittenden.com/ include/care_index.htm.

160 Guedeney, A. and Fermanian, J. (2001) 'A validity and reliability study of assessment and screening for sustained withdrawal reaction in infancy: The Alarm Distress Baby Scale.' *Infant Mental Health Journal 22*, 5, 559–575.

161 Crittenden, P.M. (1981) 'Abusing, neglecting, problematic and adequate dyads: Differentiating by patterns of interaction.' *Merril-Palmer Quarterly 27*, 1–18.

162 *Ibid.*

163 Barlow, J. and Scott, J. (2010) *Safeguarding Children in the 21st Century: Where to Now?* Totnes: Research in Practice.

164 Eyberg, S.M., Besmear, J., Edwards, D. and Robinson, E. (1994) 'Manual for the dyadic Parent–Child Interaction Coding System II.' *Social and Behavioural Sciences Documents* (MS no: 2898).

165 Biringen, Z. (2000) 'Emotional availability: Conceptualization and research findings.' *American Journal of Orthopsychiatry 70*, 104–114.

166 Harnett, P. and Dawe, S. (2008) 'Reducing child abuse potential for child abuse among families: Implications for assessment and treatment.' *Brief Treatment and Crisis Intervention 8*, 226–235.

167 *Ibid.*

168 See Jones, D., Hindley, N. and Ramchandani, P. (2006) 'Making Plans: Assessment, Intervention and Evaluating Outcomes.' In J. Aldgate, D. Jones and C. Jeffery (eds) *The Developing World of the Child.* London: Jessica Kingsley Publishers, pp.278–279. for further discussion.

169 Cleaver, H., Walker, S., Scott, J., Cleaver, D., Rose, W., Ward, H. and Pithouse, A. (2008) *The Integrated Children's System: Enhancing Social Work and Inter-Agency Practice.* London: Jessica Kingsley Publishers.

170 Cleaver, H. and Walker, S. (2004) 'From policy to practice: The implementation of a new framework for social work assessments of children and families.' *Child and Family Social Work 9*, 1, 81–90.

171 Barlow, J., Simkiss, D. and Stewart-Brown, S. (2006) 'Interventions to prevent or ameliorate child physical abuse and neglect: Findings from a systematic review.' *Journal of Children's Services 1*, 6–28.

172 Barlow, J. (2006) 'Home Visiting Programmes for Parents of Pre-School Children: The UK Experience.' In C. McAuley, P. Pecora and W. Rose (eds) *Effective Interventions for Children and Families.* London: Jessica Kingsley Publishers.

173 Bull, J., McCormick, G., Swann, C. and Mulivihill, C. (2004) *Ante-Natal and Post-Natal Home-Visiting Programmes: A Review of Reviews. Evidence Briefing (First Edition).* London: Health Development Agency.

174 MacMillan, H.L., Wathen, C.N., Barlow, J., Fergusson, D.M., Leventhal, D.M. and Taussig, H.N. (2009) 'Child maltreatment 3: Interventions to prevent maltreatment and associated impairment.' *The Lancet 373,* 9659, 250–266.

175 Olds, D.L., Henderson, C.R. and Kitzman, H. (1994) 'Does prenatal and infancy nurse home visitation have enduring effects on qualities of parental caregiving and child health at 25 to 50 months of life?' *Pediatrics 93,* 89–98.

176 Olds, D.L., Henderson, C.R., Cole, R.C., Eckenrode, J., Kitzman, H., Luckey, D., Sidora, K., Pettitt, L., Morris, P. and Powers, J. (1998) 'Long-term effects of home visitation on children's criminal and anti social behaviour: 15-year follow up of a randomized trial.' *Journal of the American Medical Association 280,* 14, 1238–1244.

177 Olds, D.L., Robinson, J., O'Brien, R., Luckey, D.W., Pettitt, L.M., Henderson, C.R., Ng, R.N., Korfmacher, J., Hiatt, S. and Talmi, A. (2002) 'Home visiting by nurses and by paraprofessionals: A randomized controlled trial.' *Pediatrics 110,* 3, 486–496.

178 Olds, D., Eckenrode, J., Henderson, C.R., Kitzman, H., Powers, J., Cole, R., Sidora, K., Morris, P., Pettitt, L. and Luckey, D. (1997) 'Long-term effects of home visitation on maternal life course and child abuse and neglect: 15-year follow up of a randomized trial.' *Journal of the American Medical Association 278,* 637–643.

179 Department of Health (2009) *op. cit.*

180 Barnes, J., Ball, M., Meadows, P., Belsky, J. and the FNP Implementation Research Team (2009) *Nurse–Family Partnership Programme, Second Year Pilot Sites Implementation in England: The Infancy Period.* London: Department for Children, Schools and Families and Department of Health.

181 MacMillan, Wathen, Barlow, Fergusson, Leventhal and Taussig (2009) *op. cit.*

182 See Nurse Family Partnership (2008) Accessed on 24 January 2011 at: http://cbpp-pcpe.phac-aspc.gc.ca/intervention_pdf/en/600.pdf.

183 See for instance Hutchings, J., Bywater, T., Williams, M.E., Shakespeare, M.K. and Whitaker, C. (2009) *Evidence for the Extended School Aged Incredible Years Parent Programme with Parents of High-Risk 8 to 16 Year olds.* Bangor: School of Psychology, Bangor University.

184 Webster-Stratton, C. and Reid, J. (2010) 'Adapting the Incredible Years, an evidence-based parenting programme, for families involved in the child welfare system.' *Journal of Children's Services 5,* 1, 25–42.

185 DeVore, E.R. and Ginsburg, K.R. (2005) 'The protective effects of good parenting on adolescents.' *Current Opinion in Pediatrics 17,* 4, 460–465.

186 Stanton, B., Cole, M., Galbraith, J., Li, X., Pendleton, S., Cottrel, L., Marshall, S., Wu, Y. and Kaljee, L. (2004) 'Randomized trial of a parenting intervention.' *Archives of Pediatrics and Adolescent Medicine 158,* 947–955.

187 Simons-Morton, B.G., Hartos, J., Leaf, W. and Preusser, D. (2006) 'The effect on teen driving outcomes of the Checkpoints Programme in a state-wide trial.' *Accident Analysis and Prevention 38,* 907–912.

Chapter 4

188 Farmer, E. and Lutman, E. (forthcoming) *Working Effectively with Neglected Children and their Families – Understanding their Experiences and Long-Term Outcomes.* London: Jessica Kingsley Publishers.

189 Ward, H., Brown, R., Westlake, D. and Munro, E.R. (forthcoming) *Safeguarding Babies and Very Young Children from Abuse and Neglect.* London: Jessica Kingsley Publishers.

190 Wade, J., Biehal, N., Farrelly, N. and Sinclair, I. (2011) *Caring for Abused and Neglected Children: Making the Right Decisions for Reunification or Long-Term Care.* London: Jessica Kingsley Publishers.

191 Cleaver, H., Unell, I. and Aldgate, J. (2011) *Children's Needs – Parenting Capacity. The Impact of Parental Mental Illness, Learning Disability, Problem Alcohol and Drug Use and Domestic Violence on Children's Safety (2nd Edition).* London: The Stationery Office.

192 Hindley, N., Ramchandani, P.G. and Jones, D.P.H. (2006) 'Risk factors for recurrence of maltreatment: A systematic review.' *Archives of Disease in Childhood 91,* 9, 744–752.

193 See also Brandon, M., Sidebotham, P., Ellis, C., Bailey, S. and Belderson, P. (forthcoming) *Child and Family Practitioners' Understanding of Child Development: Lessons Learnt from a Small Sample of Serious Case Reviews.* London: Department for Education.

194 Haringey Local Safeguarding Children Board (2010) *Serious Case Review: Child A, March 2009.* London: Department for Education, p.39.

195 Ayre, P. (1998) 'Assessment of significant harm: Improving professional practice.' *British Journal of Nursing 7*, 1, 31–36.

196 Stephenson, O. (1996) 'Emotional abuse and neglect: A time for reappraisal.' *Child and Family Social Work 1*, 1, 13–18.

197 Farmer and Lutman (2009) *op. cit.* p.105.

198 *Ibid.* p.113.

199 Mattinson, J. (1975) *The Reflection Process in Case Work Supervision.* London: Institute of Marital Studies.

200 Brandon, M., Belderson, P., Warren, C., Howe, D., Gardner, R., Dodsworth, J. and Black, J. (2008) *Analysing Child Deaths and Serious Injury through Abuse and Neglect: What can we Learn? A Biennial Analysis of Serious Case Reviews 2003–2005.* DCSF-RR023. London: Department for Children, Schools and Families, pp.72–73.

201 Ward, H., Brown, R. and Maskell-Graham, D. (forthcoming) *Young Children Suffering, or Likely to Suffer, Significant Harm: Experiences on Entering Education.* Loughborough: Centre for Child and Family Research, Loughborough University.

202 Haringey Local Safeguarding Children Board (2010) *op. cit.*

203 Holmes, L. and McDermid, S. (forthcoming) *Understanding the Costs of Child Welfare.* London: Jessica Kingsley Publishers.

204 Hannon, C., Wood, C. and Bazalgette, L. (2010) *In Loco Parentis.* London: DEMOS.

205 Scott, S., Knapp, M., Henderson, J. and Maughan, B. (2001) 'Financial cost of social exclusion: Follow up study of antisocial children into adulthood.' *British Medical Journal 323*, 191–196.

206 Ward, H., Holmes, L. and Soper, J. (2008) *Costs and Consequences of Placing Children in Care.* London: Jessica Kingsley Publishers.

207 See also Fauth, R., Jelicic, H., Hart, D., Burton, S. and Shemmings, D. (2010) *Effective Practice to Protect Children Living in 'Highly Resistant' Families.* London: C4EO.

208 Ward, Brown, Westlake and Munro (forthcoming) *op. cit.*

209 See Jones, D., Hindley, N. and Ramchandani, P. (2006) 'Making Plans: Assessment, Intervention and Evaluating Outcomes.' In J. Aldgate, D. Jones and C. Jeffery (eds) *The Developing World of the Child.* London: Jessica Kingsley Publishers.

210 Ward, H., Munro, E.R. and Dearden, C. (2006) *Babies and Young Children in Care: Life Pathways, Decision-Making and Practice.* London: Jessica Kingsley Publishers.

211 Tannenbaum, L. and Forehand, R. (1994) 'Maternal depressive mood: The role of the father in preventing adolescent problem behaviours.' *Behaviour Research and Therapy 32*, 321–325.

212 Van den Dries, L., Juffer, F., Van IJzendoorn, M.H. and Bakermans-Kranenburg, M.J. (2009) 'Fostering security? A meta-analysis of attachment in adopted children.' *Children and Youth Services Review 31*, 410–421.

213 Howe, D. (2005) *Child Abuse and Neglect: Attachment, Development and Intervention.* Basingstoke: Palgrave Macmillan.

214 Schore, A. (2010) 'Relational Trauma and the Developing Right Brain: The Neurobiology of Broken Attachment Bonds.' In T. Baradon (ed.) *Relational Trauma in Infancy: Psychoanalytic, Attachment and Neuropsychological Contributions to Parent–Infant Psychotherapy.* New York: Routledge.

215 Van den Dries, Juffer, Van IJzendoorn and Bakermans-Kranenburg (2009) *op. cit.*

216 Jones, Hindley and Ramchandani (2006) *op. cit.*

217 Skuse, T. and Ward, H. (2003) *Outcomes for Looked After Children: Children's Views, the Importance of Listening. An Interim Report to the Department of Health.* Loughborough: Centre for Child and Family Research, Loughborough University.

218 Ward, H. (2009) 'Patterns of instability. Moves within the English care system: Their reasons, contexts and consequences.' *Children and Youth Services Review 31*, 1113–1118.

219 See also Hunt, J., Waterhouse, S. and Lutman, E. (2008) *Keeping Them in the Family: Outcomes for Abused and Neglected Children Placed with Family and Friends Carers through Care Proceedings.* London: BAAF; and Farmer, E. and Moyers, S. (2008) *Kinship Care: Fostering Effective Family and Friends Placements.* London: Jessica Kingsley Publishers.

220 Hannon, Wood and Bazalgette (2010) *op. cit.*

221 Sergeant, H. (2006) *Handle with Care.* London: Centre for Policy Studies.

Chapter 5

222 Montgomery, P., Gardner, F., Ramchandani, P. and Bjornstad, G. (2009) *Systematic Reviews of Interventions following Physical Abuse: Helping Practitioners and Expert Witnesses Improve the Outcomes of Child Abuse.* Report to the Department for Children, Schools and Families. Oxford: University of Oxford.

223   Barlow, J. and Schrader McMillan, A. (2010) *Safeguarding Children from Emotional Maltreatment: What Works.* London: Jessica Kingsley Publishers.

224   For instance, MacMillan, H.L., Wathen, C.N., Barlow, J., Fergusson, D.M., Leventhal, D.M. and Taussig, H.N. (2009) 'Child maltreatment 3: Interventions to prevent maltreatment and associated impairment.' *The Lancet 373,* 9659, 250–266.

225   Compiled from Montgomery, Gardner, Ramchandani and Bjornstad (2009) *op. cit.* pp.12–15.

226   Compton, S.N., March, J.S., Brent, D., Albano, A.M.V., Weersing, R. and Curry, J. (2004) 'Cognitive-behavioral psychotherapy for anxiety and depressive disorders in children and adolescents: An evidence-based medicine review.' *Journal of the American Academy of Child and Adolescent Psychiatry 43,* 930–959.

227   March, J.S., Amaya-Jackson, L., Murray, M.C. and Schulte, A. (1998) 'Cognitive-behavioral psychotherapy for children and adolescents with posttraumatic stress disorder after a single-incident stressor.' *Journal of the American Academy of Child and Adolescent Psychiatry 37,* 585–593.

228   Webster-Stratton, C., Reid, J. and Hammond, M. (2001) 'Social skills and problem-solving training for children with early-onset conduct problems: Who benefits?' *Journal of Child Psychology and Psychiatry 42,* 943–952.

229   Dretzke, J., Frew, E., Davenport, C., Barlow, J., Stewart-Brown, S., Sandercock, J., Bayliss, S., Raftery, J., Hyde, C. and Taylor, R. (2005) 'The effectiveness and cost-effectiveness of parent training/education programmes for the treatment of conduct disorder, including oppositional defiant disorder, in children.' *Health Technology Assessment 9,* 50, 50.

230   Gardner, F., Burton, J. and Klimes, I. (2006) 'Randomised controlled trial of a parenting intervention in the voluntary sector for reducing child conduct problems: Outcomes and mechanisms for change.' *Journal of Child Psychology and Psychiatry 47,* 1123–1132.

231   Hutchings, J., Bywater, T., Daley, D., Gardner, F., Whitaker, C., Jones, K., Eames, C. and Edwards, R.T. (2007) 'Parenting intervention in Sure Start services for children at risk of developing conduct disorder: Pragmatic randomised controlled trial.' *British Medical Journal 334,* 678–682.

232   Fluke, J. (2008) 'Child protective services rereporting and recurrence: Context and considerations regarding research.' *Child Abuse and Neglect 32,* 8, 749–751.

233   Hindley, N., Ramchandani, P. and Jones, D.P.H. (2006) 'Risk factors for recurrence of maltreatment: A systematic review.' *Archives of Disease in Childhood 91,* 9, 744–752.

234   Thoburn, J. and members of the Making Research Count Consortium (2009) *Effective Interventions for Complex Families where there are Concerns About, or Evidence of, a Child Suffering Significant Harm. Safeguarding Briefing 1.* London: Centre for Excellence and Outcomes in Children and Young People's Services (C4EO).

235   See for instance Cleaver, H., Unell, I. and Aldgate, J. (2011) *Children's Needs – Parenting Capacity. The Impact of Parental Mental Illness, Learning Disability, Problem Alcohol and Drug Use and Domestic Violence on Children's Safety (2nd Edition).* London: The Stationery Office; Cleaver, H., Nicholson, D., Tarr, S. and Cleaver, D. (2007) *Child Protection, Domestic Violence and Parental Substance Misuse: Family Experiences and Effective Practice.* London: Jessica Kingsley Publishers; Kroll, B. and Taylor, A. (2003) *Parental Substance Misuse and Child Welfare.* London: Jessica Kingsley Publishers; and Tunnard, J. (2002) *Parental Problem Drinking and its Impact on Children.* Dartington: Research in Practice.

236   Parents Under Pressure. Accessed on 24 January 2011 at: www.pupprogramme.net.au.

237   Dawe, S. and Harnett, P. (2007a) 'Reducing potential for child abuse among methadone-maintained parents: Results from a randomized controlled trial.' *Journal of Substance Abuse Treatment 32,* 4, 381–390.

238   Parents Under Pressure. *op. cit.*

239   See also MacMillan, Wathen, Barlow, Fergusson, Leventhal and Taussig (2009) *op. cit.* p.255.

240   Williamson, E. and Hester, M. (2009) *Evaluation of the South Tyneside Domestic Abuse Perpetrator 2006–8.* Final Report. Bristol: University of Bristol.

241   Cleaver, Unell and Aldgate (2011) *op. cit.*

242   For further information see MacMillan, Wathen, Barlow, Fergusson, Leventhal and Taussig (2009) *op. cit.* p.259.

243   Sullivan, C.M. and Bybee, D. (1999) 'Reducing violence using community based advocacy for women with abusive partners.' *Journal of Consulting and Clinical Psychology 67,* 1, 43–53.

244   Hindley, Ramchandani and Jones (2006) *op. cit.*

245   WHO (2007) *The Cycles of Violence: The Relationship Between Childhood Maltreatment and the Risk of Later Becoming a Victim or Perpetrator of Violence.* Copenhagen: World Health Organization.

246   Kim, J. (2009) 'Type-specific intergenerational transmission of neglectful and physically abusive parenting behaviours among young parents.' *Children and Youth Services Review 31,* 7, 761–767.

247   For summary see Jones, D.P.H. (2008) 'Child Maltreatment.' In M. Rutter, D. Bishop, D. Pine, S. Scott, J. Stevenson, E. Taylor and A. Thapar (eds) *Rutter's Child and Adolescent Psychiatry (Fifth Edition)*. Oxford: Blackwell Publishing.

248   For further information see Barlow and Schrader McMillan (2010) *op. cit.* pp.68–70 and MacMillan, Wathen, Barlow, Fergusson, Leventhal and Taussig (2009) *op. cit.* p.253.

249   Sanders, M.R., Pidgeon, A.M., Gravestock, F., Connors, M.D., Brown, S. and Young, R.W. (2004) 'Does parental attributional retraining and anger management enhance the effects of the Triple P-Positive Parenting Programme with parents at risk of child maltreatment?' *Behavioural Therapy 35*, 513–535.

250   Prinz, R.J., Sanders, M.R., Shapiro, C.J., Whitaker, D.J. and Lutzker, J.R. (2009) 'Population-based prevention of child maltreatment: The US Triple P system population trial.' *Prevention Science 10*, 1, 1–12.

251   Sanders, Pidgeon, Gravestock, Connors, Brown and Young (2004) *op. cit.*

252   Triple P Programme. Accessed on 24 January 2011 at: www.triplep.net/.

253   Barlow and Schrader McMillan (2010) *op. cit.* pp.70–73; Iwaniec, D. (1997) 'Evaluating parent training for emotionally abusive and neglectful parents: Comparing individual versus individual and group intervention.' *Research in Social Work Practice 7*, 3, 329–349.

254   For further information see Barlow and Schrader McMillan (2010) *op. cit.* pp.93–94 and Montgomery, Gardner, Ramchandani and Bjornstadt (2009) *op. cit.*

255   Cicchetti, D., Rogosch, F. and Toth, S. (2006) 'Fostering secure attachment in infants in maltreating families through preventive interventions.' *Development and Psychopathology 18*, 623–649.

256   Toth, S.L., Rogosch, F.A., Cicchetti, D. and Manly, J.T. (2006) 'The efficacy of toddler–parent psychotherapy to reorganise attachment in the young offspring of mothers with major depressive disorder: A randomised preventive trial.' *Journal of Consulting and Clinical Psychology 74*, 6, 1006–16.

257   Toth, S., Maughan, A., Todd Manly, J., Spagnola, M. and Cicchetti, C. (2002) 'The relative efficacy of two interventions in altering maltreated preschool children's representational models: Implications for attachment theory.' *Development and Psychopathology 14*, 887–908.

258   Fukkink, R. (2008) 'Video feedback in widescreen: A meta-analysis of family programmes.' *Clinical Psychology Review 28*, 6, 904–916.

259   For further information see Barlow and Schrader McMillan (2010) *op. cit.* pp.98–99.

260   Benoit, D., Madigan, S., Lecce, S., Shea, B. and Goldberg, S. (2001) 'Atypical maternal behaviour toward feeding-disordered infants before and after intervention.' *Infant Mental Health Journal 22*, 6, 611–626.

261   *Ibid.*

262   For further information see Montgomery, Gardner, Ramchandani and Bjornstad (2009) *op. cit.* pp.31–32.

263   See also MacMillan, Wathen, Barlow, Fergusson, Leventhal and Taussig (2009) *op cit* p.255

264   Chaffin, M., Silovsky, J.F., Funderburk, B., Valle, L.A., Brestan, E.V., Balachova, T. *et al.* (2004) 'Parent–Child Interaction Therapy with physically abusive parents: Efficacy for reducing future abuse reports.' *Journal of Consulting and Clinical Psychology 72*, 3, 500–510.

265   See Stith, S.M., Ting Lui, L., Davies, C., Boykin, E.L., Alder, M.C., Harris, J.M., Som, A., McPherson, M. and Dees, J.E.M.E.G. (2009) 'Risk factors in child maltreatment: A meta-analytic review of the literature.' *Aggression and Violent Behaviour 14*, 3–29.

266   Binggeli, N., Hart, S.N. and Brassard, M.R. (2001) *Psychological Maltreatment of Children*. London: Sage.

267   Stratton, P. (2005) *Report on the Evidence Base of Systemic Family Therapy*. Warrington: Association for Family Therapy.

268   Carr, A. (2000) *Family Therapy: Concepts, Process and Practice*. Chichester: John Wiley & Sons Ltd.

269   Asen, E. (2002) 'Outcome research in family therapy.' *Advances in Psychiatric Treatment 8*, 3, 230–238.

270   Carr, A. (2006) 'Thematic review of family therapy journals in 2005.' *Journal of Family Therapy 28*, 4, 420–439.

271   Fraser, L. (1995) 'Eastfield Ming Quong: Multiple-Impact In-Home Treatment Model.' In L. Combrick-Graham (ed.) *Children and Families at Risk*. New York, NY: Guilford Press.

272   Kolko, D.J. (1996) 'Individual cognitive behavioural treatment and family therapy for physically abused children and their offending parents: A comparison of clinical outcomes.' *Child Maltreatment 1*, 322–342.

273   Meezan, W. and O'Keefe, M. (1998) 'Evaluating the effectiveness of multifamily group therapy in child abuse and neglect.' *Research on Social Work Practice 8*, 330–353.

274   This randomized controlled trial reported after completion of the scientific reviews but it builds on studies that were identified by Montgomery and colleagues.

275   Swenson, C., Schaeffer, C., Henggeler, S., Faldowski, R. and Mayhew, A. (2010) 'Multi-Systemic Therapy for Child Abuse and Neglect: A randomised controlled effectiveness trial.' *Journal of Family Psychology 24*, 497–507.

276 Stallman, H., Walmsley, K., Bor, W., Collerson, M.E., Swenson, C. and McDermott, B. (2010) 'New directions in the treatment of child physical abuse and neglect in Australia: MST-CAN, a case study.' *Advances in Mental Health 9*, 148–161.

277 Bronfenbrenner, U. (1979) *The Ecology of Human Development: Experiments by Nature and Design*. Cambridge, MA: Harvard University Press.

278 See Kolko (1996) *op. cit.*; Meezan and O'Keefe (1998) *op. cit.*

279 Swenson, Schaeffer, Henggeler, Faldowski and Mayhew (2010) *op. cit.*

280 Stallman, Walmsley, Bor, Collerson, Swenson and McDermott (2010) *op. cit.*

281 See Swenson, Schaeffer, Henggeler, Faldowski and Mayhew (2010) *op. cit.*

282 But see Wiggins, C., Fenichel, E. and Mann, T. (2007) *Literature Review: Developmental Problems of Maltreated Children and Early Intervention Options for Maltreated Children*. Report to Office of the Assistant Secretary for Planning and Evaluation, US Department of Health and Human Services; Macdonald, G.M. (2001) *Effective Interventions for Child Abuse and Neglect: An Evidence-Based Approach to Evaluating and Planning Interventions*. Chichester: John Wiley & Sons Ltd.

283 For further information see Montgomery, Gardner, Ramchandani and Bjornstad (2009) *op. cit.* pp.25–26.

284 Moore, E., Armsden, G. and Gogerty, P.L. (1998) 'A twelve-year follow up study of maltreated and at-risk children who received early therapeutic child care.' *Child Maltreatment 3*, 3–16.

285 For further information see Montgomery, Gardner, Ramchandani and Bjornstad (2009) *op. cit.* pp.24–25.

286 Fantuzzo, J., Sutton-Smith, B., Atkins, M., Meyers, R., Stevenson, H., Coolahan, K., Weiss, A. and Manz, P. (1996) 'Community-based resilient peer treatment of withdrawn maltreated preschool children.' *Journal of Consulting and Clinical Psychology 64*, 1377–1386.

287 See for example Campbell, R., Starkey, F., Holliday, J., Audrey, S., Bloor, M., Parry-Langdon, N., Hughes, R. and Moore, L. (2008) 'An informal school-based peer-led intervention for smoking prevention in adolescence (ASSIST): A cluster randomised trial.' *The Lancet 371*, 1595–1602; and Cuijpers, P. (2002) 'Peer-led and adult-led school drug prevention: A meta-analytic comparison.' *Journal of Drug Education 32*, 2, 107–119.

288 See for instance Leve, L., Fisher, P. and Chamberlain, P. (2009) 'Multidimensional Treatment Foster Care as a preventive intervention to promote resiliency among youth in the child welfare System.' *Journal of Personality 77*, 6 1869–1902; and Fisher, P., Chamberlain, P. and Leve, L. (2009) 'Improving the lives of foster children through evidence-based interventions.' *Vulnerable Children and Youth Studies 4*, 2, 122–127.

289 Fisher, P.A., Burraston, B. and Pears, K. (2005) 'The Early Intervention Foster Care Programme: Permanent placement outcomes from a randomized trial.' *Child Maltreatment 10*, 61–71; and Fisher, P.A. and Kim, H.K. (2007) 'Intervention effects on foster preschoolers' attachment-related behaviours from a randomized trial.' *Prevention Science 8*, 161–170. The evaluation given in Appendix 2 (Example 10) is the only MTFC evaluation identified by the scientific reviews, presumably because it met the criteria by referring explicitly to physical abuse, while others do not. Strictly speaking our discussion should therefore be restricted to this study, but it seems pointless to withhold, in the interests of academic purity, information about the wider programme that is of potential value to readers.

290 National Implementation Team (2010) *Multi-Dimensional Treatment Foster Care in England: Annual Project Report*. London: Department for Children, Schools and Families.

291 *Ibid.* p.1.

292 Holmes, L., Westlake, D. and Ward, H. (2009) *Calculating and Comparing the Costs of Multidimensional Treatment Foster Care, England (MTFCE)*. Report to the Department for Children, Schools and Families. Loughborough: Centre for Child and Family Research, Loughborough University.

293 Garland, A.F., Bickman, L. and Chorpita, B.F. (2010) 'Change what? Identifying quality improvement targets by investigating usual mental health care.' *Administration in Policy and Mental Health 37*, 15–26.

294 Chorpita, B.F. and Daleidin, E.L. (2009) 'Mapping evidence-based treatments for children and adolescents: Application of the distillation and matching model to 615 treatments from 322 randomized trials.' *Journal of Consulting and Clinical Psychology 77*, 3, 566–579.

295 Garland, A.F., Hawley, K.M., Brookman-Frazee, L. and Hurlburt, M.S. (2008) 'Identifying common elements of evidence-based psychosocial treatments for children's disruptive behaviour problems.' *Journal of the American Academy of Child and Adolescent Psychiatry 47*, 5, 505–514.

296 Jones, D.P.H., personal communication.

297 For example, see summaries based upon these by Jones, D.P.H. (2008) 'Child Maltreatment.' In M. Rutter, D. Bishop, D. Pine, S. Scott, J. Stevenson, E. Taylor and A.Thapar (eds) *Rutter's Child and Adolescent Psychiatry (Fifth Edition)*. Oxford: Blackwell Publishing, pp.431–433.

298 Jones, D.P.H. (2009) 'Child Abuse and Neglect.' In M. Gelder, J. Lopez-Ibor and N. Andreasen (eds) *The New Oxford Textbook of Psychiatry (Second Edition)*. Oxford: Oxford University Press, pp.1738–1739.

Chapter 6

299 France, A., Munro, E.R. and Waring, A. (2010) *The Evaluation of Arrangements for Effective Operation of the New Local Safeguarding Children Boards in England – Final Report.* London: Department for Education.

300 Carpenter, J., Hackett, S., Patsios, D. and Szilassy, E. (2010) *Outcomes of Inter-Agency Training to Safeguard Children.* Research Report DCSF-RR209. London: Department for Children, Schools and Families.

301 Komulainen, S. and Haines, L. (2009) *Understanding Parent's Information Needs and Experiences where Professional Concerns Regarding Non-Accidental Injury were not Substantiated. Research Report.* London: Royal College of Paediatrics and Child Health.

302 Tompsett, H., Ashworth, M., Atkins, C., Bell, L., Gallagher, A., Morgan, M. and Wainwright, P. (2009) *The Child, the Family and the GP: Tensions and Conflicts of Interest in Safeguarding Children.* DCSF-RBX-09-05-ES. London: Department for Children, Schools and Families.

303 Laming, Lord (Cm 5730) (2003) *The Victoria Climbié Inquiry: Report of an Inquiry by Lord Laming.* London: The Stationery Office; and Haringey Local Safeguarding Children Board (2010) *Serious Case Review: Child A, March 2009.* London: Department for Education.

304 Laming, Lord (Cm 5730) (2003) *op. cit.*

305 Children Art (2004) London: HMSO.

306 HM Government (2010) *Working Together to Safeguard Children: A Guide to Inter-Agency Working to Safeguard and Promote the Welfare of Children.* London: Department for Children, Schools and Families.

307 Department for Education (2010b) *More Freedom and Flexibility: A New Approach for Children's Trust Boards, Children and Young People's Plans, and the 'Duty to Cooperate'.* News release, 3 November 2010. London: Department for Education.

308 Department for Education (Cm 7980) (2010f) *The Importance of Teaching: The Schools White Paper.* London: The Stationery Office.

309 See Department for Communities and Local Government: Newsroom, 14 October 2010. Ministerial Statement by Rt Hon Eric Pickles: *Local Government Accountability*; and HM Treasury (Cm 7942) (2010) *Spending Review.* London: The Stationery Office.

310 HM Government (2010) *op. cit.* pp.60–62.

311 Royal College of General Practitioners (2009) *Safeguarding Children and Young People: A Toolkit for General Practice.* London: RCGP.

312 See Department for Children, Schools and Families (2009) *Referrals, Assessments and Children and Young People who are the Subject of a Child Protection Plan, England – Year Ending March 31 2009* (www.data.gov.uk/dataset/referrals) and Department for Education (2010d) *Children in Need in England, including their Characteristics and Further Information on Children who were the Subject of a Child Protection Plan (2009–2010 Children in Need Census, Final).* London: Department for Education.

313 Munro, E. (2010) *The Munro Review of Child Protection. Part One: A Systems Analysis.* London: Department for Education.

314 Holmes, L., Munro, E.R. and Soper, J. (2010) *Calculating the Cost and Capacity Implications for Local Authorities Implementing the Laming (2009) Recommendations.* London: LGA.

315 Munro (2010) *op. cit.*

316 HM Government (2010) *op. cit.*

317 Sanders, R., Colton, M. and Roberts, S. (1999) 'Child abuse fatalities and cases of extreme concern: Lessons from reviews.' *Child Abuse and Neglect 23*, 3, 257–268.

318 Munro, E. (1999) 'Common errors of reasoning in child protection work.' *Child Abuse and Neglect 23*, 8, 745–758.

319 Ward, H., Brown, R., Westlake, D. and Munro, E.R. (forthcoming) *Safeguarding Babies and Very Young Children from Abuse and Neglect.* London: Jessica Kingsley Publishers.

320 Ward, H., Holmes, L., Moyers, S., Munro, E.R. and Poursanidou, D. (2004) *Safeguarding Children: A Scoping Study of Research in Three Areas.* Loughborough: Centre for Child and Family Research, Loughborough University.

321 Ward, Brown, Westlake and Munro (forthcoming) *op. cit.*

322 Laming, Lord (HC 330) (2009) *The Protection of Children in England: A Progress Report.* London: The Stationery Office.

323 Holmes, Munro and Soper (2010) *op. cit.*

324 Farmer, E. and Lutman, E. (forthcoming) *Working Effectively with Neglected Children and their Families – Understanding their Experiences and Long-Term Outcomes.* London: Jessica Kingsley Publishers.

325 *Ibid.* p.185.

326 France, Munro and Waring (2010) *op. cit.* p.177.

327 *Ibid.* p.177.

328 See Leslie, B. (2005) 'Housing Issues in Child Welfare: A Practice Response with Service and Policy Implications.' In J. Scott and H. Ward (eds) *Safeguarding and Promoting the Well-Being of Children, Families and Communities.* London: Jessica Kingsley Publishers.

329 Department for Education (2010e) *Response to Public Comments on Coalition Agreement on Families and Children.* London: Department for Education.

330 Farmer and Lutman (2009) *op. cit.* p.77.

331 Laming, Lord (Cm 5730) (2003) *op. cit.* p.367.

332 *Ibid.*

333 HM Government (2010) *op. cit.* Section 4.3.

334 *Ibid.* Section 4.2.

335 Salas, E. and Cannon-Bowers, J. (2001) 'The science of training: A decade review of progress.' *Annual Review of Psychology 52,* 471–499.

336 See www.education.gov.uk/researchandstatistics/research/scri Carpenter, J., Patsios, D., Szilassy, E. and Hackett, S. (2011) *Connect, Share and Learn: A Toolkit for Evaluating the Outcomes of Inter-Agency Training to Safeguard Children.* London: NSPCC.

337 Carpenter, Hackett, Patsios and Szilassy (2010) *op. cit.*

338 Tompsett, Ashworth, Atkins, Bell, Gallagher, Morgan and Wainwright (2009) *op. cit.*

339 Royal College of Paediatrics and Child Health (2010) *Safeguarding Children and Young People: Roles and Competences for Health Care Staff. Intercollegiate Document.* London: Royal College of Paediatrics and Child Health.

340 *Ibid.*

341 Laming, Lord (HC 330) (2009) *op. cit.*

342 Children Act (2004) *op. cit.*

343 HM Government (2010) *op. cit.* Sections 3.8–3.10.

344 Chief Inspector of Social Services, Director for Health Improvement, Commission for Health Improvement and HM Chief Inspector of Constabulary (2002) *Safeguarding Children: A Joint Chief Inspectors' Report on Arrangements to Safeguard Children.* London: Department of Health.

345 Narducci, T. (2003) *Increasing the Effectiveness of the ACPC.* London: NSPCC.

346 Munro, E. (2011b) *The Munro Review of Child Protection: Final Report. A Child-Centred System.* London: Department for Education; Department for Education (2011) *A Child-Centred System: The Government's Response to the Munro Review of Child Protection.* London: Department for Education.

347 Laming, Lord (Cm 5730) (2003) *op. cit.* p.6.

348 Munro (2010) *op. cit.*

349 Laming, Lord (Cm 5730) (2003) *op. cit.* p.8.

350 *Ibid.* pp.5–6.

351 Department for Education (2010e) *op. cit.*

352 Percy-Smith, J. (2006) 'What works in strategic partnerships for children: A research review.' *Children and Society 20,* 4, 313–323.

353 Laming, Lord (Cm 5730) (2003) *op. cit.*

354 Laming, Lord (HC 330) (2009) *op. cit.*

355 HM Government (2010) *op. cit.* Paras 3.52–3.32, p.99.

356 Haringey Local Safeguarding Children Board (2010) *op. cit.*

357 Laming, Lord (HC 330) (2009) *op. cit.*

358 Haringey Local Safeguarding Children Board (2010) *op. cit.*

359 Children Act (2004) *op. cit.*

360 Hardy, B., Turrell, A. and Wistow, G. (1992) *Innovations in Community Care Management.* Aldershot: Avebury.

361 HM Government (2010) *op. cit.* Para. 3.97, p.109.

362 France, Munor and Waring (2010) *op. cit.*

363 Children Act (2004) *op. cit.*

364 Munro (2010) *op. cit.*; Munro, E. (2011a) *The Munro Review of Child Protection: Interim Report. A Child's Journey.* London: Department for Education.

365 Department of Health (2010) (cm 7881) *Equity and Excellence: Liberating the NHS.* London: The Stationery Office.

366 Royal College of Paediatrics and Child Health (2010) *op. cit.*

Chapter 7

367 Laming, Lord (Cm 5730) (2003) *The Victoria Climbié Inquiry: Report of an Inquiry by Lord Laming*. London: The Stationery Office.

368 Jones, D.P.H. (2008) 'Child Maltreatment.' In M. Rutter, D. Bishop, D. Pine, S. Scott, J. Stevenson, E. Taylor and A. Thapar (eds) *Rutter's Child and Adolescent Psychiatry (Fifth Edition)*. Oxford: Blackwell Publishing.

369 Hindley, N., Ramchandani, P.G. and Jones, D.P.H. (2006) 'Risk factors for recurrence of maltreatment: A systematic review.' *Archives of Disease in Childhood 91*, 9, 744–752.

370 For a comprehensive overview see Cleaver, H., Unell, I. and Aldgate, A. (2011) *Children's Needs – Parenting Capacity. The Impact of Parental Mental Illness, Learning Disability, Problem Alcohol and Drug Use and Domestic Violence on Children's Safety (2nd Edition)*. London: The Stationery Office.

371 See De Bellis, M. (2005) 'Psychobiology of neglect.' *Child Maltreatment 10*, 2, 150–172.

372 See Glaser, D. (2000) 'Child abuse and neglect and the brain: A review.' *The Journal of Child Psychiatry and Psychology 41*, 1, 97–116.

373 Rees, G., Stein, M., Hicks, L. and Gorin, S. (2011) *Adolescent Neglect: Research, Policy and Practice*. London: Jessica Kingsley Publishers.

374 Department of Health (2009) *Healthy Lives, Brighter Futures: The Strategy for Children and Young People's Health*. London: Department of Health and Department for Children, Schools and Families.

375 See Health Scotland. *Starting Well? What is Triple P?* Accessed on 24 January 2011 at: www.healthscotland. com/uploads/documents/swsection%208.pdf; see also the Institute for Applied Health. Accessed on 24 January 2011 at: www.gcu.ac.uk/iahr/globalprojects/triplep/.

376 Barnes, J., Ball, M., Meadows, P., Belsky, J. and the FNP Implementation Research Team (2009) *Nurse–Family Partnership Programme, Second Year Pilot Sites Implementation in England: The Infancy Period*. London: Department for Children, Schools and Families and Department of Health.

377 See for instance Hutchings, J., Bywater, T., Williams, M.E., Shakespeare, M.K. and Whitaker, C. (2009) *Evidence for the Extended School Aged Incredible Years Parent Programme with Parents of High-Risk 8 to 16 Year Olds*. Bangor: School of Psychology, Bangor University. Also see Webster-Stratton, C. and Reid, J. (2010) 'Adapting the Incredible Years, an evidence-based parenting programme, for families involved in the child welfare system.' *Journal of Children's Services 5*, 1, 25–42.

378 Further information about such programmes can be found in the two reviews of evidence: Barlow, J. and Schrader McMillan, A. (2010) *Safeguarding Children from Emotional Maltreatment: What Works*. London: Jessica Kingsley Publishers; Montgomery, P., Gardner, F., Ramchandani, P. and Bjornstad, G. (2009) *Systematic Reviews of Interventions following Physical Abuse: Helping Practitioners and Expert Witnesses Improve the Outcomes of Child Abuse*. Report to Department for Children, Schools and Families. Oxford: University of Oxford.

379 Parents Under Pressure: see Barlow and Schrader McMillan (2010) *op. cit.* pp.79–80.

380 For further information see Barlow and Schrader McMillan (2010) *op. cit.* pp.68–70 and MacMillan, H.L., Wathen, C.N., Barlow, J., Fergusson, D.M., Leventhal, D.M., and Taussig, H.N. (2009) 'Child maltreatment 3: Interventions to prevent child maltreatment and associated impairment.' *The Lancet 373*, 9659, 250–266, p.253.

381 For further information see Barlow and Schrader McMillan (2010) *op. cit.* pp.93–94 and Montgomery, Gardner, Ramchandani and Bjornstad (2009) *op. cit.*

382 For further information see Barlow and Schrader McMillan (2010) *op. cit.* pp.98–99.

383 For further information see Montgomery, Gardner, Ramchandani and Bjornstad (2009) *op. cit.* pp.31–32 and MacMillan, Wathen, Barlow, Fergusson, Leventhal and Taussig (2009) *op. cit.* pp.250–266.

384 Swenson, C., Schaeffer, C., Henggeler, S., Faldowski, R. and Mayhew, A. (2010) 'Multi-Systemic Therapy for Child Abuse and Neglect: A randomised controlled effectiveness trial.' *Journal of Family Psychology 24*, 497–507.

385 For further information see Montgomery, Gardner, Ramchandani and Bjornstad (2009) *op. cit.* pp.25–26.

386 *Ibid.* pp.24–25.

387 *Ibid.* pp.23–24.

388 Garland, A.F., Hawley, K.M., Brookman-Frazee, L. and Hurlburt, M.S. (2008) 'Identifying common elements of evidence-based psychosocial treatments for children's disruptive behaviour problems.' *Journal of the American Academy of Child and Adolescent Psychiatry 47*, 5, 505–514.

389 See, for instance, Becker, S., Sempik, J. and McCrossen, V. (2003) *Mapping Therapeutic Service Provision and Approaches Used by Learning Support Units in Nottingham City Secondary Schools: First Report – LSU Managers' Perceptions*. Loughborough: Centre for Child and Family Research, Loughborough University, and Nottingham City Education Department.

390 Farmer, E. and Lutman, E. (forthcoming) *Working Effectively with Neglected Children and their Families – Understanding their Experiences and Long-Term Outcomes.* London: Jessica Kingsley Publishers.

391 Wade, J., Biehal, N., Farrelly, N. and Sinclair, I. (2011) *Caring for Abused and Neglected Children: Making the Right Decisions for Reunification or Long-Term Care.* London: Jessica Kingsley Publishers.

392 Ward, H., Brown, R., Westlake, D. and Munro, E.R. (forthcoming) *Safeguarding Babies and Very Young Children from Abuse and Neglect.* London: Jessica Kingsley Publishers.

393 Wade, Biehal, Farrelly and Sinclair (2011) *op. cit.*

394 Forrester, D. and Harwin, J. (2008) 'Parental substance misuse and child welfare: Outcomes for children two years after referral.' *British Journal of Social Work 38,* 1518–1535.

395 Ward, H., Skuse, T. and Munro, E.R. (2005) 'The best of times, the worst of times: Young people's views of care and accommodation.' *Adoption and Fostering 29,* 1, 8–17.

396 Skuse, T. and Ward, H. (2003) *Outcomes for Looked After Children: Children's Views, the Importance of Listening. An Interim Report to the Department of Health.* Loughborough: Centre for Child and Family Research, Loughborough University.

397 Sinclair, I., Baker, C., Lee, J. and Gibbs, I. (2007) *The Pursuit of Permanence: A Study of the English Child Care System.* London: Jessica Kingsley Publishers.

398 Ward, H. (2009) 'Patterns of instability. Moves within the English care system: Their reasons, contexts and consequences.' *Child and Youth Services Review 31,* 1113–1118.

399 Stein, M. and Munro, E.R. (eds) (2008) *Young People's Transitions from Care to Adulthood: International Research and Practice.* London: Jessica Kingsley Publishers.

400 See Skuse and Ward (2003) *op cit.*

401 *Ibidem*

402 Scott, S., Knapp, M., Henderson, J. and Maugham, B. (2001) 'Financial cost of social exclusion: Follow up study of antisocial children into adulthood.' *British Medical Journal 323,* 191–196.

403 Ward, H., Holmes, L. and Soper, J. (2008) *Costs and Consequences of Placing Children in Care.* London: Jessica Kingsley Publishers.

Appendices

404 For further information see Barlow, J. and Schrader McMillan, A. (2010) *Safeguarding Children from Emotional Maltreatment: What Works.* London: Jessica Kingsley Publishers, pp.79–80.

405 See Dawe, S. and Harnett, P.H. (2007) 'Reducing potential for child abuse among methadone-maintained parents: Results from a randomized controlled trial.' *Journal of Substance Abuse Treatment 32,* 381–390.

406 Parents Under Pressure. Accessed on 24 January 2011 at: www.pupprogramme.net.au.

407 Dawe and Harnett (2007) *op. cit.*

408 Personal communication from steering group members.

409 See National Academy for Parenting Research. Accessed on 24 January 2011 at: www.parentingresearch.org.uk/Projects.aspx?ID=3.

410 For further information see Barlow and Schrader McMillan (2010) *op. cit.* pp. 68–70 and MacMillan, H.L., Wathen, C.N., Barlow, J., Fergusson, D.M., Leventhal, D.M. and Taussig, H.N. (2009) 'Child maltreatment 3: Interventions to prevent child maltreatment and associated impairment.' *The Lancet 373,* 9659, 250–266, p.253.

411 Sanders, M.R., Pidgeon, A.M., Gravestock, F., Connors, M.D., Brown, S. and Young, R.W. (2004) 'Does parental attributional retraining and anger management enhance the effects of the Triple P-Positive Parenting Programme with parents at risk of child maltreatment?' *Behavioural Therapy 35,* 513–535.

412 Prinz, R.J., Sanders, M.R., Shapiro, C.J., Whitaker, D.J. and Lutzker, J.R. (2009) 'Population-based prevention of child maltreatment: The US Triple P system population trial.' *Prevention Science 10,* 1, 1–12.

413 Iwaniec, D. (2007) *The Emotionally Abused and Neglected Child: Identification, Assessment and Intervention.* Chichester: John Wiley and Sons.

414 See Triple P Programme. Accessed on 24 January 2011 at: www.triplep.net/.

415 Stern, S.B. and Azar, S.T. (1998) 'Integrating cognitive strategies into behavioural treatment for abusive parents and families with aggressive adolescents.' *Clinical Child Psychology and Psychiatry 3,* 387–403.

416 For further information see Barlow and Schrader McMillan (2010) *op. cit.* pp.70–73.

417 Iwaniec, D. (1997) 'Evaluating parent training for emotionally abusive and neglectful parents: Comparing individual versus individual and group intervention.' *Research in Social Work Practice 7,* 3, 329–349.

418 For further information see Barlow and Schrader McMillan (2010) *op. cit.* pp.93–94 and Montgomery, P., Gardner, F., Ramchandani, P. and Bjornstad, G. (2009) *Systematic Reviews of Interventions following Physical Abuse: Helping Practitioners and Expert Witnesses Improve the Outcomes of Child Abuse.* Unpublished report to DCSF. Oxford: University of Oxford.

419 Toth, S., Maughan, A., Todd Manly, J., Spagnola, M. and Cicchetti, C. (2002) 'The relative efficacy of two interventions in altering maltreated preschool children's representational models: Implications for attachment theory.' *Development and Psychopathology 14*, 887–908.

420 For further information see Barlow and Schrader McMillan (2010) *op.cit.* pp.98–9.

421 Benoit, D., Madigan, S., Lecce, S., Shea, B. and Goldberg, S. (2001) 'Atypical maternal behaviour toward feeding-disordered infants before and after intervention.' *Infant Mental Health Journal 22*, 6, 611–626.

422 For further information see Montgomery, Gardner, Ramchandani and Bjornstad (2009) *op. cit.* pp.31–32 and MacMillan, Wathen, Barlow, Fergusson, Leventhal and Taussig (2009) *op. cit.*

423 Chaffin, M., Silovsky, J.F., Funderburk, B., Valle, L.A., Brestan, E.V., Balachova, T. *et al.* (2004) 'Parent–Child Interaction Therapy with physically abusive parents: Efficacy for reducing future abuse reports.' *Journal of Consulting and Clinical Psychology 72*, 3, 500–510.

424 Parent–Child Interaction Therapy (PCIT). Accessed on 24 January 2011 at: http://pcit.phhp.ufl.edu.

425 Parent–Child Interaction Therapy International (PCIT International). Accessed on 24 January 2011 at: www.pcit.org.

426 Child Welfare Information Gateway: Protecting children, strengthening families. Accessed on 1 December 2010 at www.childwelfare.gov.

427 Swenson, C., Penman, J., Henggeler, S. and Rowland, M. (2010) *Multisystemic Therapy for Child Abuse and Neglect.* Charleston, SC: Family Services Research Center, MUSC.

428 Swenson, C., Schaeffer, C., Henggeler, S., Faldowski, R. and Mayhew, A. (2010) 'Multi-Systemic Therapy for Child Abuse and Neglect: A randomised controlled effectiveness trial.' *Journal of Family Psychology 24*, 497–507.

429 For further information see Montgomery, Gardner, Ramchandani and Bjornstad (2009) *op. cit.* pp.25–26.

430 Moore, E., Armsden, G. and Gogerty, P.L. (1998) 'A twelve-year follow up study of maltreated and at-risk children who received early therapeutic child care.' *Child Maltreatment 3*, 3–16.

431 For further information see Montgomery, Gardner, Ramchandani and Bjornstad (2009) *op. cit.* pp.24–25.

432 Fantuzzo, J., Sutton-Smith, B., Atkins, M., Meyers, R., Stevenson, H., Coolahan, K., Weiss, A. and Manz, P. (1996) 'Community-based resilient peer treatment of withdrawn maltreated preschool children.' *Journal of Consulting and Clinical Psychology 64*, 1377–1386.

433 Head Start is a programme implemented in the US that provides comprehensive education, health, nutrition and parent involvement services to low-income children and their families. Education includes preschool education to national standards that have become de facto standards for all US preschools. Health services include screenings, health check-ups and dental check-ups. Social services provide family advocates to work with parents and assist them in accessing community resources for low-income families.

434 For further information see Montgomery, Gardner, Ramchandani and Bjornstad (2009) *op. cit.* pp.23–24.

435 Fisher, P.A., Burraston, B. and Pears, K. (2005) 'The Early Intervention Foster Care Programme: Permanent placement outcomes from a randomized trial.' *Child Maltreatment 10*, 61–71.

436 Fisher, P.A. and Kim, H.K. (2007) 'Intervention effects on foster preschoolers' attachment-related behaviours from a randomized trial.' *Prevention Science 8*, 161–170.

437 Fisher, Burraston and Pears (2005) *op. cit.*

438 That is, the probability of this happening by chance is less than 5 per cent.

439 Fisher, P.A., Stoomiller, M., Gunner, M.R. and Burraston, B.O. (2007) 'Effects of a therapeutic intervention for foster pre-schoolers on diurnal cortisol activity.' *Psychoneuroendocrinology 32*, 892–906.

440 Fisher and Kim (2007) *op. cit.*

441 Department for Children, Schools and Families (2010) *Working Together to Safeguard Children.* London: Department for Children, Schools and Families, Para. 3.22.

References

Advisory Council on the Misuse of Drugs (2003) *Hidden Harm: Responding to the Needs of Children of Problem Drug Users.* London: Home Office.

Alarm Distress Baby Scale (ADBB) Available at www.adbb.net/gb-intro.html, accessed on 3 August 2011.

Allen, G. (2011) *Early Intervention: The Next Steps.* London: HM Government.

Andrews, A.B. (1996) 'Public opinions about what a citizen can do to help abused and neglected children in addictive families.' *Journal of Community Practice 3*, 1, 19–33.

Angeles Cerezo, M. and Pons-Salvador, G. (2004) 'Improving child maltreatment detection systems: A large-scale case study involving health, social services, and school professionals.' *Child Abuse and Neglect 28*, 1153–1170.

Appleton, J.V. (1996) 'Working with vulnerable families: A health visiting perspective.' *Journal of Advanced Nursing 23*, 5, 912–918.

Asen, E. (2002) 'Outcome research in family therapy.' *Advances in Psychiatric Treatment 8*, 3, 230–238.

Asthana, A. (Policy Editor) (2010) 'Sure Start children's centres told to charge for some services.' *The Observer*, 14 November.

Ayre, P. (1998) 'Assessment of significant harm: Improving professional practice.' *British Journal of Nursing 7*, 1, 31–36.

Barlow, J. (2006) 'Home Visiting Programmes for Parents of Pre-School Children: The UK Experience.' In C. McAuley, P. Pecora and W. Rose (eds) *Effective Interventions for Children and Families.* London: Jessica Kingsley Publishers.

Barlow, J. and Schrader McMillan, A. (2010) *Safeguarding Children from Emotional Maltreatment: What Works.* London: Jessica Kingsley Publishers.

Barlow, J. and Scott, J. (2010) *Safeguarding Children in the 21st Century: Where to Now?* Totnes: Research in Practice. Available at www.rip.org.uk, accessed on 16 May 2011.

Barlow, J., Simkiss, D. and Stewart-Brown, S. (2006) 'Interventions to prevent or ameliorate child physical abuse and neglect: Findings from a systematic review.' *Journal of Children's Services 1*, 6–28.

Barnard, M. (2007) *Drug Addiction and Families.* London: Jessica Kingsley Publishers.

Barnes, J., Ball, M., Meadows, P., Belsky, J. and the FNP Implementation Research Team (2009) *Nurse–Family Partnership Programme, Second Year Pilot Sites Implementation in England: The Infancy Period.* London: Department for Children, Schools and Families and Department of Health.

Becker, S., Sempik, J. and McCrossen, V. (2003) *Mapping Therapeutic Service Provision and Approaches Used by Learning Support Units in Nottingham City Secondary Schools: First Report – LSU Managers' Perceptions.* Loughborough: Centre for Child and Family Research, Loughborough University and Nottingham City Education Department.

Benoit, D., Madigan, S., Lecce, S., Shea, B. and Goldberg, S. (2001) 'Atypical maternal behaviour toward feeding-disordered infants before and after intervention.' *Infant Mental Health Journal 22*, 6, 611–626.

Binggeli, N., Hart, S.N. and Brassard, M.R. (2001) *Psychological Maltreatment of Children.* London: Sage.

Biringen, Z. (2000) 'Emotional availability: Conceptualization and research findings.' *American Journal of Orthopsychiatry 70*, 104–114.

Boulton, S. and Hindle, D. (2000) 'Emotional abuse: The work of a multi-disciplinary consultation group in a child psychiatric service.' *Clinical Child Psychology and Psychiatry 5*, 3, 439–452.

Brandon, M., Bailey, S. and Belderson, P. (2010) *Building on the Learning from Serious Case Reviews: A Two-Year Analysis of Child Protection Database Notifications 2007–2009.* London: Department for Education.

Brandon, M., Bailey, S., Belderson, P., Gardner, R. *et al.* (2009) *Understanding Serious Case Reviews and their Impact. A Biennial Analysis of Serious Case Reviews 2005–2007.* DCSF-RR129. London: Department for Children, Schools and Families.

Brandon, M., Belderson, P., Warren, C., Howe, D. *et al.* (2008) *Analysing Child Deaths and Serious Injury through Abuse and Neglect: What can we Learn? A Biennial Analysis of Serious Case Reviews 2003–2005.* DCSF-RR023. London: Department for Children, Schools and Families.

Brandon, M., Howe, A., Dagley, V., Salter, C. and Warren, C. (2006) 'What appears to be helping or hindering practitioners in implementing the Common Assessment Framework and lead professional working?' *Child Abuse Review 15*, 390–413.

Brandon, M., Sidebotham, P., Ellis, C., Bailey, S. and Belderson, P. (2011) *Child and Family Practitioners' Understanding of Child Development: Lessons Learnt from a Small Sample of Serious Case Reviews.* London: Department for Education.

Bronfenbrenner, U. (1979) *The Ecology of Human Development: Experiments by Nature and Design.* Cambridge, MA: Harvard University Press.

Bull, J., McCormick, G., Swann, C. and Mulivihill, C. (2004) *Ante-Natal and Post-Natal Home-Visiting Programmes: A Review of Reviews. Evidence Briefing. First Edition.* London: Health Development Agency.

Campbell, R., Starkey, F., Holliday, J., Audrey, S. *et al.* (2008) 'An informal school-based peer-led intervention for smoking prevention in adolescence (ASSIST): A cluster randomised trial.' *The Lancet 371,* 1595–1602.

Carpenter, J., Hackett, S., Patsios, D. and Szilassy, E. (2010) *Outcomes of Inter-Agency Training to Safeguard Children.* Research Report DCSF-RR209. London: DCSF.

Carpenter, J., Patsios, D., Szilassy, E. and Hackett, S. (2011) *Connect, Share and Learn: A Toolkit for Evaluating the Outcomes of Inter-Agency Training to Safeguard Children.* London: NSPCC.

Carpenter, M., Kennedy, M., Armstrong, A.L. and Moore, E. (1997) 'Indicators of abuse and neglect in preschool children's drawings.' *Journal of Psychosocial Nursing and Mental Health Services 35,* 40, 10–17.

Carr, A. (2000) *Family Therapy: Concepts, Process and Practice.* Chichester: John Wiley & Sons Ltd.

Carr, A. (2006) 'Thematic review of family therapy journals in 2005.' *Journal of Family Therapy 28,* 4, 420–439.

Chaffin, M., Silovsky, J.F., Funderburk, B., Valle, L.A. *et al.* (2004) 'Parent–Child Interaction Therapy with physically abusive parents: Efficacy for reducing future abuse reports.' *Journal of Consulting and Clinical Psychology 72,* 3, 500–510.

Chester, D.L., Jose, R.M., Aldlyami, E., King, H. and Moiemen, N.S. (2006) 'Non-accidental burns in children: Are we neglecting neglect?' *Burns 32,* 2, 222–228.

Chief Inspector of Social Services, Commission for Health Improvement, HM Chief Inspector of Constabulary, HM Chief Inspector of the Crown Prosecution Service, HM Chief Inspector of Schools and HM Chief Inspector of Prisons (2002) *Safeguarding Children: A Joint Chief Inspectors' Report on Arrangements to Safeguard Children.* London: Department of Health.

Children Act (2004) London: HMSO.

Child Welfare Information Gateway: Protecting children, strengthening families. Available at www.childwelfare.gov, accessed on 3 August 2011.

Chorpita, B.F. and Daleidin, E.L. (2009) 'Mapping evidence-based treatments for children and adolescents: Application of the distillation and matching model to 615 treatments from 322 randomized trials.' *Journal of Consulting and Clinical Psychology 77,* 3, 566–579.

Cicchetti, D., Rogosch, F. and Toth, S. (2006) 'Fostering secure attachment in infants in maltreating families through preventive interventions.' *Development and Psychopathology 18,* 623–649.

Cleaver, H. and Nicholson, D. (2007) *Parental Learning Disability and Children's Needs: Family Experiences and Effective Practice.* London: Jessica Kingsley Publishers.

Cleaver, H., Nicholson, D., Tarr, S. and Cleaver, D. (2007) *Child Protection, Domestic Violence and Parental Substance Misuse: Family Experiences and Effective Practice.* London: Jessica Kingsley Publishers.

Cleaver, H., Unell, I. and Aldgate, J. (2011) *Children's Needs – Parenting Capacity. The Impact of Parental Mental Illness, Learning Disability, Problem Alcohol and Drug Use and Domestic Violence on Children's Safety (2nd Edition).* London: The Stationery Office.

Cleaver, H. and Walker, S. (2004) 'From policy to practice: The implementation of a new framework for social work assessments of children and families.' *Child and Family Social Work 9,* 1, 81–90.

Cleaver, H., Walker, S., Scott, J., Cleaver, D. *et al.* (2008) *The Integrated Children's System: Enhancing Social Work and Inter-agency Practice.* London: Jessica Kingsley Publishers.

Compton, S.N., March, J.S., Brent, D., Albano, A.M.V., Weersing, R. and Curry, J. (2004) 'Cognitive-behavioral psychotherapy for anxiety and depressive disorders in children and adolescents: An evidence-based medicine review.' *Journal of the American Academy of Child and Adolescent Psychiatry 43,* 930–959.

Coohey, C. (1996) 'Child maltreatment: Testing the social isolation hypothesis.' *Child Abuse and Neglect 20,* 3, 241–254.

Crittenden Care Index: Family Relations Institute. Available at www.patcrittenden.com/include/care-index.htm, accessed on 3 August 2011.

Crittenden, P.M. (1981) 'Abusing, neglecting, problematic and adequate dyads: Differentiating by patterns of interaction.' *Merril-Palmer Quarterly 27,* 1–18.

Cuijpers, P. (2002) 'Peer-led and adult-led school drug prevention: A meta-analytic comparison.' *Journal of Drug Education 32,* 2, 107–119.

Daniel, B., Taylor, J. and Scott, J. (2011) *Recognizing and Helping the Neglected Child: Evidence-Based Practice for Assessment and Intervention.* London: Jessica Kingsley Publishers.

Daniel, B., Taylor, J. and Scott, J. (forthcoming) *Training Resources on Child Neglect for a Multi-Agency Audience.*

Dawe, S. and Harnett, P. (2007) 'Reducing potential for child abuse among methadone-maintained parents: Results from a randomized controlled trial.' *Journal of Substance Abuse Treatment 32,* 4, 381–390.

De Bellis, M.D. (2005) 'Psychobiology of neglect.' *Child Maltreatment 10,* 2, 150–172.

Department for Children, Schools and Families (2009a) *Building a Safe, Confident Future: The Final Report of the Social Work Taskforce.* London: Department for Children, Schools and Families.

Department for Children, Schools and Families (2009b) *Referrals, Assessment and Children and Young People who are the Subject of a Child Protection Plan, England – Year Ending March 31 2009.* Available at www.data.gov.uk/dataset/referrals

Department for Children, Schools and Families (2010) *Working Together to Safeguard Children.* London: Department for Children, Schools and Families.

Department for Children, Schools and Families (2011) *Common Assessment Framework (CAF).* Available at www.education.gov.uk/childrenandyoungpeople/strategy/integratedworking/caf, accessed on 15 April 2011.

Department for Communities and Local Government: Newsroom, 14 October 2010. Ministerial Statement by Rt Hon Eric Pickles: *Local Government Accountability*.

Department for Education (2003) (Cm 5860) *Every Child Matters*. London: The Stationery Office.

Department for Education (2010a) *Reform of Children's Trusts. Safeguarding and Social Work Reform*. News release: 22 July. Available at www.education.gov.uk, accessed on 19 May 2011.

Department for Education (2010b) *More Freedom and Flexibility: A New Approach for Children's Trust Boards, Children and Young People's Plans, and the 'Duty to Cooperate'*. News release, 3 November 2010. London: Department for Education.

Department for Education (2010c) *Secretary of State for Education's Letter to Local Authorities: 4 November 2010*. London: Department for Education.

Department for Education (2010d) *Children in Need in England, including their Characteristics and Further Information on Children who were the Subject of a Child Protection Plan (2009–2010 Children in Need Census, Final)*. London: Department for Education.

Department for Education (2010e) *Response to Public Comments on Coalition Agreement on Families and Children*. London: Department for Education.

Department for Education (2010f) (Cm 7980) *The Importance of Teaching: The Schools White Paper*. London: The Stationery Office.

Department for Education and Skills (2006) *Common Assessment Framework for Children and Young People: Practitioners' Guide for Service Managers and Practitioners*. London: The Stationery Office.

Department of Health (1995) *Child Protection: Messages from Research*. London: HMSO.

Department of Health (2009) *Healthy Lives, Brighter Futures: The Strategy for Children and Young People's Health*. London: Department of Health and Department for Children, Schools and Families.

Department of Health (2009, updated 2010a) *The Pregnancy Book*. London: Department of Health.

Department of Health (2009, updated 2010b) *Birth to Five*. London: Department of Health.

Department of Health (2010) (cm 7881) *Equity and Excellence: Liberating the NHS*. London: The Stationery Office.

Department of Health, Department for Education and Employment and Home Office (2000) *Framework for the Assessment of Children in Need and their Families*. London: The Stationery Office.

Department of Health and Department for Education and Skills (2004) *National Service Framework for Children, Young People and Maternity Services*. London: Department for Education and Skills and Department of Health.

DeVore, E.R. and Ginsburg, K.R. (2005) 'The protective effects of good parenting on adolescents.' *Current Opinion in Pediatrics 17*, 4, 460–465.

Dretzke, J., Frew, E., Davenport, C., Barlow, J. *et al.* (2005) 'The effectiveness and cost-effectiveness of parent training/ education programmes for the treatment of conduct disorder, including oppositional defiant disorder, in children.' *Health Technology Assessment 9*, 50.

Durrant, J.E. (1999) 'Evaluating the success of Sweden's corporal punishment ban.' *Child Abuse and Neglect 23*, 5, 435–448.

Egeland, B. (2009) 'Taking stock: Child emotional maltreatment and developmental psychology.' *Child Abuse and Neglect 33*, 22–26.

Eyberg, S.M., Besmear, J., Edwards, D. and Robinson, E. (1994) 'Manual for the dyadic Parent–Child Interaction Coding System II.' *Social and Behavioural Sciences Documents* (MS no: 2898).

Fantuzzo, J., Sutton-Smith, B., Atkins, M., Meyers, R. *et al.* (1996) 'Community-based resilient peer treatment of withdrawn maltreated preschool children.' *Journal of Consulting and Clinical Psychology 64*, 1377–1386.

Farmer, E. and Lutman, E. (forthcoming) *Working Effectively with Neglected Children and their Families – Understanding their Experienced and Long-Term Outcomes*. London: Jessica Kingsley Publishers.

Farmer, E. and Moyers, S. (2008) *Kinship Care: Fostering Effective Family and Friends Placements*. London: Jessica Kingsley Publishers.

Fauth, R., Jelecic, H., Hart, D., Burton, S. and Shemmings, D. (2010) *Effective Practice to Protect Children Living in 'Highly Resistant' Families*. London: C4EO (www.c4eo.org.uk).

Field, F. (2010) *The Foundation Years: Preventing Poor Children from Becoming Poor Adults*. London: HM Government.

Finkelhor, D. (2008) *Childhood Victimization: Violence, Crime, and Abuse in the Lives of Young People*. Oxford: Oxford University Press.

Fisher, P.A., Burraston, B. and Pears, K. (2005) 'The Early Intervention Foster Care Programme: Permanent placement outcomes from a randomized trial.' *Child Maltreatment 10*, 61–71.

Fisher, P.A., Chamberlain, P. and Leve, L. (2009) 'Improving the lives of foster children through evidence-based interventions.' *Vulnerable Children and Youth Studies 4*, 2, 122–127.

Fisher, P.A. and Kim, H.K. (2007) 'Intervention effects on foster preschoolers' attachment-related behaviours from a randomized trial.' *Prevention Science 8*, 161–170.

Fisher, P.A., Stoomiller, M., Gunner, M.R. and Burraston, B.O. (2007) 'Effects of a therapeutic intervention for foster pre-schoolers on diurnal cortisol activity.' *Psychoneuroendocrinology 32*, 892–906.

Fluke, J. (2008) 'Child protective services rereporting and recurrence: Context and considerations regarding research.' *Child Abuse and Neglect 32*, 8, 749–751.

Forrester, D. and Harwin, J. (2008) 'Parental substance misuse and child welfare: Outcomes for children two years after referral.' *British Journal of Social Work 38*, 1518–1535.

France, A., Munro, E.R. and Waring, A. (2010) *The Evaluation of Arrangements for Effective Operation of the New Local Safeguarding Children Boards in England – Final Report.* DFE-RR027. London: Department for Education.

Fraser, L. (1995) 'Eastfield Ming Quong: Multiple-Impact In-Home Treatment Model.' In L. Combrick-Graham (ed.) *Children and Families at Risk.* New York, NY: Guilford Press.

Freisthler, B., Merrit, D.H. and LaScala, E.A. (2006) 'Understanding the ecology of child maltreatment: A review of the literature and directions for future research.' *Child Maltreatment 11,* 3, 263–280.

Fukkink, R. (2008) 'Video feedback in widescreen: A meta-analysis of family programmes.' *Clinical Psychology Review 28,* 6, 904–916.

Gardner, F., Burton, J. and Klimes, I. (2006) 'Randomised controlled trial of a parenting intervention in the voluntary sector for reducing child conduct problems: Outcomes and mechanisms for change.' *Journal of Child Psychology and Psychiatry 47,* 1123–1132.

Garland, A.F., Bickman, L. and Chorpita, B.F. (2010) 'Change what? Identifying quality improvement targets by investigating usual mental health care.' *Administration in Policy and Mental Health 37,* 15–26.

Garland, A.F., Hawley, K.M., Brookman-Frazee, L. and Hurlburt, M.S. (2008) 'Identifying common elements of evidence-based psychosocial treatments for children's disruptive behaviour problems.' *Journal of the American Academy of Child and Adolescent Psychiatry 47,* 5, 505–514.

Gaudin, J.M. (1993) 'Effective intervention with neglectful families.' *Criminal Justice and Behaviour 20,* 1, 66–89.

Gilbert, R., Kemp, A., Thoburn, J., Sidebotham, P. *et al.* (2009) 'Child maltreatment 2: Recognising and responding to child maltreatment.' *The Lancet 10,* 373, 167–180.

Gilbert, R.E., Widom, C., Browne, K., Fergusson, D., Webb, E. and Janson, S. (2009) 'Child maltreatment 1: Burden and consequences of child maltreatment in high income countries.' *The Lancet 373,* 68–81.

Glaser, D. (2000) 'Child abuse and neglect and the brain: A review.' *The Journal of Child Psychiatry and Psychology 41,* 1, 97–116.

Glaser, D., Prior, V., Auty, K. and Tilki, S. (2010) *Does Training and Consultation in a Systematic Approach to Emotional Abuse (FRAMEA) Improve the Quality of Children's Services?* Unpublished report to Department for Education.

Guedeney, A. and Fermanian, J. (2001) 'A validity and reliability study of assessment and screening for sustained withdrawal reaction in infancy: The Alarm Distress Baby Scale.' *Infant Mental Health Journal 22,* 5, 559–575.

Hannon, C., Wood, C. and Bazalgette, L. (2010) *In Loco Parentis.* London: DEMOS.

Hardy, B., Turrell, A. and Wistow, G. (1992) *Innovations in Community Care Management.* Aldershot: Avebury.

Haringey Local Safeguarding Children Board (2010) *Serious Case Review: Child A, March 2009.* London: Department for Education.

Harnett, P. (2007) 'A procedure for assessing parents' capacity for change in child protection cases.' *Children and Youth Services Review 29,* 1179–1188.

Harnett, P. and Dawe, S. (2008) 'Reducing child abuse potential for child abuse among families: Implications for assessment and treatment.' *Brief Treatment and Crisis Intervention 8,* 226–235.

Health Scotland. *Starting Well? What is Triple P?* Available at www.healthscotland.com/uploads/documents/swsection%208.pdf, accessed on 20 May 2011.

Hicks, L. and Stein, M. (2010) *Neglect Matters: A Multi-Agency Guide for Professionals Working Together on Behalf of Teenagers.* London: Department for Education. Available at http://php.york.ac.uk/inst/spru/pubs/ipp.php?id=1563, accessed 23 September 2011.

Hicks, L. and Stein, M. in collaboration with the Children's Society and the NSPCC (2010) *Neglect Matters: A Guide for Young People about Neglect.* London: ChildLine.

Hindley, N., Ramchandani, P.G. and Jones, D.P.H. (2006) 'Risk factors for recurrence of maltreatment: A systematic review.' *Archives of Disease in Childhood 91,* 9, 744–752.

HM Government (2010) *Working Together to Safeguard Children: A Guide to Inter-Agency Working to Safeguard and Promote the Welfare of Children.* London: Department for Children, Schools and Families.

HM Treasury (2010) (Cm 7942) *Spending Review.* London: The Stationery Office.

Holmes, L. and McDermid, S. (forthcoming) *Understanding the Costs of Child Welfare.* London: Jessica Kingsley Publishers.

Holmes, L., Munro, E.R. and Soper, J. (2010) *Calculating the Cost and Capacity Implications for Local Authorities Implementing the Laming (2009) Recommendations.* London: LGA.

Holmes, L., Westlake, D. and Ward, H. (2009) *Calculating and Comparing the Costs of Multidimensional Treatment Foster Care, England (MTFCE).* Report to the Department for Children, Schools and Families. Loughborough: Centre for Child and Family Research, Loughborough University.

Howe, D. (2005) *Child Abuse and Neglect: Attachment, Development and Intervention.* Basingstoke: Palgrave Macmillan.

Hultman, C.S., Priolo, D., Cairns, B.A., Grant, E.J., Peterson, H.D. and Meyer, A.A. (1998) 'Psychosocial forum. Return to jeopardy: The fate of pediatric burn patients who are victims of abuse and neglect…including commentary by Doctor M.' *Journal of Burn Care & Rehabilitation 19,* 4, 367–376.

Hunt, J., Waterhouse, S. and Lutman, E. (2008) *Keeping Them in the Family: Outcomes for Abused and Neglected Children Placed with Family and Friends Carers through Care Proceedings.* London: BAAF.

Hutchings, J., Bywater, T., Daley, D., Gardner, F. *et al.* (2007) 'Parenting intervention in Sure Start services for children at risk of developing conduct disorder: Pragmatic randomised controlled trial.' *British Medical Journal 334*, 678–682.

Hutchings, J., Bywater, T., Williams, M.E., Shakespeare, M.K. and Whitaker, C. (2009) *Evidence for the Extended School Aged Incredible Years Parent Programme with Parents of High-Risk 8 to 16 Year Olds.* Bangor: School of Psychology, Bangor University.

Institute for Applied Health. Available at www.gcu.ac.uk/iahr/globalprojects/triplep/, accessed on 3 August 2011.

Iwaniec, D. (1997) 'Evaluating parent training for emotionally abusive and neglectful parents: Comparing individual versus individual and group intervention.' *Research in Social Work Practice 7*, 3, 329–349.

Iwaniec, D. (2007) *The Emotionally Abused and Neglected Child: Identification, Assessment and Intervention.* Chichester: John Wiley and Sons.

Jones, D.P.H. (2008) 'Child Maltreatment.' In M. Rutter, D. Bishop, D. Pine, S. Scott *et al.* (eds) *Rutter's Child and Adolescent Psychiatry. Fifth Edition.* Oxford: Blackwell Publishing.

Jones, D.P.H. (2009) 'Child Abuse and Neglect.' In M. Gelder, J. Lopez-Ibor and N. Andreasen (eds) *The New Oxford Textbook of Psychiatry. Second Edition.* Oxford: Oxford University Press.

Jones, D., Hindley, N. and Ramchandani, P. (2006) 'Making Plans: Assessment, Intervention and Evaluating Outcomes.' In J. Aldgate, D. Jones and C. Jeffery (eds) *The Developing World of the Child.* London: Jessica Kingsley Publishers.

Kim, J. (2009) 'Type-specific intergenerational transmission of neglectful and physically abusive parenting behaviours among young parents.' *Children and Youth Services Review 31*, 7, 761–767.

Klee, H., Jackson, M. and Lewis, S. (2002) *Drug Misuse and Motherhood.* London: Routledge.

Kolko, D.J. (1996) 'Individual cognitive behavioural treatment and family therapy for physically abused children and their offending parents: A comparison of clinical outcomes.' *Child Maltreatment 1*, 322–342.

Komulainen, S. and Haines, L. (2009) *Understanding Parent's Information Needs and Experiences where Professional Concerns Regarding Non-Accidental Injury were not Substantiated. Research Report.* London: Royal College of Paediatrics and Child Health (Department for Education Research Brief DCSF-RBX-09-02).

Kroll, B. and Taylor, A. (2003) *Parental Substance Misuse and Child Welfare.* London: Jessica Kingsley Publishers.

Laming, Lord (2003) (Cm 5730) *The Victoria Climbié Inquiry: Report of an Inquiry by Lord Laming.* London: The Stationery Office.

Laming, Lord (2009) (HC 330) *The Protection of Children in England: A Progress Report.* London: The Stationery Office.

Leslie, B. (2005) 'Housing Issues in Child Welfare: A Practice Response with Service and Policy Implications.' In J. Scott and H. Ward (eds) *Safeguarding and Promoting the Well-Being of Children, Families and Communities.* London: Jessica Kingsley Publishers.

Leve, L., Fisher, P. and Chamberlain, P. (2009) 'Multidimensional Treatment Foster Care as a preventive intervention to promote resiliency among youth in the child welfare system.' *Journal of Personality 77*, 6 1869–1902.

Longitudinal Studies of Child Abuse and Neglect (LONGSCAN) Available at www.iprc.unc.edu/longscan, accessed on 3 August 2011.

Macdonald, G.M. (2001) *Effective Interventions for Child Abuse and Neglect: An Evidence-Based Approach to Evaluating and Planning Interventions.* Chichester: John Wiley & Sons Ltd.

MacMillan, H.L., Wathen, C.N., Barlow, J., Fergusson, D.M., Leventhal, D.M. and Taussig, H.N. (2009) 'Child maltreatment 3: Interventions to prevent child maltreatment and associated impairment.' *The Lancet 373*, 9659, 250–266.

Mahony, Cardinal R. (1998) *Creating a Culture of Life* (unpublished letter).

Main, M. and Hesse, E. (1990) 'Parents' Unresolved Traumatic Experiences are Related to Infant Disorganised Attachment Status: Is Frightened and/or Frightening Parental Behaviour the Linking Mechanism?' In M.T. Greenberg, D. Cicchetti and E.M. Cummings (eds) *Attachment in the Preschool Years.* Chicago: University of Chicago Press.

Maiter, S., Alaggia, R. and Trocme, N. (2004) 'Perceptions of maltreatment by parents from the Indian sub-continent: Challenging myths about culturally based abusive parenting practices.' *Child Maltreatment 9*, 3, 309–324.

March, J.S., Amaya-Jackson, L., Murray, M.C. and Schulte, A. (1998) 'Cognitive-behavioral psychotherapy for children and adolescents with posttraumatic stress disorder after a single-incident stressor.' *Journal of the American Academy of Child and Adolescent Psychiatry 37*, 585–593.

Mattinson, J. (1975) *The Reflection Process in Case Work Supervision.* London: Institute of Marital Studies.

McConnell, D. and Llewellyn, G. (2002) 'Stereotypes, parents with intellectual disability and child protection.' *Journal of Social Welfare and Family Law 24*, 3, 297–317.

McCrory, E., De Brito, S. and Viding, E. (2010) 'Research review: The neurobiology and genetics of maltreatment and adversity.' *Journal of Child Psychology and Psychiatry 51*, 1079–1095.

Meezan, W. and O'Keefe, M. (1998) 'Evaluating the effectiveness of multifamily group therapy in child abuse and neglect.' *Research on Social Work Practice 8*, 330–353.

Moe, V. and Slinning, K. (2001) 'Children prenatally exposed to substances: Gender-related differences in outcome from infancy to 3 years of age.' *Infant Mental Health Journal 3*, 334–350.

Montgomery, P., Gardner, F., Ramchandani, P. and Bjornstad, G. (2009) *Systematic Reviews of Interventions following Physical Abuse: Helping Practitioners and Expert Witnesses Improve the Outcomes of Child Abuse.* Report to Department for Children, Schools and Families. Oxford: University of Oxford (Department for Education Research Brief DCSF-RBX-09-08A).

Moore, E., Armsden, G. and Gogerty, P.L. (1998) 'A twelve-year follow up study of maltreated and at-risk children who received early therapeutic child care.' *Child Maltreatment 3*, 3–16.

Morrell, C.J., Spiby, H., Stewart, P., Walters, S. and Morgan, A. (2000) 'Costs and effectiveness of community postnatal support workers: Randomised controlled trial.' *British Medical Journal 321*, 593–598.

Morrison, T. (2006) *Staff Supervision in Social Care: Making a Real Difference for Staff and Service Users. Third Edition.* Brighton: Pavilion.

Munro, E. (1999) 'Common errors of reasoning in child protection work.' *Child Abuse and Neglect 23*, 8, 745–758.

Munro, E. (2006) 'What tools do we need to improve identification of child abuse?' *Child Abuse Review 14*, 374–388.

Munro, E. (2010) *The Munro Review of Child Protection. Part One: A Systems Analysis.* London: Department for Education.

Munro, E. (2011a) *The Munro Review of Child Protection: Interim Report. A Child's Journey.* London: Department for Education.

Munro, E. (2011b) (cm 8062) *The Munro Review of Child Protection: Final Report. A Child-Centred System.* London: Department for Education.

Munro, E.R., Brown, R., Sempik, J. and Ward, H. with Owen, C. (2011) *Scoping Review to Draw Together Data on Child Injury and Safeguarding and to Compare the Position of England with that in Other Countries.* Research Report DFE-RR083. London: Department for Education.

Narducci, T. (2003) *Increasing the Effectiveness of the ACPC.* London: NSPCC.

National Academy for Parenting Research. Available at www.parentingresearch.org.uk/Projects.aspx?ID=3, accessed on 20 May 2011.

National Implementation Team (2010) *Multi-Dimensional Treatment Foster Care in England: Annual Project Report.* London: Department for Children, Schools and Families.

National Mental Health Development Unit. Available at www.nmhdu.org.uk/news/multi-systemic-therapy-new-therapy-brings-results-for-troubled-young-people/, accessed on 20 May 2011.

National Working Group on Child Protection and Disability (2003) *It Doesn't Happen to Disabled Children: Child Protection and Disabled Children.* London: NSPCC.

Nurse Family Partnership (2008) Available at http://cbpp-pcpe.phac-aspc.gc.ca/intervention_pdf/en/600.pdf, accessed on 20 May 2011.

O'Hagan, K. (2006) *Identifying Emotional and Psychological Abuse.* Maidenhead: Open University Press.

Olds, D.L., Eckenrode, J., Henderson, C.R., Kitzman, H. *et al.* (1997) 'Long-term effects of home visitation on maternal life course and child abuse and neglect: 15-year follow up of a randomized trial.' *Journal of the American Medical Association 278*, 637–643.

Olds, D.L., Henderson, C.R., Cole, R.C., Eckenrode, J. *et al.* (1998) 'Long-term effects of home visitation on children's criminal and anti social behaviour: 15-year follow up of a randomized trial.' *Journal of the American Medical Association 280*, 14, 1238–1244.

Olds, D.L., Henderson, C.R. and Kitzman, H. (1994) 'Does prenatal and infancy nurse home visitation have enduring effects on qualities of parental caregiving and child health at 25 to 50 months of life?' *Pediatrics 93*, 89–98.

Olds, D.L., Robinson, J., O'Brien, R., Luckey, D.W. *et al.* (2002) 'Home visiting by nurses and by paraprofessionals: A randomized controlled trial.' *Pediatrics 110*, 3, 486–496.

Paavilainen, E., Astedt-Kurki, P. and Panounen, M. (2000) 'School nurses' operational modes and ways of collaborating in caring for child abusing families in Finland.' *Journal of Clinical Nursing 9*, 5, 745–746.

Parent–Child Interaction Therapy (PCIT). Available at http://pcit.phhp.ufl.edu, accessed on 23 May 2011.

Parent–Child Interaction Therapy (PCIT International). Available at www.pcit.org, accessed on 3 Auguest 2011.

Parents Under Pressure. Available at www.pupprogramme.net.au, accessed on 23 May 2011.

Percy-Smith, J. (2006) 'What works in strategic partnerships for children: A research review.' *Children and Society 20*, 4, 313–323.

Prime Minister's Strategy Unit (2004) *Alcohol Harm Reduction Strategy for England.* London: Cabinet Office.

Prinz, R.J., Sanders, M.R., Shapiro, C.J., Whitaker, D.J. and Lutzker, J.R. (2009) 'Population-based prevention of child maltreatment: The US Triple P system population trial.' *Prevention Science 10*, 1, 1–12.

Radford, L., Corral, S., Bradley, C., Fisher, H. *et al.* (2011) *The Maltreatment and Victimisation of Children in the UK: NSPCC Report on a National Survey of Young People's, Young Adults' and Caregivers' Experiences.* London: NSPCC.

Rees, G. and Siakeu, J. (2004) *Thrown Away: The Experiences of Children Forced to Leave Home.* London: The Children's Society.

Rees, G., Stein, M., Hicks, L. and Gorin, S. (2011) *Adolescent Neglect: Research, Policy and Practice.* London: Jessica Kingsley Publishers.

Roldan, M.C., Galera, S. and O'Brien, B. (2005) 'Women living in a drug (and violence) context: The maternal role.' *Revista Latino-Americana de Enfermagem 13*, 1118–1126.

Rose, S.J. and Meezan, W. (1995) 'Child neglect: A study of the perceptions of mothers and child welfare workers.' *Children and Youth Services Review 17*, 4, 471–486.

Rose, S.J. and Meezan, W. (1996) 'Variations in perceptions of child neglect.' *Child Welfare Journal 75*, 2, 139–160.

Rose, S.J. and Selwyn, J. (2000) 'Child neglect: An English perspective.' *International Social Work 43*, 2, 179–192.

Royal College of General Practitioners (2009) *Safeguarding Children and Young People: A Toolkit for General Practice*. London: RCGP. Available at www.rcgp.org.uk/clinical_and_research/circ/innovation__evaluation/safeguarding_children_tookit.aspx, accessed on 23 May 2011.

Royal College of Paediatrics and Child Health (2010) *Safeguarding Children and Young People: Roles and Competences for Health Care Staff. Intercollegiate Document*. London: Royal College of Paediatrics and Child Health.

Safe on the Streets Research Team (1999) *Still Running – Children on the Streets in the UK*. London: The Children's Society.

Salas, E. and Cannon-Bowers, J. (2001) 'The science of training: A decade review of progress.' *Annual Review of Psychology 52*, 471–499.

Sanders, M.R. (2008) 'The Triple P-Positive Parenting Programme: A public health approach to parenting support.' *Journal of Family Psychology 22*, 506–517.

Sanders, M.R., Pidgeon, A.M., Gravestock, F., Connors, M.D., Brown, S. and Young, R.W. (2004) 'Does parental attributional retraining and anger management enhance the effects of the Triple P-Positive Parenting Programme with parents at risk of child maltreatment?' *Behavioural Therapy 35*, 513–535.

Sanders, R., Colton, M. and Roberts, S. (1999) 'Child abuse fatalities and cases of extreme concern: Lessons from reviews.' *Child Abuse and Neglect 23*, 3, 257–268.

Schore, A. (2010) 'Relational Trauma and the Developing Right Brain: The Neurobiology of Broken Attachment Bonds.' In T. Baradon (ed.) *Relational Trauma in Infancy: Psychoanalytic, Attachment and Neuropsychological Contributions to Parent–Infant Psychotherapy*. New York: Routledge.

Scott, S., Knapp, M., Henderson, J. and Maughan, B. (2001) 'Financial cost of social exclusion: Follow up study of antisocial children into adulthood.' *British Medical Journal 323*, 191–196.

Sergeant, H. (2006) *Handle with Care*. London: Centre for Policy Studies.

Sidebotham, P. (2003) 'Red skies, risk factors and early indicators. Invited comments on early indicators of child abuse and neglect: A multi-professional Delphi study by Catherine Powell.' *Child Abuse Review 12*, 41–45.

Simons-Morton, B.G., Hartos, J., Leaf, W. and Preusser, D. (2006) 'The effect on teen driving outcomes of the Checkpoints Programme in a state-wide trial.' *Accident Analysis and Prevention 38*, 907–912.

Sinclair, I., Baker, C., Lee, J. and Gibbs, I. (2007) *The Pursuit of Permanence: A Study of the English Child Care System*. London: Jessica Kingsley Publishers.

Skuse, T. and Ward, H. (2003) *Outcomes for Looked After Children: Children's Views, the Importance of Listening. An Interim Report to the Department of Health*. Loughborough: Centre for Child and Family Research, Loughborough University.

Social Work Reform Board (2010) *Building a Safe and Confident Future: One Year On*. London: HM Government.

Stallman, H., Walmsley, K., Bor, W., Collerson, M.E., Swenson, C. and McDermott, B. (2010) 'New directions in the treatment of child physical abuse and neglect in Australia: MST-CAN, a case study.' *Advances in Mental Health 9*, 148–161.

Stanton, B., Cole, M., Galbraith, J., Li, X. *et al.* (2004) 'Randomized trial of a parenting intervention.' *Archives of Pediatrics and Adolescent Medicine 158*, 947–955.

Stein, M. and Munro, E.R. (eds) (2008) *Young People's Transitions from Care to Adulthood: International Research and Practice*. London: Jessica Kingsley Publishers.

Stephenson, O. (1996) 'Emotional abuse and neglect: A time for reappraisal.' *Child and Family Social Work 1*, 1, 13–18.

Stevenson, O. (2007) *Neglected Children and their Families. Second Edition*. Oxford: Blackwell.

Stern, S.B. and Azar, S.T. (1998) 'Integrating cognitive strategies into behavioural treatment for abusive parents and families with aggressive adolescents.' *Clinical Child Psychology and Psychiatry 3*, 387–403.

Stith, S.M., Ting Lui, L., Davies, C., Boykin, E.L. *et al.* (2009) 'Risk factors in child maltreatment: A meta-analytic review of the literature.' *Aggression and Violent Behaviour 14*, 3–29.

Stratton, P. (2005) *Report on the Evidence Base of Systemic Family Therapy*. Warrington: Association for Family Therapy.

Sullivan, C.M. and Bybee, D. (1999) 'Reducing violence using community based advocacy for women with abusive partners.' *Journal of Consulting and Clinical Psychology 67*, 1, 43–53.

Swenson, C., Penman, J., Henggeler, S. and Rowland, M. (2010) *Multisystemic Therapy for Child Abuse and Neglect*. Charleston, SC: Family Services Research Center, MUSC.

Swenson, C., Schaeffer, C., Henggeler, S., Faldowski, R. and Mayhew, A. (2010) 'Multi-Systemic Therapy for Child Abuse and Neglect: A randomised controlled effectiveness trial.' *Journal of Family Psychology 24*, 497–507.

Tannenbaum, L. and Forehand, R. (1994) 'Maternal depressive mood: The role of the father in preventing adolescent problem behaviours.' *Behaviour Research and Therapy 32*, 321–325.

Tanner, K. and Turney, D. (2006) 'Therapeutic Interventions with Children who have Experienced Neglect and their Families in the UK.' In C. McAuley, P. Pecora and W. Rose (eds) *Enhancing the Well-Being of Children through Effective Interventions: International Evidence for Practice*. London: Jessica Kingsley Publishers.

The Bridge Consultancy (1995) *Paul: Death through Neglect*. The Bridge Consultancy.

Thoburn, J. and members of the Making Research Count Consortium (2009) *Effective Interventions for Complex Families where there are Concerns About, or Evidence of, a Child Suffering Significant Harm. Safeguarding Briefing 1*. London: Centre for Excellence and Outcomes in Children and Young People's Services (C4EO).

Thornberry, T.P., Ireland, T.O. and Smith, C.A. (2001) 'The importance of timing: The varying impact of childhood and adolescent maltreatment on multiple problem outcomes.' *Development and Psychopathology 13*, 4, 957–979.

Tompsett, H., Ashworth, M., Atkins, C., Bell, L. *et al.* (2009) *The Child, the Family and the GP: Tensions and Conflicts of Interest in Safeguarding Children.* DCSF-RBX-09-05-ES. London: Department for Children, Schools and Families.

Toth, S., Maughan, A., Todd Manly, J., Spagnola, M. and Cicchetti, C. (2002) 'The relative efficacy of two interventions in altering maltreated preschool children's representational models: Implications for attachment theory.' *Development and Psychopathology 14,* 887–908.

Toth, S.L., Rogosch, F.A., Cicchetti, D. and Manly, J.T. (2006) 'The efficacy of toddler–parent psychotherapy to reorganise attachment in the young offspring of mothers with major depressive disorder: A randomised preventive trial.' *Journal of Consulting and Clinical Psychology 74,* 6 1006–16.

Triple P Programme. Available at www.triplep.net/, accessed on 31 May 2011.

Tunnard, J. (2002) *Parental Problem Drinking and its Impact on Children.* Dartington: Research in Practice.

Tunnard, J. (2004) *Parental Mental Health Problems: Key Messages from Research, Policy and Practice.* Dartington: Research in Practice.

Tunstill, J., Allnock, D. and The National Evaluation of Sure Start Team (2007) *Understanding the Contribution of Sure Start Local Programmes to the Task of Safeguarding Children's Welfare.* London: HMSO.

Twardosz, S. and Lutzker, J.R. (2010) 'Child maltreatment and the developing brain: A review of neuroscience perspectives.' *Aggression and Violent Behavior 15,* 59–68.

Van den Dries, L., Juffer, F., Van IJzendoorn, M.H. and Bakermans-Kranenburg, M.J. (2009) 'Fostering security? A meta-analysis of attachment in adopted children.' *Children and Youth Services Review 31,* 410–421.

Vazsonyi, A.T., Hibbert, J.R. and Snider, J.B. (2003) 'Exotic enterprise no more? Adolescent reports of family and parenting processes from youth in four countries.' *Journal of Research on Adolescence 13,* 2, 197–207.

Wade, J., Biehal, N., Clayden, J. and Stein, M. (1998) *Going Missing: Young People Absent from Care.* Chichester: Wiley.

Wade, J., Biehal, N., Farrelly, N. and Sinclair, I. (2011) *Caring for Abused and Neglected Children: Making the Right Decisions for Reunification or Long-Term Care.* London: Jessica Kingsley Publishers.

Ward, H. (2009) 'Patterns of instability. Moves within the English care system: Their reasons, contexts and consequences.' *Children and Youth Services Review 31,* 1113–1118.

Ward, H., Brown, R. and Maskell-Graham, D. (forthcoming) *Young Children Suffering, or Likely to Suffer, Significant Harm: Experiences on Entering Education.* Loughborough: Centre for Child and Family Research, Loughborough University.

Ward, H., Brown, R., and Westlake, D. (2012) *Safeguarding Babies and Very Young Children from Abuse and Neglect.* London: Jessica Kingsley Publishers.

Ward, H., Holmes, L., Moyers, S., Munro, E.R. and Poursanidou, D. (2004) *Safeguarding Children: A Scoping Study of Research in Three Areas.* Loughborough: Centre for Child and Family Research, Loughborough University.

Ward, H., Holmes, L. and Soper, J. (2008) *Costs and Consequences of Placing Children in Care.* London: Jessica Kingsley Publishers.

Ward, H. and Jones, H. (2009) 'Le système de protection en Angleterre.' *Santé, Societé et Solidarité 1,* 181–192.

Ward, H., Munro, E.R. and Dearden, C. (2006) *Babies and Young Children in Care: Life Pathways, Decision-Making and Practice.* London: Jessica Kingsley Publishers.

Ward, H., Skuse, T. and Munro, E.R. (2005) 'The best of times, the worst of times: Young people's views of care and accommodation.' *Adoption and Fostering 29,* 1, 8–17.

Webster-Stratton, C. and Reid, J. (2010) 'Adapting the Incredible Years, an evidence-based parenting programme, for families involved in the child welfare system.' *Journal of Children's Services 5,* 1, 25–42.

Webster-Stratton, C., Reid, J. and Hammond, M. (2001) 'Social skills and problem-solving training for children with early-onset conduct problems: Who benefits?' *Journal of Child Psychology and Psychiatry 42,* 943–952.

Westat Inc (1993) *A Report on the Maltreatment of Children with Disabilities.* Washington DC: National Center on Child Abuse and Neglect.

WHO (2007) *The Cycles of Violence: The Relationship Between Childhood Maltreatment and the Risk of Later Becoming a Victim or Perpetrator of Violence.* Copenhagen: World Health Organization.

Wiggins, C., Fenichel, E. and Mann, T. (2007) *Literature Review: Developmental Problems of Maltreated Children and Early Intervention Options for Maltreated Children.* Report to Office of the Assistant Secretary for Planning and Evaluation, US Department of Health and Human Services.

Williamson, E. and Hester, M. (2009) *Evaluation of the South Tyneside Domestic Abuse Perpetrator Programme 2006–8.* Final Report. Bristol: University of Bristol.

Wooster, D. (1999) 'Assessment of nonorganic failure to thrive: Infant–toddler intervention.' *The Transdisciplinary Journal 9,* 4, 353–371.

Zahn-Waxler, C., Duggal, S. and Gruber, R. (2002) 'Parental Psychopathology.' In M. Bornstein (ed.) *Handbook of Parenting: Social Conditions and Applied Parenting.* New Jersey: Erlbaum.

Subject Index

Author Index

Allnock, D. 23, 23–4, 55–70, 124–5, 189–90
Ashworth, M. 23, 24, 116–37, 187–8
Atkins, C. 23, 24, 116–37, 187–8
Auty, K. 22, 24, 179–80

Bailey, S. 23, 24–5, 44, 124, 169–70
Barlow, J. 22, 24, 32, 34–6, 44, 49–50, 55–70, 94–112, 165–6
Belderson, P. 23, 24–5, 38, 42–4, 46–7, 50, 76, 167–8, 169–70
Bell, L. 23, 24, 116–37, 187–8
Biehal, N. 22, 24, 27, 73–90, 107, 109–11, 123, 124–6, 146, 191–2
Bjornstad, G. 22, 24, 94–112, 183–4
Black, J. 23, 24–5, 38, 42–3, 46–7, 50, 76, 167–8, 169–70
Brandon, M. 23, 24–5, 38, 42–4, 46–7, 50, 76, 124, 167–8, 169–70
Brown, D. 22
Brown, R. 22, 24, 27, 40–2, 47, 49, 60–1, 67, 69, 73–90, 99, 108–10, 119–20, 124–6, 128, 193–4

Carpenter, J. 22, 24, 116–38, 171–2

Daniel, B. 22, 24, 26, 29–51, 173–4
Dodsworth, J. 23, 24–5, 38, 42–3, 46–7, 50, 76, 167–8

Farmer, E. 22, 30–1, 34, 36, 73–90, 82–4, 86–9, 108–10, 122–5, 175–6
Farrelly, N. 22, 24, 27, 73–90, 107, 109–11, 123, 124–6, 146, 191–2
France, A. 23, 24, 27, 116–37, 177–8

Gallagher, A. 23, 24, 116–37, 187–8
Gardner, F. 22, 24, 94–112, 183–4
Gardner, R. 23, 24–5, 38, 42–4, 46–7, 50, 76, 167–8, 169–70
Glaser, D. 22, 24, 179–80
Gorin, S. 22, 24, 29–51, 55–70, 185–6

Hackett, S. 22, 24, 116–38, 171–2
Haines, L. 22, 24, 116–37, 171–2

Hicks, L. 22, 24, 29–51, 55–70, 185–6
Howe, D. 23, 24–5, 38, 42–3, 46–7, 50, 76, 167–8

Komulainen, S. 22, 24, 116–37, 171–2

Laming, Lord 11
Lutman, E. 22, 30–1, 34, 36, 73–90, 82–4, 86–9, 108–10, 122–5, 175–6

Montgomery, P. 22, 24, 94–112, 183–4
Morgan, M. 23, 24, 116–37, 187–8
Munro, E.R. 12, 16, 22–4, 27, 40–2, 47, 49, 60–1, 67, 69, 73–90, 99, 108–10, 116–37, 177–8, 193–4

Patsios, D. 22, 24, 116–38, 171–2
Prior, V. 22, 24, 179–80

Ramchandani, P. 22, 24, 94–112, 183–4
Rees, G. 22, 24, 29–51, 55–70, 185–6

Schrader McMillan, A. 22, 24, 32, 34–6, 44, 49–50, 55–70, 94–112, 165–6
Scott, J. 22, 24, 26, 29–51, 173–4
Sidebotham, P. 23, 24–5, 44, 124, 169–70
Sinclair, I. 22, 24, 27, 73–90, 107, 109–11, 123, 124–6, 146, 191–2
Stein, M. 22, 24, 29–51, 55–70, 185–6
Szilassy, E. 22, 24, 116–38, 171–2

Taylor, J. 22, 24, 26, 29–51, 173–4
Tilki, S. 22, 24, 179–80
Tompsett, H. 23, 24, 116–37, 187–8
Tunstill, J. 23, 23–4, 55–70, 124–5, 189–90

Wade, J. 22, 24, 27, 73–90, 107, 109–11, 123, 124–6, 146, 191–2
Wainwright, P. 23, 24, 116–37, 187–8

Ward, H. 22, 24, 27, 40–2, 47, 49, 60–1, 67, 69, 73–90, 99, 108–10, 119–20, 124–6, 128, 193–4
Waring, A. 23, 24, 27, 116–37, 177–8
Warren, C. 23, 24–5, 38, 42–3, 46–7, 50, 76, 167–8, 169–70
Westlake, D. 22, 24, 27, 40–2, 47, 49, 60–1, 67, 69, 73–90, 99, 108–10, 119–20, 124–6, 128, 193–4